The Church
Helping or Hurting?

2nd Edition

**Making Individuals and Churches
Safe and Effective for
Helping Wounded People Heal**

A Guide to Practical Christianity

Based on the Genesis Process for Personal Change

Michael Dye, CADC, NCAC II
Founder and Author of the Genesis Process

Copyright © 2015 by Michael Dye

All rights reserved, including the right of reproduction in whole or in part in any form. No portion of this book may be reproduced in any form whatsoever, except for brief quotations in reviews, without the written permission of the publisher.

ISBN: 978-0-615-98629-6

Cover and interior design and layout by Rose Island Bookworks

Manufactured in the United States of America

DEDICATION

This book is dedicated to my son,
Joah Michael Dye
(June 9, 1977–May 1, 2013).
Joah was a gentle, special needs giant who had more of the attributes
of Jesus than anyone I know. From the day he was born,
he challenged me to be a better person.

I would also like to dedicate this book to all of the people I have
worked with who struggle with self-destructive behaviors.
They have taught me so much of what is put forth in this book.
May it bring hope to those who are struggling now.

ACKNOWLEDGMENTS

I would like to thank my wife, Cathy, for listening to all my ideas and speeches and hanging in there with me for thirty-three years. I couldn't have done this without you.

Thanks to Rona Getty for helping organize all the stories people wrote in. Thank you to Amy Muia, Director of the Tierra Nueva women's program in Mount Vernon, Washington, for her help in organizing my thoughts and getting them down on paper. Your help with this book is invaluable. Also thanks to my daughter in-law Mallory Dye for her help with this 2nd edition.

FORWARD TO THE 2ND EDITION

Upon getting feedback from the 1st edition I realized that some of the concepts needed future amplification and clarification. So I rewrote many of the key points and added a few clarifying stories. Also several people who know me ask why I didn't include my speech about the "Fear of God" as they felt it would be an important understanding for the church. So it is now Chapter 10. The goal of this book is to help individuals and churches look at how effective our practices and theologies are at helping or hindering our ability and willingness to see broken people heal. This book is now pretty much the best of what I have learned over the past 45 years as to helping wounded and addicted people heal. It is my hope that it will encourage you and your church/agency to be more effective conduits for change and healing.

TABLE OF CONTENTS

PART I: FOUNDATIONS xiii

Introduction: Changing the World One Safe Person at a Time 1
Trying to Find Truth 2
New Opportunities 4
Initiating Change 6
Author's Notes 8

Chapter One: Foundational Principles of Genesis 13
Principle 1: The Empty Place 14
Principle 2: Some of Us Only Learn (Wisdom) from Experience 16
Principle 3: The Mystery of Change 18
Principle 4: Why We Do What We Don't Want to Do 21
Principle 5: Relationships–The Missing Piece of the Puzzle 23
Principle 6: The Church's Role in Restoration 25
    Morals 26
    Values 28
    Relationships 29
    Restoration and Grace 32

PART II: WHAT'S BROKEN 35

Chapter Two: What's Broken? 37
The Mystery of Our Self-Destructive Behavior 37
    Selena's Frustration 39
    How Can We Help? 42
    Sam's Story 42
Understanding Brain Basics 43
    Introducing the Limbic System 44
    Damage Starts Early 47
    Story of a Broken Heart 49
Healing Heart Wounds 50
    The Survival Brain 52
    Defensive Personalities 56

    Cravings Drive Good and Bad Behaviors............................ 58
    Self-Justification 60
    John's Story.. 60
    Out-Running Myself 61
    Getting Up the Hill.. 61
The Neurochemicals of the Brain... 63
    Got To Have It! Dopamine.. 63
    I've Had Enough! Serotonin... 64

Chapter Three: Learning to Trust Again 67
A Mother's Role... 68
A Father's Role 71
Relearning to Trust.. 74
Healing Power of Joy... 76
    Jane's Story... 77

Chapter Four: Addiction–Is it Sin or Disease?................. 81
When the Church Hinders Recovery.. 81
Addiction—Is it Sin or Disease?.. 84
    Disease is the Result of Sin... 88
    Art's Story... 89
    The Craving Brain 90
    Shame vs. Grace.. 92
    Rejection and Love: Grace at Work.................................... 99
12-Step Programs 102

Chapter Five: Secrets and Freedom 109
What is a Secret?... 110
    Mike's Story.. 111
The Damage Secrets Do.. 112
    Secrets Damage Relationships 113
    Secrets are Infectious... 114
    Secrets Diminish Our Potential....................................... 116
    Stan's Story... 117
Safe Church Practices 118
    Sharing Testimonies 118
    Recovery Focused Small Groups...................................... 119

Leader Accountability...120
Communicate a Simple, Accessible Message.................... 121
Summary of Part II: What's Broken?............................... 125

PART III: WHAT WORKS 125
Introduction to What Works?................................ 129
Evangelism Through Recovery.. 130
Chapter Six: Freedom from Spiritual Stagnation 133
The Spiritually Stagnant 133
   Laurie's Story... 135
   Made for a Purpose.. 137
   A Common Story.. 140
The Dilemma of Free Will... 141
Breaking the Power of Spiritual Stagnation 143
   The Fifth Gospel.. 143
   Rena's Story 148
Spiritual Immaturity vs. Maturity 148
   Give to Grow... 149
   Fear Keeps Us Stagnant 152
   Beware of Complacency 153
   Redirecting Priorities 155
More Than a Program... 156
Redeeming Our Pain... 160
Summary 164

Chapter Seven: Freedom from the Pharisaical Spirit............ 167
Defining the Pharisaical Spirit 167
   Pharisees Don't Bear Fruit 169
   Pharisees Aren't Safe 170
   Pharisees Are Performance Driven............................ 171
   Tims' Story... 172
   Pharisees Are Hypocritical... 173
   Forbidden Fruit 177
   A Struggle with Pornography.................................... 179
   Pharisees Create Wounds with Guilt and Shame 180

Sending the Wrong Message 181
Overcoming Shame 183
A Pastor's Story 184
Steps Toward Change 185
Defeat Denial 186
One Sin Doesn't Fit All 187
Avoid the Trap of Judging Others.. 188
Let Go of Having to Be Right... 191
Mary's Story... 195

Chapter Eight: Extending Grace 199
Two Essentials: Grace and Competency 200
What is Authentic Grace?.. 202
Grace is Humble, Not Proud... 202
Grace is Unconditional 204
Grace Sees the Heart... 206
Grace is Acceptance, Not Enabling 207
Grace is Spirit-Driven, Not Law-Driven 209
Grace Is Sacrificial and Others-Centered 213
Grace Is an Action, Not a Theological Concept................. 215
Grace is Tolerance... 217
Gratitude... 218
A Story of Grace in Action... 220
Importance of Modeling Grace 221

Chapter Nine: Restoring Hope.. 223
The Power of Hope 223
The Hope Formula... 225
Isabel's Story... 226
What Works? Heart Change... 227
Understanding Thoughts and Beliefs................................... 228
Our Role in Heart Change.. 230
We Ask Jesus to Fill Our Hearts 231
Foster a Personal Relationship 232
Cooperate with the Holy Spirit 233
A True Story of What Hurts and What Helps.................... 234

What Can Safe and Effective Churches Do to Restore Hope? 236
Value the Person More Than the Rules 236
   Outside the Box 238
   Offer Acceptance and Support 239
   In a Safe Church it is OK to Question............................ 240
   Accetance Can be Hard.. 241
   A What Works Story... 241
   Investing Time is What Heals 243
   Partner with God 244
Applying What Works 245
Practical Examples.. 246
Stress: A Relevant Topic for Many People Today 247
Encourage Fun 247
Educate on the Importance of Integrity................................ 248
Another "What Works" Story 249

Chapter Ten: Fear 253
Fear.. 256
   Rose's Story 258
Love and Desire 259
   Desire for Money 261
Resentment and Hate 261
Resentments Are Unforgiveness 262
   Control from the Grave... 264

Chapter Eleven: The Pastor's Role 267
We Are Always Looking for a Leader 268
   Pastoring as a Father Figure 268
   Pastoring from a Place of Security 270
   John's Story... 272
   Pastoring as a Counselor 273
   Susan's Story.. 275
   Pastoring with Authenticity...................................... 276
   Jim's Story.. 279
   Pastoring with Accountability 280
   Jill's Story... 281

Chapter Twelve: Revival through Unity 265
The Power of Revival. 285
   A True Revival Story 286
Promoting Revival. 287
   Loving One Another is the Key. 287
   Freedom from Religion 289
   Examine Ourselves. 291
   Kathy's Story 292
What Hinders Unity and Revival?. 293
Church Splits. 294
   Mary's Story. 296
The Power of Belief Systems 297
   Jim's Story. 300
   Denominational Divides. 301
   Insecurity. 302
   Nick's Story 303
Christ and Him Crucified 304

Chapter Thirteen: The Joy Center: Healing the Heart 306
Joy Impacts Our Development. 306
The Power of Joy 309
   Disgust Communicates Rejection 311
   Joy Expresses Value. 313
   Joy is Face-to-Face. 314
The Power of Acceptance 315
Summary 316

Final Thoughts 321

Notes. 325

PART I   FOUNDATIONS

Introduction: Changing the World, One Safe Person at a Time
Chapter One: Foundational Principles of Genesis

INTRODUCTION

CHANGING THE WORLD, ONE SAFE PERSON AT A TIME

*"Everyone thinks of changing the world,
but no one thinks of changing himself."*
~ Leo Tolstoy

I have always been a constant researcher and problem solver. As a kid, I had to take everything apart to try to improve it. I am still that way. Unsolved mysteries bug me—so, of course, I am usually bugged all of the time. The main mystery that has bugged me for the last forty-five years is this: Why are human beings so self-destructive? Though we want to change, why aren't we able to change? Why do we continue to do the very things we do not want to do? Providing insights into these types of questions is my goal in writing this book.

It turns out that the Apostle Paul was also perplexed about this very issue. In Romans 7, he pondered the question, "Why do I do what I hate?" It is this same question that has continued to bug me, essentially, "What's broken in us humans?"[1] Over the past forty-five years (thirty-five as a Christian), my search for truth has led me to some interesting conclusions, resulting in some new understandings about how to help hurting people recover. We will look at this mystery of human self-destructive behavior from biblical, neurochemical, social, and just plain common sense perspectives. My hope is that these new understandings will make you and your church a safer and more effective place to help wounded people heal.

My current personal recovery began years ago when God spoke to me one morning. He said, "Michael, you're a man like Paul." My first reaction was, "Cool!" Paul did mighty things and wrote most of the New

Testament, so I figured I must have some great things ahead of me! When I got done flattering myself, I realized that what God really meant was that I was like Paul—when he was still Saul—a Pharisee in need of a deep heart change. I had a heart and calling to help messed-up people, but God was telling me that my main hindrance to being effective was myself—I was a Pharisee. If I was to become safe and effective at helping those who God would bring to me, I had to change my heart first.

From that point on, He began showing me that it was this Pharisaical, or religious, part of me that was sabotaging my efforts to be the person I wanted to be and was hindering my effectiveness at what He called me to do. I began to understand that being judgmental, critical, self-righteous, and theologically "correct" (i.e., religious), was making me an unsafe person and frustratingly unfruitful in my calling. This process has been the hardest personal change I have ever attempted. Just try not to judge anyone for a whole day and you'll see what I mean! I still relapse many times a day, but the fruit of this discovery and the work I've done to change has allowed God to use me, like Paul, in ways I could not have imagined. I had to be willing to change who I am before He would trust me to do something for Him. This was hard because I am a doer-type of person.

This book is an attempt to bridge the gap between the church and wounded people by making individuals and churches safe, accepting, and effective. As Christians, we need both grace and competency to see lives changed. Offering love without judgment and demonstrating the know-how to provide practical solutions that work in real life will draw hurting people to us for help. If we can't provide these things, then they will look elsewhere.

TRYING TO FIND TRUTH

My first encounter with Christ took place in 1979. Prior to that, I spent thirteen years entrenched in the "hippie movement" of the 1960s–70s, looking for God in all the wrong places. I practiced most of the world religions that the era had to offer: Hinduism, Buddhism, metaphysics, the occult, shamanism, and all the New Age philosophies. I studied with some of the biggest gurus, and traveled around the world seeking truth and enlightenment, I also tried all the mind-expanding drugs available. Like so many in that period, I was looking for "THE TRUTH" that would fill my deep longing to understand the meaning of life and where I fit in (i.e., my purpose).

The gurus taught me that once I had experienced "cosmic consciousness," or "nirvana," then I would be at peace, and the emptiness inside me would go away. I worked very hard and had many "enlightenment experiences," but they faded after a week or two. Soon the empty longing returned and I started searching again. The intensity of my search nearly killed me many times. Since my dangerous adventures did not succeed in killing me, I began to realize that God (whoever He was) must have intervened and saved my life. In my heart, I knew that He must have some sort of plan for my life—it took me another ten years to meet Him personally.

From those thirteen years of searching, I learned one key thing: no matter how hard I tried, I could not change on my own. Sure, I could change some of my behaviors, like not eating meat. And I even acquired certain disciplines, like fasting and meditation. However, the person I was deep inside my heart remained the same. The lonely, secret part of me, the part that I did not like, went untouched. I refer to this as the *empty place*. This is a place well known by those who struggle with self-destructive behavior. It is the unconscious, lonely, and painful part of a person that drives them to do things that are harmful to themselves and others.

Being self-destructive (often characterized by addiction) is simply a loss of control. It is the inability to change the way we feel and act in some way, or to stop doing something harmful on our own. As Paul states in Romans 7, there seems to be something within us, that is stronger than our will—something that drives and controls what we feel and do. Unraveling this mystery was the foundational principle that led to the writing of my first book, *The Genesis Process for Relapse Prevention*, designed to help those with life-threatening addictions.[2]

It really began one night in 1979, after years of trying to outrun the emptiness in my heart, I realized I was out of things to try that would fill the void inside me. It was my prodigal moment. I had already explored New Age esoteric versions of Christianity several times and dismissed them as "not for me." I had never read the Bible or been to church, except for get ting married in one once—but I was on acid at the time, so it probably didn't count. That night, lying there in the dark, I realized the only thing I had not tried in my search for truth was Jesus.

For a 60s hippie, the worst thing that I could do was to sell-out, conform, and become a Christian. Out of desperation, I prayed, "Jesus, if you are who you say you are, and you can make me into the person I have always wanted to be, I'll dump all this other stuff and follow you." Right then, something hit me. At the time I didn't know what it was, but when I got up the next morning, I knew I was done searching. I was different. The painful emptiness that felt like a thirst I had not been able to quench, or an itch I could not scratch, was gone. God filled the empty place with Christ in answer to my prayer.

NEW OPPORTUNITIES

At the time of this writing, I am 68 years old, which means I am part of what is called the *baby boomer* generation. My generation has experienced the fastest changing period in the history of mankind. Sixty years ago, we didn't have computers, cell phones, jet aircraft travel, television, or Prozac. As our world gets more complex and stressful, our ways of coping have also become more intense and destructive. The more affluent we are, the more self-destructive we have become. Rightly, we have been called the "me" generation.

People of every age are searching for a life that has meaning, purpose, and value. At the same time, they are engaging in increasingly self-destructive coping behaviors to anesthetize the emptiness they feel. With almost every negative statistic on the rise—crime, drugs, mental illness, disease, ADD, divorce, global warming, violence, obesity, and sex addiction—we are becoming a society that turns to pharmaceuticals before looking to God and each other to solve our problems. We are the most affluent society and also the most self-destructive. Why?

Looking at how to solve this overwhelming tide of need, I have come to the conclusion that it is only the local church that has the resources to effectively help those searching for help. Now is the opportune time for Christians to step up and provide answers to the complex problems plaguing our world by engaging in real and effective ways to help. We can do this by what I simply call *practical Christianity*—a Christianity that is relevant to the issues our society struggles with.

Even though I don't think society looks at Christianity as being relevant to provide real help for real-life struggles, as evidenced by the fact that statistically people are becoming less and less religious,[3] I do believe that the church has the greatest potential to help wounded people experience real and lasting freedom. We will look into this topic in more depth later.

Though I am writing from a Christian perspective, the principles in this book are for every human being who wants to understand the mystery of why we keep doing the things that are harmful to others and ourselves— the mystery of human change. Most of my ministry has been spent working with wounded people who have become habitually self-destructive (wounded people are usually also addicted people whose means of coping have become habitual). Over the last few years, my focus has shifted to helping Christians and churches become more effective at helping wounded people heal. In order to actually help them, though, we first have to become safe.

I have worked for thirty-four years with people in crisis and I can tell you that not many people come to God when everything is going well for them. They usually seek Him in times of crisis. Many of these people, including myself, have not had good experiences with feeling safe and welcome in the church. Typically, many churches and Christians simply look at self-destructive coping behaviors as sinful, and can be very judgmental and condemning of those seeking help. What they don't understand, however, is that a changed life is the best kind of evangelism, as it demonstrates the power of God.

Grace is the power of effective Christianity, and grace is revealed in the gratitude we have for our own changed lives extended to others. This kind of gratitude makes us naturally more tolerant of others. If Christians are going to see their faith impact society, it will only be through safe, grace-based churches—those that are healing, relevant, and effective for helping broken people by meeting their needs successfully. Of course, the safest and most effective people to help others will be those who are openly and honestly dealing with their own issues. Church people in real recovery will be a powerful force.

Fortunately, there is ample evidence that the church is doing good things in our society. In fact, if you took Christianity and all the help it provides out of this country, I think we would see our society collapse quickly. For example, I would guess that at least eighty percent of the free residential recovery programs are Christian-based. Also, think of the homeless feeding programs, and the many local helps ministries done by the churches. Many, many lives are impacted for the better, yet we don't hear much about those in the news compared to the times when we mess up.

My intention is not to bash the church, but rather to challenge those within the church to examine their faith in a practical way. Many churches are doing a great job of providing help—perhaps yours is. But the church as a whole still has a long way to go. Unfortunately, some churches are actually hurting more than healing.

My hope is that this book will spur you on to help others in the most effective way possible, and that it has the following effects:

1. It will affirm that what you are already doing is right on.
2. It will challenge you to make changes in yourself and in your church.
3. Some of both.

> *"Be the change that you wish to see in the world."*
> ~ Mahatma Ghandi

INITIATING CHANGE

Lasting recovery requires heart change, which is the main theme of this book and the New Testament. A few years ago, I realized that in the long-term, the recovering people I've worked with were much more successful in life if they were involved in a good church. We want to be the kind of (safe) church that not only draws recovering people to us, but keeps them coming back. The transition to becoming a safe and effective church involves not only having the right answers, but also asking the right questions. Change begins by asking honest and fearless questions. Self-examination can be uncomfortable because it can challenge our basic belief systems. Yet, change begins from being made to feel uncomfortable.

Throughout this book, we will explore the power and consequences of changing belief systems. I think you will be amazed at how much our beliefs drive so many of the mysteries of how we act and feel. I ask you to read this book with an open mind. Some of the concepts may be a challenge for you, but one of my goals in writing this book is to show you that it's okay to think outside the box. Oftentimes, it is outside the box where change begins.

"The world as we have created it is a process of our thinking. It cannot be changed without changing our thinking."
~ Albert Einstein

Since positive change comes from asking the right questions, you can't get good answers unless you ask good questions. Therefore, I have provided *Self Discovery Questions* at the end of each chapter to hopefully help you experience the fruit of asking difficult questions. I sometimes call them *change questions*. I encourage you to explore them prayerfully and fully. Some of you may want to use this book and the questions for group discussions, which I guarantee will be lively. My desire is that you will use this book to discover the answers to these sometimes difficult questions, which are designed to promote change. The following are a few of the questions we will explore:

- Is my church's teaching and focus relevant to the issues that people in my community and in my church struggle with?
- Do we have effective programs that go along with what we are teaching?
- As a Christian, am I a safe person for wounded people? Can God trust me with desperate people who are seeking help?
- Is my church a safe and effective place for hurting and addicted people to seek help?

- Do those of us in the church demonstrate that we have Christ's heart for broken people? Why or why not?

It is my hope that you will be open to the challenge and grab hold of the courage it takes to look at yourself and your church in a new and honest way. I invite you to expand your thinking as we explore what may be hindering you and your faith community from being effective. The fruit of this (sometimes) painful process will be real change—change in our families, our community, our world, and ourselves. It is not my goal to get you to see things my way, but to challenge you to examine the way you see them. Changing the world begins with one safe person at a time.

AUTHOR'S NOTES

Many of the principles in this book are taken from *The Genesis Change Group Process*. This book may challenge you and raise questions such as, "Where do we go from here?" For further information, I encourage you to investigate *The Genesis Process for Change Groups*, which contains practical solutions for many of the problems addressed in this book.[4]

To get the most out of this book, I suggest that you take it in small bites—read a section and then contemplate it before moving on to the next one. The book is divided in to three parts:

PART I: This section explains the foundations of the principals presented.

PART II: This section delves into *what is broken* in human beings that cause us to be so self-destructive and what it takes to heal. We will explore the mystery of human change.

PART III: This section is about *what works* and what hinders the restoration of wounded people.

The stories in this book are true. They come from a response to a survey I sent out asking for good and bad stories about experiences people have had when they sought help for serious problems at their church. Many of the stories are from people who are going through the *Genesis Change*

Groups and refer to their experience in the groups. Several of the stories are about struggles with sex addictions, which has become so pervasive in the Christian community. I have changed the stories enough to protect the innocent and the guilty. The quotes, or what I call *Key Thoughts*, are mine unless attributed. Biblical references are taken from the *New American Standard Bible* unless designated otherwise.

Some have given feedback from the 1st Edition that the book is to long. This book is not a causal reading book. I suggest you take it in small doses, at most one chapter at time.

SELF-DISCOVERY QUESTIONS

Honestly rate yourself and your church.

1. Is my church's teaching and focus relevant to the issues that people in my community and in my church struggle with?

   _____
   _____
   _____
   _____

2. Do we have effective programs that go along with what we are teaching?

   _____
   _____
   _____
   _____

3. As a Christian, am I a safe person for wounded people? Can God trust me with desperate people who are seeking help?

   _____
   _____
   _____
   _____

4. Is my church a safe and effective place for hurting and addicted people to seek help?

5. Do those of us in the church demonstrate that we have Christ's heart for broken people? Why or why not?

CHAPTER ONE

FOUNDATIONAL PRINCIPLES OF GENESIS

"He who has found his life will lose it, and he who has lost his life for my sake will find it." Matthew 10:39

To appreciate this book, it is important to understand the basic principles upon which the *Genesis Process* has been built. I am convinced that if biblical principles are sound, they will work at a practical level. The origin of the *Genesis Process* is the story of how God brought me to this ministry of helping people change—it is a story about finding a "practical Christianity" that works in changing people's lives. As you will see, I went through many junctures and dead ends before finding some basic truths that got to the heart of what hurting/addicted people need in order to change. As I look back now, it all makes sense, but at the time I didn't have a clue what I was learning.

> *"The easiest kind of relationship for me is with 10,000 people. The hardest is with one."*
>
> ~ Joan Baez

KEY thought: We all have a void that drives us to seek intimacy with God and each other.

PRINCIPLE 1: THE EMPTY PLACE

It was during my transition from eastern religions to Christianity that I first discovered the existence of what I call the *empty place*. It became a foundational understanding in my quest to help stuck people change. In a short period of time, I got divorced, became a Christian, and remarried. I had always been drawn to hurting people, so along with my fearless new wife, Cathy, we began to minister in a variety of situations, including a full-lockup mental hospital and several convalescent homes. We also started a soup kitchen/coffee house for street people in Santa Cruz, California, where many of the homeless are not only alcoholics, but also dual-diagnosis, mentally ill addicts. They taught us a lot about people who were stuck.

Next, I developed a process to de-program those involved in eastern religions, New Age cults, and other similar practices of which I had recently come out of. We went into witchcraft and New Age fairs and set up a booth called the *Spiritual IQ Test* to get people to think outside the box of their current beliefs. This early ministry turned out to be very fruitful since those attending these fairs were spiritual seekers and open to new concepts, and I spoke their language. At one point, we even mortgaged our house to buy a tent that held 600 people for evangelism services (we will look at the lessons from the tent in the chapter on revival). This was all within the first three years of being Christians—we learned everything through experiences.

Finally, we got involved in a local residential drug and alcohol rehab program, and it was here that I found my calling. Many of the people we worked with would say things like: "What's wrong with me?" "Why am I this way? I hate it!" "Why can't I change?" "There is some kind of void in me that I can't fill. I don't even know what it is." Through this experience, I discovered that we all have an awareness of a void (i.e., *the empty place*); it is a kind of loneliness that causes us to say, "There must be something more. What am I missing?"

In 2007, *60 Minutes* anchor, Steve Kroft, interviewed Tom Brady (All-Pro NFL Quarterback for the New England Patriots) after his third Super Bowl victory for the Patriots. Kroft noted Brady's tremendous success and was struck by Brady's desire for something more. "He has dated actresses and supermodels and makes millions of dollars a year.

He has been called America's most eligible bachelor. By most popular standards, he has it all. That is why I was struck by hearing him make the following statement during the interview:"

> "Why do I have three Super Bowl rings and still think there's something greater out there for me? I mean, maybe a lot of people would say, 'Hey man, this is what it's all about.' I reached my goal, my dream. I think, 'God, it's got to be more than this.' I mean this isn't, this can't be what it's all cracked up to be." When Kroft asked him, "What's the answer?" Brady responded, "I wish I knew. I wish I knew . . . I love playing football and I love being quarterback for this team. But at the same time, I think there are a lot of other parts about me that I'm trying to find."[1]

Just like Tom Brady, it really doesn't matter who we are, or how successful we become, there is still an awareness of "something more" that keeps us seeking. That's because God designed human beings to be healthy, by developing meaningful relationships, and to serve a greater purpose than our own needs and desires. He gave us a *heart*, a central place inside of us that can only be fulfilled by a purposeful connection with Him and with others.

> **KEY thought** All of our habitual self-destructive behaviors primarily do the same thing. They temporarily anesthetize the awareness of the empty place.

Intimate relationships are a foundational necessity for being a healthy human being. From years of working with hurting and addicted people, I have come to understand a common root that drives our self-destructive coping behaviors. Human addictive coping behaviors are simply ways to temporarily anesthetize the awareness of *the empty place*, which feels like a deep loneliness. This empty place can only be filled by intimacy with God and people. Understanding this concept enables those with self-destructive behaviors to get to the root of what is driving the behavior (i.e., what the behavior is there for), rather than just trying to control it. For those who want to help hurting people, this is an important principle to understand. We are designed to function as human beings through relationships, which is the only true way to fill *the empty place*. We will explore this principal throughout this book.

> **KEY thought** — There are basically two types of people in the world—regular people and prodigals.

PRINCIPLE 2: SOME OF US ONLY LEARN WISDOM FROM EXPERIENCE

During this period I learned another important insight that later translated into helping others—it was the realization that I am a prodigal. This came about over the next couple of years, as I tried to help self-destructive people, yet saw very little change in them. They just weren't getting it. I began to realize that most of the people we were trying to help were prodigals. Typically, prodigals do not learn well from information only; rather, they learn from experience. They are also impulsive and learn through trial and (mostly) error. This key insight became one of the first foundational principles of the *Genesis Process*, which is based on helping people change through new experiences, not just information. In Chapter 2, we will see that our coping behaviors are driven by the experiential part of the brain. It takes new and opposite experiences to change what drives destructive behaviors.

The main difference between prodigals and regular people is how they learn life's lessons. Think of the *Parable of the Prodigal Son* in Luke 15. What is the difference between the good son and the prodigal son? The good son saw that giving in to temptation would end up being bad for him, and so he chose not to. But the prodigal son did not accept information by itself. He had to learn from personal experience in order to accept what was true. No one could have taught him the lesson he learned from the pigs. He had to learn it himself in his own way.

Because much of our Christian learning in today's churches and rehab centers is informational and not experiential, many prodigals coming into Christianity simply do not get it. They need to experience Christianity in order to accept its truth, grow, and change. Just like in Bible times, when people encountered Jesus, they went away with profound experiences that changed their lives and behaviors. The day of Pentecost gives another good example of a transforming experience, as well as Paul's personal transformation on the road to Damascus.

In my own personal search for truth, I first had to test new ideas and then eliminate everything false on the basis of my experiences before I could come to believe and trust "The Truth." I am still that way. I do not trust information until it proves true in reality. Prodigals not only don't learn well from information, but we tend to rebel against it. On the journey to find my place in ministry, I had to eliminate everything that was not quite right in order to find what was. It can be a long and frustrating process for us prodigals. Prodigals usually have to experience and eliminate what is not true for them before they can discover what is true, especially when it comes to learning to live as a Christian. This means that those who are trying to help them have to allow them to make mistakes and try things that may not be fruitful. We must always accept them with compassion and grace and try not to rescue or judge them. At the same time, we can try to lead them towards learning experiences to find the truth.

> *"If they had a social gospel in the days of the prodigal son, somebody would have given him a bed and a sandwich and he never would have gone home."*
> ~ Dr. Vance Havner [2]

I have found that most people with compulsive and impulsive personalities are prodigals. I think we are born that way. We have a mysterious compulsion to explore life's limits. Some kids will not even climb onto the first branch of a tree, while others will not stop until they reach the highest branch possible. They have to know what it will feel like, to see if there will be a rush. These are the "go for it" kids. As a prodigal, I have been in the hospital—a lot. As I said, we have to try things for ourselves! The good news is that when prodigals do finally "get it" they can become amazing Christians. When they finally find their truth, they are all in.

The prodigals I have worked with are very much this way. They are not afraid to take risks and try new things; in fact, they make great missionaries! Since they typically don't like to stay inside the box and aren't generally confined by rules, they can actually become pioneers—real change agents in the Church, if we let them. Those who do not like change, or need to be in control, prodigals can be very threatening. Not everyone likes change, so throughout history change agents have typically had a hard time.

> *"When patterns are broken, new worlds emerge."*
> ~ "Tuli" Kupferberg [3]

PRINCIPLE 3: THE MYSTERY OF CHANGE

Cathy and I spent the next seven years volunteering at a drug rehabilitation center in Santa Cruz, trying to learn how to help addicts get well. The main thing I learned was that all of the people we tried to help had one thing in common—they had all become someone they didn't want to be, and ended up somewhere they hadn't intended to go. Whether mental patients, drug addicts, those in cults, homeless street people, food addicts, or even rageaholics (those addicted to anger), they all wanted to change, but were not able to. In trying to solve this mystery, I realized that understanding begins by asking the right question. As human beings, when we want to change, why we are not able to change?

After nine years of pioneering ministries and working alongside other agencies trying to help hurting people, I realized I still had no clue how to really help those who wanted to change, be able to change. Some, of course, met Christ and had a miraculous transformation, but most were still struggling to get free. Bible study, prayer, or just getting them off the streets wasn't enough. Something was still missing.

> **KEY thought** — God will free us from our judgments, prejudices, and fears by moving us towards them.

In 1987, we were called to missions. We sold most everything we owned and joined Youth With A Mission (YWAM). Just before leaving, I was having doubts about whether God was really calling us to do this. Our life was going pretty well where we were and we had just adopted a new baby. Being a prodigal, I was worried about what my future learning curve might look like. So, I made this deal with God. I told Him, "Okay God, I'll go. But this is the deal—I'm an introvert with ADD, so don't put me in a large city. I hate big cities. I'm an evangelist; so don't put me in any kind of counseling ministry, because I don't want to listen to people snivel all day. You know I work construction and race motorcycles, so don't put me in anything that has to do with homosexuals, because I can't relate."

He didn't say anything, so I figured He acquiesced to my request! Well, we ended up in the inner city of London counseling homosexuals. I learned an important lesson about working with God—He will free us from our judgments, prejudices, and fears by moving us towards them. I would have rather been healed and delivered, but when we are just delivered we don't learn much about how to help or gain empathy for those who still struggle. This experience taught me a very important prodigal lesson—we have to be careful about rescuing people from their trials, because their trials may be freeing lessons from God. I needed to learn that lesson in order to progress in the ministry of helping hurting people change.

After going through the basic missionary training schools, we worked with prostitutes in the Philippines and addicts in Singapore. We smuggled Bibles into China and finally ended up in inner city London. I believed that since we had made so many sacrifices to become missionaries, God was going to anoint us with some special power. I believed that if we prayed for people and led Bible studies, then they would be healed and delivered from their problems. Like so many Christians, we thought we could just love people out of their self-destruction. Not only did we not see much fruit from our efforts, many of those we were trying to help either died or ended up in prison.

> *"Energy and persistence conquer all things."*
> ~ Benjamin Franklin

Confused and very discouraged, I concluded that what I needed was more education. I went back to the States and went through the YWAM Addictive Behavior Counseling School and later graduated from the Bethany College Addictions Counselors Program. I passed the state and national exams and became a certified addictions counselor. Finally, with all of this education, we felt we were ready to open our own rehabilitation center. YWAM had a building in Santa Barbara, California, that was offered to us to start a residential drug and alcohol rehabilitation program. There was a lot at stake, as it was the first one of its kind for YWAM.

At the rehab, we worked with some of the most difficult addicts in the area. Most were under California's "Three Strikes Law," which meant that if they were convicted of one more felony, they would serve a mandatory prison term of twenty-five years. Many of the women we worked with had children that were in protective custody. One more relapse meant that they would lose their children permanently. These clients had the most consequential pressure that society could place on them and they should have been very motivated to change and not relapse. Yet once again, we saw very little lasting recovery and real freedom. Many of them relapsed; some died, or went back to prison. It was very discouraging.

The turning point for our ministry came one night when I got a phone call from one of my ex-clients. She was loaded on drugs and started cussing me out, telling me how stupid we were. She ended the call by informing me that most of the addicts in our program were using. We tested everyone and found it was true. Most of our clients and one of our staff members tested positive. We felt so humiliated, naïve, and stupid! We had to start all over again. So much hard work and sacrifice—we felt it was all for nothing.

> *"Men's best successes come after their disappointments."*
> ~ Henry Ward Beecher [4]

PRINCIPLE 4: WHY WE DO WHAT WE DON'T WANT TO DO

The day after discovering the widespread drug use in our program, I went down to the beach to tell God all the things He wasn't doing right. I was very confused, frustrated, and angry. I wondered why He would call us into this ministry when it seemed like we were doing more harm than good. The people who came to us for help weren't getting better. I told God that if He didn't give me something that worked, I was not going to do this anymore. He answered my empty threat with a question, "Michael, why do people do the very thing they do not want to do?" I replied, "I don't know." I waited for Him to answer, but that was all He said. I was back at square one with the mystery of Romans 7—what keeps us from being able to change our self destructive behaviors? Being a prodigal, I started to understand that this was the way it was going to be for me—failing and then trying to figure out why.

> **KEY thought** We learn more from our failures than our successes. It is the difficult trials in our lives that define us.

> *"Affliction is a spiritual physic for the soul, and is compared to a furnace, for as gold is tried and purified therein, so men are proved and either purified from their dross, and fitted for good uses, or else entirely burnt up and undone forever."*
> ~ Wellins Calcott [5]

As I wrestled with that question for a couple of days, I began to see that until we could answer the question, "Why do we as human beings continue to do the very thing that we don't want to do," we would not be able to come up with an effective treatment program for self-destructive behavior. How could we, if we did not even understand what was broken? I was back to where I started from: people want to change, but are unable to.

The fourth principle is based on Romans 7 and the question, *"Why do*

I do the very thing I don't want to do?" Even Paul suffered from this dilemma. Essentially he said, "In my mind I want to serve the law of God and do what is right. But in my behavior I keep doing the very thing I do not want to do." Paul's conclusion in Romans 7:20 is that if he was doing the very thing he didn't want to do, then it wasn't him doing it. Paul is saying that this phenomenon is a mystery. He realized that there was something stronger than his conscious self and his good intentions, something he called "sin" that was causing him to do the very thing he did not want to do. In Greek, the word for sin (*hamartia*) simply means, "missing the mark." Imagine shooting an arrow at a target, but instead of hitting the target, the arrow goes wildly off course every time you shoot it. You literally end up shooting yourself in the foot. Paul was perplexed with the struggle between the two natures that fought within him—the one that desired to do good, and the other that wanted to sin.

I like ideas and Scriptures that challenge my theology and make me think outside the box—Romans 7 is one of them. This text messes up a lot of our theology because Paul had some of the most powerful attributes that God gave to mankind to overcome sin (destructive behavior). Paul had tremendous discipline, intelligence, willpower, good intentions, faith, and a solid relationship with God. Many of our Christian ideas about rehabilitation are based on the above attributes. However, in spite of all these strengths, he kept doing the very thing he did not want to do—sinning. In other words, he had an addiction—a loss of control. So, if Paul couldn't overcome his self-destructive (addictive) behavior with his outstanding strengths and attributes, then what is the answer for us? I began to probe for the answers to this mystery with a new zeal.

After much study and trial and error, I began to find the keys I was looking for within the world of brain research, where I gained more insight into understanding the Bible than I ever had before. For the first time being we are able to look into the brain (through brain scans) to understand what going on—which is enabling insight into what is broken and what works to bring about changes. Before we were guessing as to what is causing problems. Like trying to figure out what is the matter with a car without opening the hood. New understanding about the brain continues to confirm what the Bible has told us all along: transformation and freedom come from the renewing of our mind and deep changes in our heart. It has been a very rewarding journey. We will look deeper into this heart/brain connection in the next chapter.

I believe all of us have an addiction of some kind. All of us do things we know are not good for us—drugs and alcohol, food, sex, workaholism, TV, computers, stress, being fearful and controlling, anger, religiosity, lying, or just being judgmental and critical. If you know something is not good for you and it negatively affects those around you, then why don't you just stop? It turns out that our self-destructive coping behaviors are driven by a survival part of the brain that we have limited control of; we will learn more about the brain in the following chapter.

> *"Call it a clan, call it a network, call it a tribe, call it a family. Whatever you call it, whoever you are, you need one."*
> ~ Jane Howard [6]

PRINCIPLE 5: RELATIONSHIPS–THE MISSING PIECE OF THE PUZZLE

One night in a group session, as clients were telling their stories, I realized that I couldn't recall ever having met an addict with healthy relationships. Even the ones that had grown up in a fairly normal family had repressed painful memories and trauma. I was usually able to find what the client's addictive coping behaviors were anesthetizing. I began to wonder if what was driving self-destructive behavior had something to do with an inability to have healthy relationships. As I began looking into the field of brain research, I tried to see if I could find a correlation between addiction and relationships. What I discovered took me back to what I had started with in 1979—it's all about *the empty place*.

> "Now may the God of hope fill you with all joy and peace in believing, so that you will abound in hope by the power of the Holy Spirit." Romans 15:13

It was beginning to come together. Even though I knew that our destructive behaviors anesthetize the awareness of *the empty place*, I now had the scientific and biblical evidence to begin to understand "what is broken." Human beings don't function well when they are alone, isolated, and independent because God designed us in His own image for relationships—not just casual relationships, but intimate, close ones. You can be around a lot of people and still be lonely.

> **KEY thought** — Whatever we try to substitute for love and relationships we can never get enough of.

I believe isolation and loneliness is the root of what drives our self-destructive behavior. In other words, we were not made to be alone, yet there is an epidemic of loneliness in our country and world. Only when we have true intimacy with God and another person does our empty place begin to be filled, which results in functioning as a human being again. When our ability to give and receive love (intimacy) gets damaged, we have to find a way to cope with being alone and isolated, which results in living in a way we were not designed to.

Intimacy is achieved when someone understands your inner world with acceptance—a real understanding of what it's like to be you. We all need it, but few have it. Who really knows you—that is, your inner world? When we don't have genuinely close relationships with God or people, how do we cope? This is where a safe, open, and honest church can bring so much healing to people who are struggling with *the empty place*. A good church can help them develop and build true, intimate relationships, which will result in healing.

> *"I feel the need of relations and friendship, of affection,*
> *of friendly intercourse. I cannot miss these things without feeling,*
> *as does any other intelligent man, a void and a deep need."*
> ~ Vincent van Gogh

In 1996, I was offered the position of director of the recovery programs at the Santa Barbara Rescue Mission. I had a large budget and a staff of twenty-five, with fifty-five male clients and thirty-five female clients, who were some of the most relapse-prone addicts. The rescue missions are pretty much the last rungs on the ladder for help. This was my chance to apply all that I was learning about addiction from both a biblical and neurological perspective. It was my opportunity to unravel this mystery of self-destructive addictive behavior and relapse in what would be akin to the intensive care ward at a hospital.

It was in this setting that my first book, *The Genesis Process for Relapse Prevention*, was written. I was able to apply what I had been re-searching and get direct feedback from both staff and clients as to what was working. In the clinical trials, we experienced remarkable results with fifty relapse-prone clients—our recovery rates went from less than 3 percent to 68.5 percent. We knew we were finally on the right track and had something that worked. The program was so successful that I left the rescue mission to train others full-time in 2001. That brings us to the next principle in my journey, which is how the church fits into the process of restoring broken human beings.

* "And those are the ones on whom seed was sown on the good soil; and they hear the word and accept it and bear fruit, thirty, sixty, and a hundredfold." Mark 4:20

> *"The purpose of human life is to serve, and to show compassion and the will to help others. Life becomes harder for us when we live for others, but it also becomes richer and happier."*
> ~ Albert Schweitzer [7]

PRINCIPLE 6: THE CHURCH'S ROLE IN RESTORATION

While on my morning prayer walk in 2004, I believe God spoke to me again. He said, "Michael, the people that you care about (the hurting and addicted), are not going to be successful without the church." At first I tried to put it out of my mind, because many of the people I worked with (including my wife and I) often felt judged and out of place in church. Most of my clients gravitated toward 12-step meetings, where they not only felt safe and accepted, but also gained real help, grace, and understanding for their problems. Many of us in the rehabilitation ministry feel that there are those of us in the trenches (the Para-church organizations), and those in the churches who help support us—other than that, we really haven't work much together.

As I thought about it for the next couple of weeks, I began to see that God was right—He always is. I knew that people with addictions struggle for the first three or four months with a craving to return to their old coping behaviors. But once they have some success in sobriety, they are in the same boat with the rest of us—doing the harder work of learning to function and grow as a human being. Growing into our full potential and true identity as human beings is the main theme of the New Testament.

> **KEY thought** — Humans struggle with morals, values, and relationships.

Whether we are addicts or not, humans struggle in three main areas: morals, values, and relationships. I observed with my clients that a setback in any of these three areas could ignite the craving for relapse. I needed to find a community-based program that had good teaching, support, and accountability in these areas. I only found one—the church. This brings me back to the goal of this book: equipping churches to be *safe and effective* for helping wounded people heal. Let's look at each area in more depth.

> ". . . in that they show the work of the Law written in their hearts, their conscience bearing witness and their thoughts alternately accusing or else defending them." Romans 2:15

MORALS

We all struggle with morals—doing the right thing, being honest, and prioritizing God's principles in our lives. We can struggle with our moral principals and integrity in just about every aspect of life—within our families, our businesses, and our relationships to money and sex. Thankfully God provided something to help us in the area of morals—a conscience. Our conscience is basically an internal impulse to self-correct. I believe our conscience is the main way God speaks to us. Mine is always telling me to do the opposite of what I want to do, so it must not be me! Repetitive sin, secrets, and addictions numb our conscience, which can lead to denial and confusion about what is right and what is wrong.

> *About morals, I know only that what is moral is what you feel*
> *good after and what is immoral is what you feel bad after.*
> ~ Ernest Hemingway

Part of the Holy Spirit's healing role in our process of recovery is to restore our conscience in order for God to guide our lives and re-establish what is morally right and wrong for each one of us individually. Guilt and shame are the main active emotions of the conscience, motivating us to self-correct. Guilt is a bad feeling that God uses to help us become aware when we are doing something that is not good for us. Of course we have to be able to differentiate between false guilt and real guilt. For example, false guilt is the main emotion that drives co-dependency. Guilt and shame, like other painful emotions, alert us when something we are doing is wrong. We can choose to respond to or ignore our conscience, but if we ignore it for very long, it will no longer function. Paul talks about it as "having our conscience seared as with a branding iron" (1 Timothy 4:2). It is like scar tissue with no feeling.

A healthy conscience plays a key role in the process of recovery. We all struggle with morals in varying degrees of success, and some days are better than others. Safe individuals and churches understand and participate with the Holy Spirit's role in restoring a person's conscience, rather than trying to make people feel guilty by shaming them into wanting to change. It is a matter of conviction versus condemnation. Change comes from the inside out. We will look deeper into the role of religion and guilt later.

> "The kingdom of heaven is like a treasure hidden in the field, which a man found and hid again; and from joy over it he goes and sells all that he has and buys that field. Again, the kingdom of heaven is like a merchant seeking fine pearls, and upon finding one pearl of great value, he went and sold all that he had and bought it." Matthew 13:44–45

VALUES

Our values are one of the most powerful, overlooked areas in our lives that if neglected can cause us to lapse into destructive coping behaviors. Values also play a major role in the process of restoration. Simply defined, values are the things that are important to us. Consider for a moment what life would be like if we didn't have something of value to invest ourselves into. As Christians, what is valuable to us? The New Testament says that we are to invest our lives into the Kingdom of God. It tells us that the Kingdom is made up of things that fire cannot burn up and that everything else is wood, hay, and stubble (1 Corinthians 3:11–13). Of course, the only things that cannot burn up are eternal things, like people. We are to invest ourselves into people because God values them above all else. Life is good when our values and God's are the same.

> *When your values are clear to you,*
> *making decisions becomes easier.*
> ~ Roy E. Disney

Without clear values and knowing how to apply them, we tend to go through life feeling like we have no meaning or purpose. Once again the result is an emptiness. Over the years, I observed that the people I worked with who came out of darkness and pursued a life of meaning, purpose, and value were also the ones who had very little potential for relapse. In contrast, those who didn't find something important to invest their lives in (who just went through the motions every day), had a slim chance of staying sober long-term. We all need to find something to invest our life in to that is more important than ourselves. It brings out the best in us, and without it, we can easily fall into confusion, blaming, midlife crises, and a variety of empty pursuits. The church can be the place where lost people find their true identity and gifting by providing opportunities to invest themselves into others and leave what we all long for—a legacy. Ironically, we find ourselves through giving ourselves away. We will go in-depth into this important principle in the chapter on Spiritual Stagnation.

"Do not store up for yourselves treasures on earth, where moth and rust destroy, and where thieves break in and steal. But store up for yourselves treasures in heaven, where neither moth nor rust destroys, and where thieves do not break in or steal; for where your treasure is, there your heart will be also." Matthew 6:19–21

> **KEY thought** — Where one will fall, two will stand.

RELATIONSHIPS

The third area that we all struggle with is relationships. When I do the weekend personal change seminars, I always ask the question, "How many of you have no current struggles in your personal relationships?" Not one person ever raises their hand. Relationships are the most important thing in life and also the hardest.

> *Friend, there's no greater investment in life than in being a people builder. Relationships are more important than our accomplishments.*
> ~ Joel Osteen

In all these years of working with hurting, addictive people, I have found that the number one cause that drives self-destructive behaviors and relapse is poor relationships. Being involved in a destructive, painful relationship, or having no close relationships at all, leads to isolation and loneliness, which is always at the root of what drives us to not act like ourselves and do things that are not good for us. God designed us to get our needs met through healthy relationships with Him and others, so when we live in ways we are not designed to live; we have to find ways to cope, which can become habitual and destructive.

I was faced with a problem. If morals, values, and relationships are the areas my clients struggle with the most, and difficulties in any one area can cause them to relapse, then what program can I send them to that has the teaching, support, and accountability in all of these areas? There is only one that I know of—the church. I began to ask myself, "Whose problem is this?" I realized that if those of us in the helping ministries want our clients to be successful long-term, then it's up to me, and all Christians with a heart for wounded people, to create safe and effective churches. Those of us in the recovery world have the knowledge and experience to help people heal, and the church has the long-term resources. Together we can be effective. This sounds like a good partnership, doesn't it?

> **KEY thought** Programs by themselves don't work. What works in healing a broken person is when one person invests himself into another.

"Trying to do the Lord's work in your own strength is the most confusing, exhausting, and tedious of all work. But when you are filled with the Holy Spirit, then the ministry of Jesus just flows out of you."
~ Corrie ten Boom [8]

Only the church has the resources for the kind of one-on-one investment that it takes to restore a broken person. The rehabilitation of wounded people is a community project. Sobriety means to abstain—not to do it anymore—and this is the first part of recovery. Alcoholics Anonymous (AA) and other 12-step fellowships do a good job of supporting people to stay sober. But true recovery is returning to a former healthy state (i.e., back to the person you were before you were wounded by yourself and others). People who maintain sobriety, but don't really change, are called "dry drunks." If we give up an addictive coping behavior, but don't heal the underlying root cause, we have to find a new way to cope by trading one addiction for another. People in the recovery field call this "changing seats on the Titanic."

It is God, through Christ, who "restoreth my soul," and He mainly does that through His body, the church. While teaching the *Genesis*

Counselor Training Seminars at recovery agencies all over the world, I have consistently observed that program graduates who get involved in a church do much better long-term than those who don't. The best way to measure real "recovery" is by the health of our personal relationships.

The problem is a big one, but God is moving. Everywhere I go I meet one or two pastors who say that God has given them a heart to help hurting people and are eager to know how. Hurting people are often addicted people and can be the hardest to love. Yet, they are the ones who need it most. They don't trust anyone. When you think about it, our sin—our self-destructive, addictive behaviors—causes the pain that motivates most of us to seek Christ in the first place. That is where the church comes in. God will bring us people who are at the point of their greatest pain and shame. Do we have the grace, knowledge, and ability to help them?

> **KEY thought** — The hardest people to love can be the ones who need it most.

> *"Let us not be satisfied with just giving money. Money is not enough, money can be got, but they need your hearts to love them. So, spread your love everywhere you go."*
> ~ Mother Teresa

Viewing the church as a type of hospital can be difficult for many of us. It challenges the way some of us see Christianity and the role of the church. The church was not meant to be just a social get together for people who don't have any problems, but an effective hospital for broken people. Jesus tells us that He came not for the righteous, but for sinners. What an exciting place to be—where God is changing lives. When we grasp this concept, it challenges us to turn our churches into safe and *effective* places for God to send those who are the most desperate for help. To do that, we have to be honest with ourselves about what we believe and how it affects others and ourselves.

> **KEY thought** — It is not who we are—or even what we say we believe—that defines us. It is what we do.

In the next couple of chapters, we will look at the root of what drives destructive behavior and how some of our false beliefs may be hindering the healing process. If we want to be successful, we have to see hearts changed—both the hearts of seekers, and our own. Heart change is the foundational promise of the New Testament. It is a mystery and a miracle that we will explore throughout this book.

Change begins by asking the right questions. If we pretend that everything is just fine the way it is, we won't ask the right questions. It takes courage to ask the right questions, but it is the answers to hard questions that will bring the positive change that is so desperately needed. Believe me, there are more people in your church that need help than you probably realize. At the end of each chapter there are several questions for you to think about and answer—alone or in a group. While profound questions can make us uncomfortable, keep in mind that change begins from feeling discomfort. It takes courage to be brutally honest—it is a step of faith and God honors steps of faith.

> *"When you have no helpers, see your helpers in God.*
> *When you have many helpers, see God in all your helpers.*
> *When you have nothing but God, see all in God.*
> *When you have everything, see God in everything.*
> *Under all conditions, stay thy heart only on the Lord."*
> ~ Charles H. Spurgeon [9]

RESTORATION AND GRACE: A TRUE STORY

Dear Michael,

After my divorce, people in my church changed toward me even though I had been established in the ministry for many years, especially with children. That denomination believes that divorce is never okay except for adultery. It was the unforgivable sin. My husband was very abusive both physically and sexually and did not want to change. When I needed them the most, my old friends became distant and cool to me. I'm not sure what hurt worse—the divorce or the rejection by my church and friends. I began to search for a safe place to heal. I found a church with a divorce care group and after attending became aware of a restoration program and a singles conference at another church. I went and my eyes were opened! I was amazed at how the teaching there mirrored my own experience of shame and my need for grace. I joined a small group led by the singles pastor and began the Genesis Process experience. I was blessed to get my breakthrough fairly early in the process. I think it was the atmosphere of unconditional acceptance and support that made the biggest difference.

That was six years ago. I now facilitate a *Change Group*, and with God's help have seen many wonderful changes in others and myself in my group. I don't know where I'd be if I hadn't found this church that accepted me where I was and had a program to minister to my wounds. It has changed me completely. My ministry to singles continues. Last year I was married to a wonderful supportive man.

Thank you Michael,

Linda

SELF-DISCOVERY QUESTIONS

1. Why is it so hard to change our problem behaviors? What are some of yours? What have you done to try and change?

2. Discuss the idea that all addictions primarily do the same thing: they temporarily anesthetize the awareness of *the empty place*.

3. Why are some people so hard to love and help? Think of someone. If you could see their hearts, what might be behind their behaviors?

4. How are you investing your life into what is valuable to you?

PRACTICAL APPLICATION

Think of someone in your life who is difficult and struggling. Go and find a way to extend acceptance and friendship to them.

PART II: WHAT'S BROKEN

Chapter Two: What's Broken?
Chapter Three: Learning to Trust Again
Chapter Four: Addiction–Sin or Disease?
Chapter Five: Secrets and Freedom
Summary of What's Broken?

CHAPTER TWO

WHAT'S BROKEN?

"Being unwanted, unloved, uncared for, forgotten by everybody, I think that is a much greater hunger, a much greater poverty than the person who has nothing to eat."
~ Mother Teresa

> **KEY thought** Human beings are the only creatures in the observable universe that continue a self-destructive behavior regardless of the consequences.

"When you can stop, you don't want to, and when you want to stop, you can't..."
~ Luke Davies [1]

THE MYSTERY OF OUR SELF-DESTRUCTIVE BEHAVIOR

It seems to be part of our human nature to harm our selves, whether consciously, or unconsciously. We overeat, overwork, over-medicate, over-sex, overspend, and stress ourselves with worry and anxiety seemingly without concern about how we are affecting our selves and those around us. We tend to doubt or ignore medical research and the negative signals from our own bodies. Our consciences warn us, as well as those who care about us, but we ignore their warnings, continuing in self-destructive behaviors, sometimes to the point of death. Even ants and rats are smarter than that! If an ant does something that is painful or unproductive to itself or colony, it will learn and stop doing it. Similarly, rat poison only works for a short time. Rats quickly learn to avoid self-destruction and will stop eating the poison no matter how good it tastes.

As people, we tend to look down on some behaviors more than others. I think a good example is how Christians and society in general think about food addiction compared to drug, alcohol, or sex addiction. It is just as destructive as alcohol, drugs, or tobacco, and is also substance abuse, only with food. Obesity (food addiction) is now the number one killer in the United States. Approximately 33 percent of adults in the U.S. are considered overweight, and an additional 42 percent are medically obese. That adds up to about 75 percent of all adults who are self-destructive with food. Also about one fifth of elementary school children now considered medically obese.[2] Sadly, the United States is now the most obese country in the world.

Obesity is a very long, slow, painful, shameful, and expensive way to die. It also leads to other illnesses such as arthritis, heart disease, hypertension, bypass surgery, certain cancers (pancreas, kidney, prostate, endometrial, breast, and colon), and is the leading cause of Type 2 diabetes. The result is that it has the potential to bankrupt our nation's insurance and medical care systems, with the estimated annual cost at 190 billion dollars.[3] The real cost is actually many times that when you consider things like loss of productivity and the cost to the disability/welfare system. But, in spite of all this overwhelming information, we continue to overeat! Why?

What is broken in us that we continue to be so self-destructive? As you will see, "what's broken" is the same in all of us. Admitting that "I am a food addict," or being honest about any other kinds of self-destructive behavior begins the process of change. The first step is to break through denial and self-justification. It is also the beginning of being able to help others without judgment. It seems so simple—why don't we learn to just stop and ask for help?

Many well-intentioned people don't understand why self-destructive people can't just "stop it." We scratch our heads and wonder why they don't simply make better choices, or why they continue to fall back into self-destructive lifestyles, despite good advice, Bible teaching and repeated prayer for deliverance. When our best efforts to help fail, we often blame the struggling individual, claiming that he or she simply lacked enough faith, or didn't want healing badly enough. In our hearts, we may even harbor judgments that the hurting person is weak and/or lacks intelligence. However, it is not that simple, as you can see from Selena's story.

SELENA'S FRUSTRATION

Dear Michael,

Thank you for the Change Groups. I have made real change, but have been told by people in my church that I don't need support groups like Genesis or Celebrate Recovery because God delivered me from meth and alcohol when I got saved. This is coming from people who love me, but don't understand addiction and how a person can't JUST STOP USING! They told me addicts/alcoholics don't even need medical detoxification, just prayer. It's kind of funny because the ones telling me this are very overweight and can't even stick with a diet!

Anyway, I was forbidden to continue my Genesis Group. In fact, I was a Genesis facilitator and was told that if I come to church, while also attending Genesis sessions, I would be under two different "authorities," and that would cause me confusion. Don't get me wrong, I am firmly planted in my church, but their lack of understanding astounds me sometimes. For some reason, I feel like they don't want to understand. If anyone could claim they were delivered it would be me, but I know that I can't just name it and claim it.

I am coming up on six years of sobriety. I was a hardcore drinker/meth user and I still have "moments" where I get weak, but I know I can't really go to anyone in the church about it. I know I need support when the cravings come back. I've found other avenues—one was my local Rescue Mission, where I know the staff understands me and have the tools to get me through. There are a lot of hurting people in ALL the churches that need understanding, and we can't just sweep it under the "delivered" carpet.

In Him, One step-at-a-time,
Selena

> **KEY thought** Safe churches are those that understand "what's broken" in hurting, self-destructive people.

Unfortunately, Selena's story is quite common. In order for us to become safe, non-judgmental, effective helpers, we need a deeper understanding of what is actually broken. We ask ourselves, "What kind of monster would steal from loved ones, lie about almost everything, use drugs in front of their children, commit crimes against society, eat themselves to death, and betray the fragile hopes of their families over and over?" Well, wounded people—who are also often addicted people—ask the same sort of questions about themselves. Add to that the guilt they feel over not being able to keep their promises to God and you can imagine their painful inner world of shame and isolation. In order to find freedom, they need a deeper understanding of what's really broken.

To work with wounded and addicted individuals, we must understand that their problems involve more than just a lack of character, will power, or faith. There is actually a biological problem; a part of their brain is malfunctioning. To truly help people in the process of recovery, we must understand (and help them understand) how their brains are betraying them. When someone who is addicted understands what is malfunctioning in their brain and how it is driving them to do the things they hate, their sense of shame is greatly reduced. This is a crucial step in the recovery process because it has been my observation that recovery is increased as shame is decreased. These struggling individuals are now able to see that they are not monsters or stupid, weak people—instead, they are someone whose brain is not working properly. They are individuals who long to do good things in their lives, yet struggle against overwhelming urges that their brain is telling them are necessary for their survival.

This is not a new problem. In the Bible, Romans 7:15–26 shows us that Paul struggled with this very thing. In this passage, he asks himself some hard questions around this theme, "Why do I do the very thing I don't want to do?"

"For what I am doing, I do not understand, for I am not practicing what I would like to do, but I am doing the very thing I hate. But if I do the very thing I do not want to do, I agree with the Law, confessing that the Law is good. So now, no longer am I the one doing it, but sin, which dwells in me. For I know that nothing good dwells in me, that is, in my flesh; for the willing is present in me, but the doing of the good is not. For the good that I want, I do not do, but I practice the very evil that I do not want. But if I am doing the very thing I do not want, I am no longer the one doing it, but sin which dwells in me. I find then the principle that evil is present in me, the one who wants to do good. For I joyfully concur with the law of God in the inner man, but I see a different law in the members of my body, waging war against the law of my mind and making me a prisoner of the law of sin which is in my members. Wretched man that I am! Who will set me free from the body of this death? Thanks be to God through Jesus Christ our Lord! So then, on the one hand I myself with my mind am serving the law of God, but on the other, with my flesh the law of sin."

Essentially, Paul said, "In my mind I want to serve the Law of God and do what is right, but in my actions, I keep doing the very thing I do not want to do." Paul's conclusion in Romans 7:20 is that if he was doing the very thing he didn't want to do, then it wasn't him doing it. There was something within him that was stronger than his conscious self and his good intentions. It was "sin" that caused him to do the very thing he did not want to do. He was perplexed with the struggle between the two natures that battled within him.

> **KEY thought** — Safe people are open and honest about their own struggles.

HOW CAN WE HELP?

Naming addictive behaviors for what they are is imperative for making churches and individuals "safe" for struggling people. As long as we pretend "everything is fine," as many Americans have done in regards to obesity and other non-drug addictions, we won't affect positive change. Many of us are afraid to say anything because it might offend somebody. The truth is that all people with addictions will be offended (or at least become defensive) when confronted about their problem. They will feel judged and think we are being critical. But how many obese Christians look down on alcoholics or those who struggle with sex addiction? Biblically, are those behaviors worse than gluttony? Looking down or judging is the main behavior that makes us unsafe for people to seek us for help.

When we in the church are truly open and honest about our own problems, it makes us safe for others who struggle. Being honest without being judgmental is the most important characteristic of safe/effective people. My point is that we ignore some sins and come down hard on others. This kind of thinking is what the Bible refers to as "self-righteousness" and "hypocrisy." Who taught us to think this way? If I'm an alcoholic and you're 200 pounds overweight—what's the difference? We are both low-functioning human beings, dying of substance abuse.

Chronic overeating and obesity, like every other self-destructive behavior, ultimately points to *the empty place*, the place that can only be filled with loving relationships. Our churches won't be safe if we won't be open and honest about our own struggles. Of course, being open and honest must also include *effective* help and support. The two go together.

SAM'S STORY

Dear Michael,

My name is Sam and I had a problem with food. I was diagnosed as medically obese, about 150 pounds overweight. I tried unsuccessfully to lose weight for many years. My addiction to food caused me to become very depressed and isolated. I always felt that God had a calling and a ministry for me, yet I wouldn't step out because of shame and my physical limitations. I wanted to help others who, like me, were caught in behaviors that were sabotaging their lives. But how could I help them when I was not free myself?

Then my church started the Genesis Change Groups and I decided to take a chance. I came to realize that food was only the symptom, not the cause. As you say, it was filling emptiness. I would stuff myself until the empty feeling went away. It was subconscious. My change began from asking the right questions and a willingness to hear the answers. I can't tell you how frightening that was. But the group accepted me. I didn't feel judged and they supported me in stepping out, one fearful step at a time.

I found out that everyone has issues. Mine was just more obvious than most. I began to change, facing my fears. My craving for junk food began to decrease as I filled the "empty place" with relationships and service. I have lost 95 pounds so far and feel like I have my real life back. I am now running groups and teaching what I have learned at a local rehab. I've learned that God works through people, and I can't change alone.

Sam

> *"We cannot solve our problems with the same thinking we used when we created them."*
>
> ~ Albert Einstein

UNDERSTANDING BRAIN BASICS

In this section, I want to explore with you how the brain malfunctions to create addictions. Whether teaching about the brain or the Bible, I have learned that the simpler I make something, the more effective it is. So, let me try to make this as simple as possible. I have several suggested readings in the Notes section for those of you that want to explore the neuroscience of addiction on a deeper level.

In the many years that I have been working with severely self-destructive people, this understanding of "what's broken" has by far been the most helpful in inspiring successful recovery. But first we must define a few terms:

Addiction: To continue to do a self-destructive behavior in spite of the consequences; an inability to stop, a loss of control.

Sobriety: To abstain from an addictive behavior.

Recovery: To return to a former healthy state (i.e., "Who were you before you were hurt by yourself and others?"). Many people use the term "recovery" when they are actually in "sobriety."

INTRODUCING THE LIMBIC SYSTEM

Although several parts of the brain are involved with our conscious and subconscious survival behaviors, the part that causes us to do the very thing we don't want to do is called the limbic system. The limbic system is crucial in controlling the behaviors needed for our survival, I will often refer to it as our "survival brain."

The limbic system is located at the center of our brain. It is involved with our deepest beliefs and emotions. It controls our experiential memories, emotions, unconscious emotional learning, dreaming, attention, and our ability to feel pleasure and reward. The limbic system controls arousal and the expression of emotional, motivational, sexual, and social behavior, including the formation of loving attachments. It also controls our cravings for pleasure inducing drugs, food, sex, gambling, and other real or imagined survival needs. The limbic system is pretty much the source of how we feel and act.[4]

Psychology has been trying to solve this mystery of "why we do what we don't want to do" for over a hundred years. Psychologists affirm that there is a subconscious part of us that seems to control our behavior, reactions, emotions, and even our relationships. It is stronger and more powerful than the conscious mind, which reasons and makes decisions. This mysterious part of us is powerful enough to override our conscious mind, including our willpower, causing us to not act like ourselves. Trying to understand this mystery has been the challenge and the goal of my work with addicts.

The limbic system can be very difficult to re-program. For my clients, the consequence of not being able to change what drives their behaviors can result in a relapse leading to death or imprisonment. Change is not optional for them; it is life or death. Understanding the limbic survival system is critical to helping people change and experience real freedom, and for making churches safe and effective to help them. Through a scientific understanding of the limbic system, we gain new insight into how God works to change lives.

> **KEY thought** — If you want to change your self-destructive behaviors, you must change your heart.

"The best and most beautiful things in the world cannot be seen or even touched. They must be felt with the heart."
~ Helen Keller

A CHANGE OF HEART

The limbic system is also a large part of what the Bible calls "the heart." Pause and think about what comes to mind in Scripture, poetry, and songs about "the heart." We hear that we should follow our hearts, but we know if we're not careful, it might get broken. When someone says, "they had a change of heart," what was it that changed? Obviously, they are not talking about the muscle that beats in our chest; rather, it's about this mysterious center of ourselves from which our true self emanates.

• The Bible teaches a lot about the heart—the word is used about 735 times. For example, Jesus tells us that "the heart" can be desperately wicked, and Paul says the Word of God can change the thoughts and intentions of our heart. He also gives us an important understanding about the heart's role in the process of change. In Romans 10:9–10, he says, "If you confess with your mouth Jesus as Lord, and *believe* in your *heart* that God raised Him from the dead, you will be saved; for *with the heart a person believes*, resulting in righteousness, and with the mouth he confesses, resulting in salvation."

This important Scripture is key to understanding how we change our destructive behaviors. Paul says that with our hearts we believe, and what we believe results in how we act—righteousness.

In other words, if you want to change your behavior, you have to change your beliefs, which reside in your heart. One reason we have had so little success in changing self-destructive behavior is that we have tried to change it through our head using logic and information. It's this limbic system (our heart) that causes us, like Paul, to do the very thing we don't want to do. It is our survival brain. It doesn't respond very well to words only experiences. Science is now helping us understand the logistics of New Testament transformation.

"Despite everything,
I believe that people are really good at heart."
~ Anne Frank

The Old Testament focused on changing behaviors by adhering to the Laws of Judaism. The rules, rituals, and sacrifices were human efforts to be righteous before God. The thinking was that if they did everything right, God would bless them and answer their prayers. Most religions function on this precept of pleasing God by following the rules. It sounds like a good idea, except no one can do it 100 percent of the time. The Old Testament contains many examples of good human beings who were unable to change their hearts through self-effort.

The prophet Ezekiel foretold of a new edict that would be put into effect at some future time: "Moreover, I will give you a new heart and put a new spirit within you; and I will remove the heart of stone from your flesh and give you a heart of flesh (Ezekiel 36:26). This new Law, the New Covenant, was fulfilled through the coming of Jesus. When Jesus came to earth, he came with a new plan and message to humanity, which was essentially this: "Come to me just as you are, full of your sinful behaviors. You don't have to do anything. Simply ask me into your heart (limbic system) and I will begin to change your beliefs, which will begin the process of becoming free from the sinful, painful behaviors that drove you to seek me."

Changing the unconscious beliefs in our hearts that drive our self-destructive behavior usually begins with a spiritual awakening. The problem is that the beliefs driving our self-destructive behaviors and emotions are mostly subconscious and are almost impossible to see or change with our own self-effort.

Most of these limbic beliefs came from experiences, especially those in early childhood, and they can be very resistant to change. These early beliefs are like the rules or mandates we set up to run our life by. They are much like what the Bible calls vows. Knowledge and information are not very effective in changing limbic (heart) belief systems—only new experiences can change deep-rooted beliefs. The limbic system is programmed experientially, and thus must be reprogrammed (healed) experientially. In order to effectively help hurting people, it is important to have a basic understanding of how this limbic damage happens. In the next section, let's look at some of the origins of what drives self-destructive behavior.

> **KEY thought** Early childhood brain development can have a direct influence on what you struggle with later in life.

*"A torn jacket is soon mended,
but hard words bruise the heart of a child."*
~ Henry Wadsworth Longfellow

DAMAGE STARTS EARLY

In the first years of your life (especially the first year), the part of your brain that is developing deals with your ability to bond, trust, and relate to others. It is your survival brain—the limbic system. It learns from experiences, mostly with your caregivers, but also from your environment. During this period (mostly the first nine months), the brain makes a very simple decision—whether the world is safe, or dangerous—and wires itself accordingly.[5]

As a baby, you are completely dependent on others to survive and have your needs met. If you cry out and the need gets met in a comforting way, you will come to believe (limbicly) that having needs (being vulnerable) is a good thing because it results in a good experience. You have learned to believe that the world is safe. You can let your guard down and are able to receive comfort and gratification from others. Thus, your brain wires itself into a creative, exploratory brain, investigating the world around you.

However, if you are born into a dysfunctional, abusive, or addicted family, where your needs are not met, you will experience the world as unsafe, resulting in stress and fear. Researchers call this an environment of chronic inescapable stress—generating abuse, neglect, or both. Neglect (a lack of good things) can actually be worse on the developing brain than experiencing bad things. Fear and insecurity activates the unconscious survival brain (the limbic system), whose job it is to find ways to make the stress go away so that you can feel normal or okay. Remember, having needs makes you vulnerable. When crying out results in abuse or neglect, your brain learns that it is less painful to just take care of yourself. You come to subconsciously believe that others won't be there for you or don't like you, which results in what is called a survival (or hyper-vigilant) brain. The brain starts searching for anything that can make you feel normal or free of stress and attaches to it. Some psychologists call this "fear-bonding" versus "love" or "trust-bonding."

The developing brain has many more neurons than it needs. Its main job in the early years is to prune those neurons that are either not used or cause stress. The brain uses a steroid hormone called cortisol, which is a stress-related hormone that has many important functions in our bodies, but cortisol also seeks out and prunes unused or unwanted neurons. Mostly cortisol's role has to do with our "fight or flight" stress responses. Cortisol is released to help calm us down and minimize the damage done from adrenaline. As cortisol goes into the developing brain to calm it down, it also searches out and cuts off the neurons that are causing the stress.

In the case of the abused or neglected child, the limbic system will search for the source of the discomfort—in this case, relationships—and can decide that trusting relationships are bad because they cause fear and pain. Subsequently, the cortisol can prune off those neurons that give us the ability to bond, trust, and attach with others. Essentially, it is creating a survival belief that says, "If I don't need or trust anyone, then I won't be vulnerable and hurt." Psychology calls this kind of early relationship damage *Reactive Attachment Disorder*. (For on early childhood attachment see Note 4 from Chapter 13).

There have been many studies done on the children who come from neglectful orphanages in third world countries. Research has found that neglect can be more damaging than abuse. Many of these children have an attachment disorder, an inability to trust and bond with others. They can't give or show affection or appreciation. Children in these orphanages are mostly very quiet. They don't voice their needs. Their ability to have close relationships, trust, bond, and experience intimacy can be damaged for life. Probably the most affected emotion that gets damaged during this period is joy. Joy is our most powerful natural desire. Joy is produced when others—including God—are glad to be with us. Most people with an attachment disorder have a difficult time feeling emotions, like joy, love, empathy, happiness or even sincere remorse. Their self-identity and ability to have healthy relationships can be affected for life. We will look deeper into joy in the last chapter. All of this information is important in understanding what is broken, how it got broken, and how we can help wounded people get well.

STORY OF A BROKEN HEART

Several years ago, my wife and I were trying to adopt. Because we were counselors and thought we knew so much about attachment disorders, we felt that we would be able to effectively help and raise an abused child. Susan was a little girl we brought into our family through a foster-to-adopt program. She was five years old and had been satanically abused since birth. She had no ability to trust, bond, or give affection.

When we first met her, she seemed very sweet. We discovered the sweetness was an act she used to get her needs met. Our family would quickly learn how deep and devastating early childhood wounding can be. Susan got expelled from kindergarten because she was a threat the other children and the teacher couldn't handle her. She hoarded and hid food in her room because she didn't trust that anyone would take care of her. She had learned to survive on her own, trusting no one.

As a preschool teacher, my wife tried everything she knew to get Susan to respond. Susan could pretend to receive love, but her ability to give was broken. The effect on our family was devastating, and we began to doubt our ability to help her. With many tears, we realized we did not have what it would take to give her what she needed. It would take a miracle of God working through very patient, skilled, and loving people for her to recover to be the person God intended her to be. The damage was so deep she could only react to the world, rather than be part of it.

At the time, I was the director of a large recovery program, and was amazed at how Susan exhibited so many of the behaviors and attitudes of some of the worst addicts I had worked with—and she was only five years old. I remember giving her some lip balm for her chapped lips. She became instantly addicted to it and would lie and steal to get it, as if it were crack cocaine. Like Susan, many of the wounded and addicted people who seek help from agencies and churches have some degree of an attachment disorder. They have lost their ability to trust. They need a safe, grace-based atmosphere to learn to trust again.

> **KEY thought** Heart wounds don't just resolve themselves.

"Here bring your wounded hearts, here tell your anguish;
Earth has no sorrow that Heaven cannot heal."
~ Thomas More

HEALING HEART WOUNDS

Trusting and subsequent betrayal causes the initial damage. The bad news is that much of the trauma that is still controlling the lives of self-destructive people today happened in the first few years of their life, before they had the ability to process it.[6] The trauma became ingrained in their limbic (subconscious) survival brain in the form of a protective belief system. In the Genesis program, we call them "survival lies." Survival lies manifest themselves in protective or defensive personalities. By studying the brain, we have come to realize that time, by itself, doesn't heal these kinds of trauma memories, belief systems, and reactions. Heart or limbic wounds don't just go away by themselves. *The goal is to be able to move on in life through leaving the trauma behind, but glean the wisdom from it.*

"The mind replays what the heart cannot delete."
~ Unknown Author

Heart wounds have to be resolved. Because the limbic system (heart) learns from to experiences, it will take an opposite experience of safety and love to heal. Think about all the songs, books, music, movies, and poetry that are about trying to recover from betrayal, a broken heart, and learning to trust again. Are you beginning to see why creating churches full of safe, accepting individuals, along with effective programs, is so important?

> **KEY thought** — All addiction is self-gratification.

"True happiness . . . is not attained through self-gratification, but through fidelity to a worthy purpose."
~ Helen Keller

Trauma and abuse early in life creates an unconscious limbic reactive belief system that can continue to drive our emotions and behaviors as adults. This limbic system doesn't have a sense of time; it really doesn't know the difference between yesterday and forty years ago. It continues to react to events that are similar to the original traumatic experience, so we can continue to struggle with things like anxiety, anger, depression, and especially, self-control.[7] It is like having an invisible "button" that people can push to make you not act like yourself. Ever heard the term, "They really pushed my button"? In Genesis we have an exercise called, "Name That Button," where healing and freedom come from naming and removing the button.

This struggle of finding ways to cope is what predisposes us to self-gratifying coping behaviors. If you are unable to bond with, trust, and receive gratification from others, you have to learn to gratify yourself. This self-gratification is the very root of all addiction. If you want to understand self-destructive behavior and what it takes to get free, this statement is important: *All addiction is self-gratification.* This simple statement can be life changing for those who struggle. It is one of my essential bottom lines.

> "But I say, walk by the Spirit, and you will not gratify the desires of the flesh. For the desires of the flesh are against the Spirit, and the desires of the Spirit are against the flesh, for these are opposed to each other, to keep you from doing the things you want to do." Galatians 5:16–17

However, we can't just give up a coping self-gratification behavior and leave a void. If all addiction is self-gratification, then all recovery will require re-learning how to get one's needs met through relationships with God and others. God designed us to seek comfort, *gratification*, safety, understanding, and to grow through relationships with Him and other people, so that when we are down, lonely, lost, angry, or afraid, we are not trying to cope alone. Safe, fulfilling relationships give us what we need to heal the heart, the limbic system.

Understanding the brain science of addiction is important for the church because wounded people are often addicted people and the church is full of them. Their coping mechanisms have become habitual. In order for their limbic brains (hearts) to heal, they need opposite experiences from what wounded them. They need experiences of grace, acceptance, love, and safety. Remember that recovery is not becoming somebody new, but returning to a former healthy state—the person we were before we were wounded and found ways to cope with and avoid fear and pain.

> **KEY thought** Pain and fear, avoid it. Pleasure and reward, do it again. So goes the addictive brain.

THE SURVIVAL BRAIN

The survival brain has a separate and very different memory system from the conscious part of the brain. The limbic system records experiences that have to do with pleasure and reward, as well as pain and fear. These experiential memories are very important to our ability to survive. The limbic system sets up very powerful cognitive, emotional, and behavioral responses to avoid pain and fear. It tells us to simply avoid things that have caused fear and pain, and repeat things that give us pleasure and reward. This increases our ability to function and survive. When we do something that takes away stress and pain in order to function normally, the limbic system can associate such behavior with survival. It becomes part of the "do it again" craving, pleasure, and reward system. Once the brain has attached itself to a survival need, it is somewhat permanent. Addicts with years of sobriety say that even slight associations can bring back their cravings.

For example, if a particular person has hurt me, the limbic system will create the emotion anxiety telling me to be careful or to avoid what might hurt me again—in this case, a person. Similarly, if a dog bites me, I might have fear or get anxious around dogs until I have new experiences with nice dogs. It may take a while for me to trust people and dogs again, but with enough positive experiences, I'll get there. Even such mysterious behaviors, such as committing self-harm by cutting, and compulsive cleaning, can "limbicly" become associated with pleasure if those behaviors temporarily diminish emotional pain. When that happens, we are compelled to "do it again."

In my experience, there are five basic emotions that are so painful that the limbic heart can associate them with death and create powerful subconscious strategies to avoid them. They are shame, panic, abandonment, depression/hopeless despair, and rage. These emotions are especially powerful in our formative years and can feel like a total loss of control—death. For example, many of the anger/rageaholics I have worked with discovered that their anger is a protection to avoid shame. You can't be vulnerable or wrong when you are angry. Anger also keeps people at a distance so that they can't get close enough to see what is behind the anger—the fear of vulnerability and shame. In most cases, there was a time (for some reason in, my experience, around eight years old) where they experienced shame and made a subconscious vow that "I will never feel that again," thus anger. Have you ever heard someone say, "I was so embarrassed (ashamed) I thought I was going to die?" Many people who work in the field believe that shame is at the core of what drives self-destructive behavior.

Abandonment is another emotion from our childhood that can come from things like neglect or divorce and produce a powerful limbic survival imprint of not being able to survive alone. It can explain why women stay in abusive relationships, as the fear of abandonment can be greater than the fear of abuse or even death. Limbicly, the greater fear usually wins. Freedom from these kinds of emotional survival experiences and reactions requires heart healing.

> "Peace I leave with you; My peace I give to you; not as the world gives do I give to you. Do not let your heart be troubled, nor let it be fearful." John 14:27

Without this understanding of how self-destructive behaviors are connected to survival in the brain, it can be easy to pass judgment upon those who seem to repeatedly make bad choices. A common phrase addicts use to describe their experience is "use or die." This is indeed how addiction can feel—*if I don't numb the pain and fear, I won't survive.* A part of us believes we need "it" to survive. We need "it" to push these primal fears out of our awareness to feel normal and functional again. This is why we become so attached to self-destructive behaviors. It also explains why addicted people are also isolated and lonely people, as they don't want anyone to interfere with their coping behavior. There is a part of us that subconsciously *believes* that we will not survive without the coping addictive behavior. All that we are actually aware of is an overwhelming craving to just do it. This helps to explain why we do the very thing we don't want to do.

When we don't know what is broken in people, we can't understand how to help them. We usually resort to legalism and punishment, thinking this is the answer. However, punishment in and of itself doesn't work to make heart (limbic) changes. If it did, then prison would work. Failure to understand this truth leads to fear, abuse, control, and especially legalism, whereas understanding can lead to grace.

At times, we can feel helpless when dealing with broken individuals and their recurring self-destructive patterns. Sometimes, well-intending people use shame as a way to motivate others to change, but this is like trying to put out a fire with gasoline. In fact, shame can generate more of the very cravings we are trying to prevent! Of course there are natural consequences for our choices. The path to real healing is the removal of shame through compassionate understanding. Jesus is our role model for this. Read through the gospels and notice how Jesus interacted with broken (sinful) people. He removed their shame through love, hope, and compassion, and confronted those who tried to shame them. In helping wounded and addicted people, He is our model to follow.

> "It's the repetition of affirmations that leads to belief. And once that belief becomes a deep conviction, things begin to happen."
> ~ Muhammad Ali

He sent away the men who accused a woman of adultry / wrote in the sand (their sins)?

KEY thought — Survival belief systems are at the core of our self-destructive behaviors.

It is imperative to understand that it is not primarily the traumas of the past that continue to affect us. It is the distorted belief systems that the limbic system creates that are behind much of what drives our destructive emotions and behaviors. Let me give you an example. When I was 2½ years old, I was in a wagon racing another kid who was on a tricycle. My foot got caught in his front spokes, resulting in a spiral fracture of my femur. I was in traction for four months, during which time my mother and grandmother had to work, leaving me alone for most of the day. In those days, they didn't give kids pain medication, so I had to tough it out. After four months, they discovered that the doctors had set my leg wrong and had to re-break it. I had to go through the whole thing all over again.

Being alone at that young age and in pain forced me to find a way to cope. When I called out for help, no one came, which made me feel worse. So, I had to learn to manage by myself. What I (subconsciously) told myself in order to survive was, "I don't need anybody." In fact, my exact belief system was, "I'm all alone, no one cares, and I have to take care of myself." This belief system helped me survive and cope as a child by not being needy and disappointed. However, when I married, it sabotaged my capability for intimacy. I didn't need anybody. It's impossible to have intimacy without vulnerability.

In the Genesis Process, we call this a "limbic belief," or a "survival lie." I didn't discover this unconscious belief until I was in my forties. It helped me understand some of my self-sabotaging adult emotions and behaviors. It especially explained my fierce need for independence and inability to rely on others, or ask for help. The number one survival lie I have observed in those I work with is, "I don't need (trust) anyone." These belief systems form out of (real or imagined) trauma from abuse, neglect, and betrayal; i.e. pain, they affect our ability to live out of our true selves. One of the goals of the *Genesis Process Workbooks* is to identify these sabotaging survival lies and bring healing by replacing them with the truth from God. It is truly *The Truth* that sets us free—a healing of experiential memories.

> "And do not be conformed to this world, but be transformed by the renewing of your mind, so that you may prove what the will of God is, that which is good and acceptable and perfect." Romans 12:2

Uncovering and changing these predominantly subconscious survival beliefs is what can free us from the coping behaviors and reactions they produce. If you subconsciously (deep in your heart/limbic system) believe the survival lie, "I'm all alone, no one cares, and I have to take care of myself," how do you think it would affect you? How would you act and feel? In my case, I became extremely independent and couldn't ask for help, which caused ongoing problems with personal relationships. These survival belief systems are at the core of our self-sabotaging behaviors.

DEFENSIVE PERSONALITIES

Later in life, these survival beliefs can appear as false, or protective, personalities[8] and can manifest themselves as: anger, being invisible or emotionally numb, having an "I'm just fine" attitude, independence, self-righteousness, becoming a workaholic, or even becoming very religious—like a Pharisee.

We develop protective personalities to shield ourselves. In actuality, these false personalities are defense mechanisms designed to help us cope with the fear of trusting and being betrayed. They may manifest differently in different people, but they all do the same thing—they keep us from being vulnerable and hurt by others. Anger and defensiveness are the most common signs of someone exercising a defensive/protective personality.

I have discovered about a dozen of these defensive personalities in myself. Most of the time we don't realize that these protective personalities are there, because they are subconscious. They can negatively impact the people around us, especially when someone confronts us about how the personality is affecting them. You can probably think of personal incidences when you have tried to talk to someone about their behavior and got a defensive reaction that was not typical for them (i.e., you pushed their button). Understanding how these belief systems work can help you become more accepting with more grace towards difficult people by simply asking yourself, "What would that person have to believe to make them act that way?"

I remember a client named Jamie. When Jamie first began her recovery program with us, she had a protective personality of anger. At the core, Jamie was usually very sensitive and compassionate, but she had been sexually and physically abused throughout much of her childhood. To protect herself from having to trust people, Jamie could "turn on" anger at a moment's notice. She would "pop her cork" multiple times per day. Anger was a very effective tool for keeping others at arm's length. Everyone in her household was afraid to confront Jamie or correct her, which kept her safe from the shame of having made a mistake.

As Jamie learned to trust the staff and other women in the house, her anger subsided. Interestingly, another protective personality emerged. As the "Angry Woman" disappeared, "Saccharine Lady" appeared. When confronted, Jamie would no longer explode with anger. Instead, she would become sickly-sweet and kind of shy—an even more effective tool to protect her from being vulnerable. Her "sweetness" caused others to let her off the hook, which kept her safe from issues that Jamie wasn't ready to face. She discovered these were both childhood survival tools.

If you grow up in situations that result in "chronic, inescapable stress," the limbic system's radar searches for ways to reduce the stress to make you feel okay and able to function again. Addictions are not about feeling good or getting high, even though they may feel that way at the time. They are about finding ways to be free of stress and pain to gain a temporary feeling of normalcy and functionality. Feeling "normal" is associated with function and survival. *Addiction is not about feeling, it is about not feeling.*

You may be thinking, "What does all this have to do with the church?" Hang in there with me. You have to understand *what is broken* to be able to understand *what works* and *what doesn't* to bring change and healing.

> **KEY thought** Sin and addiction are driven by a unique survival emotion called a "craving."

CRAVINGS DRIVE GOOD AND BAD BEHAVIORS

Brain imaging research has identified three life areas that the limbic system is responsible for: food, sex, and safety. Can you think of any addictions that do not involve one or more of these areas? These three areas have to do with survival. The limbic system creates a unique emotion called a "craving" that focuses your attention until the survival desire, or need, is satisfied. Cravings are always associated with areas of survival, either real or imagined. Food and sex are obvious survival needs. If we cease to eat, we die. If we as a species don't procreate, we cease to continue. Safety is also a survival need, as it involves our ability to function and cope, which can become associated with such things as drugs, alcohol, money, overwork, anger, control, relationships, isolation, and religion. When you satisfy a craving for one of these things, a temporary sense of normalcy and peace emerges. So the brain says, "Do it again ... I need this to cope."

> *"Every habit he's ever had is still there in his body, lying dormant like flowers in the desert. Given the right conditions, all his old addictions would burst into full and luxuriant bloom."*
> ~ Margaret Atwood [9]

> **KEY thought** — Addictive coping behaviors are ways to temporarily feel normal.

The conscious mind can collaborate with the limbic system to help you avoid giving up a self-destructive coping behavior by using things like procrastination, denial, and even confusion. These behaviors can also become habitual because they reduce the fear and stress of having to change, or take action, making a person temporarily feel okay. Attempting to give up a coping behavior creates fear or anxiety, and the limbic system's job is to avoid them. Denial keeps an individual from acknowledging the problem at all. Procrastination avoids doing anything about the problem "now," thus temporarily reducing anxiety or fear. Confusion keeps an individual in a state of constantly seeking answers, rather than taking action. Are you beginning to see why we act the way we do?

To find freedom, we need to discover the root of our destructive coping behavior by asking and answering the questions:

- "What is the coping behavior there for?"
- "What do I get from this behavior?"
- "What triggers my acting this way?"
- "What would I experience if I gave up the behavior or substance?"

Once you discover and name the root of the behavior, there are many tools for treatment and healing. Real recovery begins when you can name what your coping behavior is there for.

> **KEY thought** — The biggest hindrance to change is self-justification.

SELF-JUSTIFICATION

Self-justification is the gatekeeper to recovery. Self-justification is a lot like denial, preventing you from starting the process of recovery. It is basically a lie that we choose to believe, preventing us from owning that we have a problem in the first place. For example, a "rageaholic" justifies his/her behavior by saying something like, "I wouldn't be angry if my wife would just get off my back," or, "If people would just leave me alone, I wouldn't have a problem." Or the classic for abusers is, "You made me do this to you."

Whether on a global or personal level, self-justification is like a wall that we cannot see beyond. It validates destructive behavior by employing a protective belief system. Whether it is addiction, cruelty, abuse, greed, or selfishness, self-justification endorses our right to do it. Self-justification usually appears as pride, but it is really about fear. We all know someone who can't apologize—it is always someone else's fault. Both sides of every conflict (including wars) are self-justified. The first step on the road to personal change is to ask for help to be able to see our self-justifications. We usually can't see it for ourselves. It can be a fearful process because self-justification protects us from having to give up our coping behaviors, which make us vulnerable, and is something we all try to avoid. It takes a safe person or group to make us *willing and able* to take this first step.

JOHN'S STORY

Hi Michael,

Remember me? My name is John and I am a chronic procrastinator. I have a long list of things I procrastinate about, but the main ones are smoking, exercise, and trying to work less. I make a plan to change and then I come up with what seems like a perfectly good reason to put it off. In my group, I have come to realize what I get from procrastination. I get a temporary sense of peace. I am anxious about changing and when I postpone change it is like taking a tranquilizer. I have become addicted to procrastination. I had no idea. I have a ways to go but the group keeps me accountable to do what I committed to do and I am moving forward.

The group has also helped me understand how my self justifications for my behaviors are a big part of my procrastination rituals. I had no idea how subconscious this whole process was.

Sincerely,

John

> **KEY thought** All addictions do primarily the same thing—they push unwanted thoughts, feelings, and memories temporarily out of our awareness.

OUTRUNNING MYSELF

Things we avoid wanting to feel, think about, or remember can cause emotions like anxiety, depression, anger, guilt, fear, and shame. These emotions interfere with our ability to function normally and the limbic system's job is to find ways to push the pain and fear out of our conscious awareness so we can function and get things done. Emotions, whether good or bad, can give you energy, change the way you feel, and become addictive. Getting energy from emotions can result in exhaustion.

Anything that changes the way you feel can become addictive. For example, in the brain, anxiety is neurochemically similar to cocaine—it speeds you up. Just like cocaine, anxiety can become addictive. This concept may come as a surprise. Most of us would say that we don't like anxiety and wish it wasn't there. Yet, many of us consistently set ourselves up to produce anxiety through worrying, stress, procrastination, perfectionism, expectations, or co-dependent rescuing. Anxiety can give us the energy to push away unwanted thoughts, memories, and fears. Anger is an even more powerful energy-producing emotion than anxiety. (See *The Faster Scale* in the Notes, Chapter 5, for more about how we get anesthetizing energy from emotions and how it leads to relapse).

GETTING UP THE HILL

A good example of getting energy from emotions is what Cathy and I call, "*getting up the hill.*" I was on a bike ride one day and not feeling very good.

We live in the mountains so everything is up or down. I was about half way up this long climb and decided go to the next bend and turn around; I just didn't have it that day. Well this little dog (some kind of Doberman sub-species) started running along side me behind a fence, yapping. It finally got out and came up and bit me. I got off my bike a tried to stomp it, but it was really fast and I had my carbon bike shoes on that are hard to walk in. Finally the owner came out and got the dog, begging me not to sue her. I was mad as my leg was bleeding and my new socks where all stained, so I told her to take the dog and lock it up. I got back on my bike and all of a sudden I was at the top of the hill and was feeling pretty good and decided to go ahead and climb up to the next town. About twenty minutes later, when the anger wore off, I was starting to feel bad again right in the middle of the last climb. Well I started thinking, "on the way back if that little dog just happened to run out in the road (after I did a little whistle) I have these skinny super hard tires that could cut that nasty little dog in half and it wouldn't be my fault because it was in the road." All of as sudden I was up the hill at Starbucks. So now when we are having a bad day and need some energy we say, "who did you use to get up the hill today." We have several favorite resentments (people or situations that we are still angry about) we can always pull up to help us get the energy to push through. We laugh because even knowing all this we don't realize we are doing it at the time. Getting energy and anesthetizing pain with emotions is usually subconscious and can become habitual.

One of my clients was a woman named Maryanne. Even though Maryanne was solid in her sobriety and had several months of "clean time" from pain pills and meth, she was addicted to caffeine-loaded energy drinks. She used her very limited welfare money to buy them, and she hid them to ensure that no one questioned her about it. One day, a staff member was driving her to a counseling appointment with her therapist. Maryanne asked the staff member to pull into the gas station so she could buy an energy drink. Instead, the staff member asked her, "Have you noticed when you seem to crave energy drinks the most?"

Maryanne suddenly realized that she craved caffeine the most when she was about to discuss her past, which had been quite traumatic. Every time she had to delve into frightening memories or face feelings, she felt an overwhelming urge for caffeine. "But why would I want caffeine, which causes even more anxiety?" she asked. "I don't get it." She soon recognized how her limbic brain was attempting to keep her "safe" by creating a craving for caffeine, which sped her up—so that scary thoughts and memories were temporarily pushed out of her awareness. She realized that speeding up with caffeine gave her a feeling of confidence just like her meth did. Once she identified this pattern, she was able to deal with her fears in more positive ways, by slowing down, asking herself what was really bothering her, and talking about her feelings with safe people, who took care not to overwhelm her. Her craving for caffeine is nearly gone. We got to what it was there for.

> **KEY thought** Anything that speeds up the body dulls the awareness of physical and emotional pain.

THE NEUROCHEMICALS OF THE BRAIN

For most people, getting energy from their emotions is totally subconscious because the parts of our brain that control these chemicals and the emotions they produce are subconscious. Knowing how these neurochemicals function will give you a basic understanding of what drives individuals to self-destructive behavior, which will lead you to being able to help. People will trust you if they think you know what you are talking about. There are two main neurochemicals that we subconsciously manipulate to accomplish this process of self-anesthetizing: dopamine and serotonin.

"GOT TO HAVE IT!" DOPAMINE

Most habit-forming drugs like alcohol, cocaine, caffeine, nicotine, and carbohydrates—as well as emotions, like anxiety, fear, anger, and stress—increase dopamine. Dopamine (DA) enhances attention and arousal, helping us to feel quicker, sharper, focused, in control, and confident. It's what produces much of our feelings of pleasure and reward. We all love dopamine. It makes us feel good. The more dopamine we have in our system, the more intense our experience. When DA raises enough, it releases adrenalin, which gives a rush that can be even more addicting.

Dopamine levels rise anytime our real or imagined survival is at stake. It focuses our attention on what is important for survival, and pushes back the awareness of information that is not wanted or needed. The hungrier we get, the more we can't think about anything but food. Dopamine says, "Got to have it to survive!" When our dopamine levels are low, we feel disconnected, unable to focus, and depressed, with a diminished sense of pleasure and reward. Dopamine speeds us up, making us feel alive and confident with an abundance of energy.

For example, sex and food can produce approximately 150 units of dopamine. Cocaine produces about 350 units, while Methamphetamine can produce up to 1,200 units of dopamine—six times more than the body can produce on its own. The more dopamine, the more the limbic system says, "Do it again." This new high level of functioning becomes our new normal. Anything that speeds up the body dulls the awareness of physical and emotional pain. Drugs, like cocaine and caffeine, speed us up, but so does stress, gambling, pornography, anger, anxiety, resentment, conflict, workaholism, worrying, fantasizing, video gaming, habitual profanity, perfectionism, food addiction, and even religiosity. All of these can raise dopamine levels and can become addictive.

"I'VE HAD ENOUGH!" SEROTONIN

If dopamine says, "Got to have it," serotonin says, "I've had enough!" Serotonin regulates the five senses, as well as sleep, aggression, and hunger. Low serotonin causes compulsivity to increase, resulting in insatiable cravings, an increase in anxiety, and especially depression. Raising serotonin decreases cravings by decreasing dopamine. Serotonin lets background information come forward into our attention. When our survival (real or imagined) feels threatened, the brain suppresses serotonin and keeps dopamine high (anxiety), so we can focus on what needs to be dealt with.

While dopamine keeps us up and focused; serotonin says, "Let's relax and think about other things." Recovery circles call this "running from the bear." We have this "bear" chasing us that is full of unwanted thoughts, feelings, and memories that we don't want to, or are not able to, deal with. So we speed up with dopamine to outrun them, and suppress serotonin to keep them out of our awareness. Think about how stressed and busy our society is. In some of my seminars I ask the question, "How many of you know you need to simplify your life?" About 80 percent of the participants raise their hands. Then I ask, "How many of you feel powerless to do so?" About the same number raise their hands. We have become addicted to stress (which speeds us up), and it is killing us, but there is a price to pay for getting energy from emotions. This unhealthy pattern of coping by speeding up is causing us to become serotonin depleted, resulting in a huge demand for SSRI's—Selective Serotonin Reuptake Inhibitors—like Prozac.

> **KEY thought** Understanding leads to empathy and effectiveness. Ignorance leads to condemnation and fear.

Remember, hurting people are often addicted people trying to cope with fear, pain, and depression. Having this knowledge can help make individuals and churches safe and effective. When people believe you really understand what is going on inside of them without judgment, they will begin to trust you. We can earn the right to introduce people to Christ because we are like Him. This trust is the first step to healing and recovery. It is a partnership. God usually heals people through people. An example of brain chemistry understanding is something my wife and I say to each other when we need some slack. When we are irritable or stressed we say, "I am out of coping chemicals." It helps us understand and extend grace.

"Trust is the fruit of a relationship in which you know you are loved."
~ Wm. Paul Young, *The Shack*

SELF-DISCOVERY QUESTIONS

1. Discuss the concept, "Why do we do the very things we don't want to do." What are the things you do that you wish you wouldn't do? Why don't you stop?

   _____
   _____
   _____
   _____

2. If you have a protective personality that keeps you from being vulnerable, what would it be called? How would you describe it?

   _____
   _____
   _____
   _____

3. What do you do to get energy that might be masking pain or fear (i.e., anxiety, stress, anger, etc.)? What do you do to cope?

   _____
   _____
   _____
   _____

PRACTICE APPLICATION

Think of someone you know that is self-destructive and share the things you have learned about "what is broken."

CHAPTER THREE

LEARNING TO TRUST AGAIN

> **KEY thought** The thing we need most is relationships.
> The thing we fear most is relationships.

To recap what we learned in the previous chapter, addictions and most self-destructive coping behaviors, do basically the same thing—they are anesthetics that dull the awareness of pain and fear. Most, if not all, of the pain and fear that drives addiction comes from relationships. The most common "double bind" that all humans experience is this: I need people, but people hurt me. Relationships that have resulted in abuse, neglect, and betrayal set up the brain to search for ways to cope and avoid getting hurt again. To avoid getting hurt again, the brain creates a craving to repeat whatever we did to cope (feel better) at the time. The limbic system is programmed to avoid pain and fear, learning from experience, not information. Thus, it creates defense systems to avoid relationships because they have produced pain and fear. Needing others, including God, makes us vulnerable and at risk for hurt and disappointment, so we learn to try and meet our own needs by self-gratifying. Most of us have limited, if any, awareness of this self-protective part of ourselves.

The parents of my generation (the baby boomers) were greatly influenced by the philosophies of Dr. Benjamin Spock and others. Dr. Spock's philosophy taught that infants were not to be "spoiled" by too much attention. Crying infants were to be ignored until their scheduled time to be cared for or fed. There are several popular Christian books that still follow this flawed philosophy. Think about it. How can you "spoil" an infant with too much love and care? It is no coincidence that our society has become much more self-destructive since the ascendance of this type of child-rearing philosophy. Drugs, divorce, violence, health issues, obesity, crime, sex, abortion, negative emotions, and mental illness have all increased exponentially. We have increasingly become a self-centered and self-gratifying society.

Babies cry because they are in some kind of discomfort. If they don't receive comfort (gratification) by their caregiver, then they learn to comfort themselves (self-gratify). This self-gratification can continue into adulthood. Many researchers and counselors now believe that it is during this early period that the foundation of our ability to have healthy relationships is formed. Trauma during this early formative period can predispose us to destructive, addictive behaviors. Remember, addictions are simply self-comforting survival behaviors.

Part of understanding "what's broken" in addicted and self-destructive individuals involves examining the core wounds that stem from relationships with the principal caregivers in our lives. Remember, the limbic system learns from experiences and must have new positive experiences to change its beliefs and reactions. Changing these survival beliefs is what sets us free from the negative behaviors that we created to cope. The church being a type of family can have a powerful effect on healing early family of origin wounds. Let's take a look at the role that mothers and fathers have in the lives of their children and how it can affect them as adults.

> "All that I am or ever hope to be, I owe to my angel mother."
> ~ Abraham Lincoln

A MOTHER'S ROLE

It is the mother's role in the first years of life to teach her children about how to give and receive love and affection. She teaches us how to bond, trust, and attach, which results in our willingness and ability to give and receive love. Her input is crucial to the formation of our ability to be vulnerable so we can get our needs met by trusting and reaching out to others. Much of our ability to feel and express empathy comes from our relationship with her. If we grow up in a home where her ability to nurture us was hindered, then later in life our ability to experience intimacy (being able to give and receive affection) and have healthy relationships is going to be, to some degree, impaired. I realized a few years ago that my daredevil risk taking personality came out of a need for my mother's attention and affection. I was constantly doing high-risk behaviors and getting hurt. It was a win-win situation for me. If I "made it" the reward was the rush, if I didn't, I got hurt and got my mother's affection and attention. We all need nurturing to be to grow into healthy adults. If we didn't get it we may have a hard time giving it.

God could not be everywhere, and therefore he made mothers.
~ Rudyard Kipling

Factors that can hinder a mother's ability to nurture include addiction, mental, emotional or physical illness, painful relationships, being single, or simply having to work. Her own needs may have been so overwhelming that she could not fully respond to her child's needs. During the first couple of years, a child's ability to communicate needs is limited. If a baby's cries are repeatedly met with abuse or neglect, rather than loving care, then the child will learn to self-gratify. This kind of self-taught survival gratification comes out of a diminished ability to depend on others, as well as an inability to give and receive affection. In psychological terms, this is called an "Attachment Disorder," which is simply a reduced ability to trust and care about others. Much of this limbic (heart) damage happens in the first year of life. Of course not all self-gratification is bad. Part of the maturing process is to develop ways to self-regulate and take care of ourselves. Much of this self-regulation takes place from two to three years old, sometimes known as the terrible two's.

As the percentage of both parents working and single mothers increase, the percentage of children in early childcare also increases. To some degree, these children will have to compete with others in order to get their needs met from someone other than their mother. As a result, their ability to give and receive affection, trust others, and bond in relationships is going to be affected. No matter how good the substitute care, it cannot adequately replace the mother's love and attention during these first two formative years. Both genetics and our home environment play a part in how much we are affected.

In the United States, we are undergoing a transformation of the family unit that is greatly affecting the lives of children—our next generation. For example, the percentage of children growing up in a home other than with their natural parents has been rising steadily. In addition, once largely limited to poor women and minorities, motherhood without marriage has settled deeply into middle-class America. According to Child Trends, a Washington D.C. research group that analyzes government data, the fastest growth in single motherhood over the last two decades has occurred among white women in their twenties, who have some college education, but no four-year degree.[1] The surge of births outside marriage among younger women—nearly two-thirds of children in the United States—are born to mothers under 30. Only 59 percent of women of all ages are married when they have children, meaning that 41 percent are now born out of wedlock. Sadly, of the children born to single mothers under the age of thirty, 53 percent are on welfare.

What does that mean for us as Christians and as a society? Researchers have consistently found that children born outside of marriage face elevated risks of falling into poverty, failing in school, suffering emotional and behavioral problems, and becoming involved with drugs and other high-risk behaviors. In other words, there will be a huge increase in people with self-gratifying problems. Why is this happening? Some of it comes from the fall-out of the feminist movement in the 60s, and is the resulting generational impact on women and their attitudes towards home and family. Today, many women are independently raising children, stemming from a hardened belief that they don't need to rely on men anymore. According to an article in the *New York Times*, one single mom was quoted saying, "Women used to rely on men, but we don't need to anymore. We support ourselves, and we support our kids." Does she really understand what she is saying? So many men and women have had such bad experiences trying to have committed relationships that they have simply given up. What will they do to cope, living in a way they are not designed to?

How is the Church going to respond effectively to this overwhelming tide of fatherless children and the growing lonely independence of single mothers stated above? How is the church going to counter this trend in a practical way to help? It's something we need to think about and plan for—with a relevant and effective Christianity. How would Jesus respond?

> "One father is more than a hundred schoolmasters."
> ~ George Herbert (1593–1633)[2]

"Moreover, we have all had human fathers who disciplined us and we respected them for it. How much more should we submit to the Father of spirits and live! They disciplined us for a little while as they thought best; but God disciplines us for our good, in order that we may share in his holiness. No discipline seems pleasant at the time, but painful. Later on, however, it produces a harvest of righteousness and peace for those who have been trained by It." Hebrews 12:9–11 (NIV)

A FATHER'S ROLE

Although the roles of mothers and fathers overlap in many areas, there are a few basic values (gifts) that only a father figure can give a child. It is a father's role, through love, discipline, and mentoring, to release us into our identity. In primitive cultures, this is called the "rite of passage." Men mentor and release boys into manhood through trials that allow them to face and overcome their fears. They also identify a boy's natural talent and train him in it. It is the father's job to help a child (both boys and girls), especially around puberty, to identify his or her special talents and gifts. Fathers naturally encourage children to "go for it," to take chances, while mothers are more protective, saying things like, "be careful." It is in taking risks and working hard that children discover their identity and potential. It is the father's role to recognize their children's attributes, as well as encourage and discipline them in the development of their talents and natural gifting.

> **KEY thought** ★ Discipline in love causes growth, but discipline in anger diminishes.

We can all identify with how important it is to have our father's approval. So, if you grow up without a father, or with a dysfunctional, abusive, disinterested, perfectionist, or emotionally absent one, you're likely to suffer uncertainty about the person you are and what you are worth. You may experience confusion about your identity, value, and special talents. As I stated above I became a risk taker. My biological father left when I was three and my stepfather was disinterested. I tried to find myself by having to constantly overcome fear. It became who I was, how I wanted others to value me. Think about the proliferation of high-risk and extreme activities just over the last decade.

Self-destructive behaviors (addiction), like drugs and sex, almost always begin at puberty; some things, like obesity and anti-social behavior, can begin much earlier. All of our unresolved childhood issues can begin to manifest when our hormones hit, along with the emotions they produce. Father-less young men and women at this age can avoid a life of pain by simply having a "big brother" type of mentor involved in their life during this crucial period. This is another area where the church can play such a vital role in intervening in a life of self-destructiveness. If most addiction begins at puberty, a program to mentor kids at this age with one-on-one "fathering" can help put a kid on a positive path. Big brother programs really do work, but unfortunately in our day and age there has to be good supervision to prevent inappropriate behavior.

> *"It is a wise father that knows his own child."*
> ~ William Shakespeare

KEY thought: If you don't know who you are or what you are worth, you will look for someone or something to tell you.

No matter how good a mother is she can never completely replace the role of a father. Many of the clients I've worked with, who did not have a father that released them into their identity, have spent their life looking for themselves in all the wrong places. I have a friend who teaches junior high school. I asked him what he believes to be the main thing that kids at that age struggle with. He answered, without hesitation, that they are seeking someone to tell him or her who they are. They will do almost anything to fit in and to have a sense of identity.

Remember, the limbic system records experiences both good and bad, pain and pleasure. It keeps an active file on our relationship experiences, especially with male authority figures. Therefore, those who have had hurtful fathers may have a history of conflict with authority, and may find it more difficult to trust God. God is usually presented as a male authority figure. The limbic system can put Him in the same file with our earthly male authority figures. I ask my clients, "When you think of male authority figures, do you come first come up with good or bad memories?" Many realize that they don't trust men or God. If you don't know who you are or what you're worth, it is easy to sell yourself cheaply. God can use us to help people find their worth.

Most of the clients I've worked with have a history of painful relationships, especially the women. I tell them that their "picker" is broken. They don't seem to have the ability to choose healthy people. I've facilitated many groups with women I call "Bad Boys and the Girls That Love Them." We explore why they are attracted to men who are not capable of intimacy or commitment. It seems to always come back to some sort of betrayal by male authority figures. In the group, they discover that "bad boys" are actually safe because they only have to give them their body, whereas a nice guy scares the hell out of them because they will have to trust them with their heart. They realize they will do anything to feel needed, which makes them easy to be taken advantage of. Of course "bad boys" are always in need of being saved from themselves.

> **KEY thought** Recovery is a process of learning to trust again.

"Learning to trust is one of life's most difficult tasks."
~ Isaac Watts [3]

RE-LEARNING TO TRUST

Remember, recovery is not becoming somebody new, but returning to a former healthy state. Ultimately, my "bottomist" bottom line for understanding the process of recovery is this: *Recovery is a process of learning to trust again.* When a person is learning to trust again, they are on the road to recovery. It was trusting followed by betrayal that started the process of fear and self-gratifying. Only when trusting is followed by reward will our hearts be healed.

> **KEY thought** — We can't change alone; we are designed for relationships.

The "survival brain" resists moving towards real or imagined fears unless there is a measure of safety. Facing these kinds of limbic fears (conscious or unconscious) alone is not safe. This is why so many people get stuck in the process of restoration. Change requires risk, which is very difficult to achieve without the support of God and others. Isolation is characteristic of most people with compulsive addictive behaviors. They have many fears and secrets.

Do you see why a seeker's first experience with church is so important? If they come to church and feel judged or rejected, they won't come back or experience the healing that Jesus promises. If they are to take the risk to face the issues and fears that drive their destructive behaviors, they must feel safe, supported, and encouraged, without the fear of judgment and rejection. Trying to control self-destructive behaviors without dealing with the underlying issues that drive them can be an exercise in futility and relapse. People usually just find a new way to cope, trading one addiction for another. They need grace and competency from a person or a church if they are to begin to trust again. Trusting is a huge risk.

> *"Change comes from taking risks, and the greatest risk is to be honest with yourself and others."*
> ~ Rick Warren, *The Purpose Driven Life*

This is why the Church is so important for the long-term rehabilitation of hurting and self-destructive people. Learning to trust again not only takes time, but it requires a focused and intentional plan to achieve real healing. In truth, none of us trusts God or people completely. We didn't start out that way—we learned not to trust. Recovery is the process of alleviating the fear of being hurt so that we can take the risk of trying to trust again. Nothing else really works.

> **KEY thought** The first step of healing wounds of betrayal, begins with God.

Since the limbic system (heart) is programmed through experiences, it doesn't respond to words very well. Healing the limbic system, along with the survival emotions and reactions it produces, can only come through opposite experiences—healing relationships. The traditional 12 Steps are a good example: the first three steps are about trusting God; the next two are about trusting a person (a sponsor), but programs in and of themselves don't work.[4] Recovery (healing what's broken) comes from one person investing himself into another person. Investing our time and resources into someone shows that he or she has value, which begins to rebuild the person's sense of worth. God does that through people. It is a process that takes long-term commitment.

Let's look at some interesting research that shows how important a safe community is in helping self-destructive people heal and experience freedom. Back in the 1970s, a man named Bruce Alexander challenged the hypotheses that addictions are merely a physical disease. Thousands of studies had been done claiming that addiction is solely a disease of the brain, mostly by putting rats in a cage with some drugs and noting that they'll repeatedly push the lever to take the drugs, even if it means starving to death.

→ Bruce Alexander was skeptical about these results. He noticed that the rats in the experiments were put alone in a boring cage with little else to do. "If I was trapped down alone in a cage," he thought,

"I'd probably want to get high too." So he built a *rat park*—a large, intricate, brightly painted, and heavily padded structure to actually make the rats happy. He put half the rats in the isolated cages and half in the park, giving both groups equal access to drugs. The rats in the isolated cages got addicted, while the rats in the park after trying the drugs stayed away. Then, even more strikingly, he took the rats in the cages that had fifty-seven days to get addicted to the drugs and put them in the park. The rats, even though they'd been addicted in the cage, suddenly stayed away from the drugs. They all voluntarily detoxed themselves—trembling and shaking, but still staying off the drugs. His conclusion: addiction is primarily a social disease.[5] Once again, it is all about the empty place. Like it or not, we are designed for relationships and we will self-destruct in some way when isolated and alone.

> • *"What should young people do with their lives today? Many things, obviously. But the most daring thing is to create stable communities in which the terrible disease of loneliness can be cured."*
>
> ~Kurt Vonnegut [6]

HEALING POWER OF JOY

I know from experience that a safe healing community can diminish the cravings for self-destructive behavior, but it takes a focused commitment. Just like in the "Rat Park," when we are living how we were designed to live, we don't need coping behaviors. It takes one caring person to invest their lives into another. Only the Church has the people—resources for that kind of investment. So, how can we make our churches and ourselves safe and effective to help hurting people heal? We need to find a way to give and receive the healing power of joy. Here is an excerpt taken from a new book called *Joy Starts Here* explaining the foundation of joy. I would recommend this book as a source of practical ways for individuals and churches to create an atmosphere of healing joy.

"A quick look at how our brain develops gives us a hint of why God rewards us with joy. Joyful interactions with our mothers, those who feed us, fathers and other primary caregivers shape the structure, chemistry and function of the brain. The foundation of joy that is built in our first year of life profoundly influences our identity and relationships throughout our lifespan. The capacities and chemistry that we use as infants become the dominant systems for our brains. If we start our life in fear, we will feel anxious about almost everything. But the brain is biased toward joy. Joy is our most powerful desire, and we are designed to seek joyful interactions automatically from birth. If we cannot find joy, we may try hard to bury our desire, but we can never escape joy's power. God built us this way." [7]

The church can be a community that heals a wounded heart by providing the experience of joy. In practical terms, joy is experienced when we feel that others are genuinely glad to be with us; when we feel appreciated and valued. We will look deeper into this principle in Part III "What Works." The next few chapters will focus on factors that can hinder the restoration process.

JANE'S STORY—LEARNING TO TRUST AGAIN

Dear Mr. Dye,

I was sexually abused by my grandfather when I was eight years old and by my minister when I was twelve years old. Then, when I was seventeen years old, another minister sexually abused me. I married at twenty-one years old and had four children. It was not until I was thirty-six that I could not keep things together anymore. I went forward in a church service because I absolutely hated my husband, and I felt that everything was my fault. Instead of the pastor shaking my hand and praying over me, he asked to talk with me after the service. He gave me a Taylor/Johnson Temperament Analysis[8] and had me fill it out during the afternoon.

I had a lot of anxiety around pastors, but I decided to take a chance, since I didn't get any sexual vibe from him. I met with him the next week. He talked for a long time and I could not figure out where he was going with the conversation. Eventually he said, "I can tell from the assessment that you have had some abuse in your life." I thought, "Who hasn't?" But he went on. At that point I had not remembered my grandfather's behavior or the first pastor's. I just felt I was very immoral for having relations with my second pastor.

During that weekend, I began to remember the memories about my grandfather. Now, at this point, I barely left my house, I avoided people and shopping all I could. I had panic attacks in the checkout lanes. My pastor would call me faithfully twice a week. He would just talk about anything. It wasn't counseling, but looking back, I knew he was really working hard at helping me stay with reality. I began to believe he really cared without wanting something.

I found a lady counselor at a rescue mission. She took me as a client for free because we did not have insurance to cover counseling. I was her last community client that she ever took. She directed me to a local recovery group. Those people were great. I would come in and stand at the back because the emotions were so great in me. When they broke up for small group, I would leave. No one crowded me or pushed me—they just let me be, and slowly I was able to join in, staying for the break out groups. They accepted me in spite of how I felt about myself. I eventually led a group myself, which was a big part of my healing. It was not one church that helped my recovery, but several. I thank God for His healing and how he had the right safe people, at the right place, and at the right time in my recovery. It all started by one person really caring. Thank you for letting me share this with you.

Jane

SELF-DISCOVERY QUESTIONS

1. How do you think your ways of coping during childhood are still affecting you today?
   _____
   _____
   _____

2. Do you trust men or women more? Why?
   _____
   _____
   _____

3. Who in your life has had the most positive influence on you? Why? What was it about them that made you trust them?
   _____
   _____
   _____

4. Rate your capacity for joy from 1 to 10, _10_. Where and when do you feel most appreciated?
   _____with my all girls small group_____
   _____
   _____

→ PRACTICAL APPLICATION

Seek out someone you know who is wounded and isolated with the intention of "being glad to be with them." See if you can bring "joy" into their life.

CHAPTER FOUR

ADDICTION: IS IT SIN OR DISEASE?

"Disease: A condition of the living animal or plant body or of one of its parts that impairs normal functioning and is typically manifested by distinguishing signs and symptoms."
~ Webster's Dictionary

As a recovering Pharisee, I try to avoid controversial theology. However, this is one area that needs to be addressed, as it can have a huge impact on those seeking help. In this chapter, I will show that there are certain religious doctrines that can hinder us from being effective in helping people heal. Some of these doctrines are inconsistent with the heart of the Gospel, which calls us to reach out and help those God brings to us. They can cause us to have a "my way or the highway" legalistic attitude, which can be a wall to those seeking help. Here is a story of how churches can sometimes turn away hurting people in need of help because of their strict adherence to their religious ideologies.

WHEN THE CHURCH HINDERS RECOVERY

Dear Michael,

After a ripping binge, I decided to go to an AA meeting and heard various people share their stories about how God had miraculously relieved a drink obsession that was beyond their control. I came with enough desperation, humiliation, and hopelessness to get on my knees and seek a God I did not believe in, and I received the radical miracle of sobriety, the Christian community would call this deliverance; I did not know that yet.

My drink and drug obsession, and the bondage to both, was lifted. I had a new strength that I could not explain. Immediately, I returned to the program to learn the tools that would help me maintain my sobriety and my sanity. Within a couple of years, my resentments toward God were lifted and I was introduced to Christ. At the age of twenty-seven, I found myself in church for the first time. Almost immediately I was told that I needed to leave those 12-step meetings because there were people there that would rob me of my faith, and that it wasn't Christian. I politely informed my new church mentor that the 12-step program I was in was the very tool God had used to introduce Himself to me and lead me to Christ. I felt that in turn I was now a missionary to the very organization that had saved my life. I was labeled as "rebellious" and told that I probably wasn't really saved. As I read the Bible, I became more confused, because Jesus wasn't like this.

I have been a Christian for twenty years and in my own personal recovery for twenty-two years. I am free to testify what God has done for me, but still careful about telling others that I attend 12-step meetings. My caution was confirmed at a church where I'd been bringing newcomers to hear the message of Christ. One of the leaders pulled aside a woman I'd brought with me and told her she didn't have to do "those meetings" anymore. Shortly afterwards, my protégé told me that she had Christ now and didn't need "those meetings" anymore. I cautioned her that if she did not get a solid foundation, including learning how to stay clean and sober and reaching out to get the support she needed, the chances were less than average that she would stay sober. Within a few months, this poor soul was drunk, divorced her husband, and has not been heard from since. It breaks my heart that the ignorance of this church and their leaders played a part in her destruction. I have heard many similar stories, and now I am very cautious about whom I bring to church.

Speaking of secret shame, I personally don't know anyone in a Protestant Christian church that is well equipped to listen to some of the degrading stories or confessions that addicts need to share to gain freedom from their addictions. Most church folk are shocked at the depth of depravity an addict will go to get their drugs or alcohol once truly addicted. I remember sharing my guilt over a past sin with one of my Bible study teachers. Her shock was so obvious. A wall of separation erected as I saw disgust written all over her face. Once more, I was feeling shamed for a crime I'd already suffered enough guilt and shame for. I learned not to share true confessions with anyone in the church that did not have a recovery background.

Frank

> **KEY thought** Safe churches are open to new understanding.

Frank's story is unfortunately all too common—I've heard it many times. I know many good churches that are able to work together with outside agencies as a part of a person's restoration process, but there are also many who have a one-dimensional view of how God is supposed to work. There are many "our way or the highway" churches that end up hurting the very people they are trying to help. I am a "whatever works" kind of guy. I've found in most cases that restoring a broken/addicted person is a community project. Let's look at one of the main Christian religious dogmas that can prevent grace and understanding.

> **KEY thought** There are doctrinal and denominational theologies that can hinder hurting people from getting well.

"Just cause you got the monkey off your back doesn't mean the circus has left town."

~ George Carlin, Comedian

ADDICTION—IS IT SIN OR DISEASE?

Over the past few years, I have worked with many churches and Christian agencies about how to help hurting and addicted people experience successful recovery. I have noticed that there is a religious perception that continues to come up, one that can sabotage the healing process for those struggling with self-destructive behaviors. The question is about whether addiction is a sin or a disease. Christians seem to be the only ones who have a problem with the idea that addiction is also a disease. If you go to any doctor in the world and admit that you are an alcoholic, he will say that you have a disease that will kill you in predictable ways and that he has no cure for you. He will tell you that addiction to alcohol has affected your brain, heart, and liver, and because you are becoming more and more damaged, you will eventually die from it. The problem is not proving that addiction is a disease scientifically; the problem is that many Christians don't want to admit that addiction is a disease out of fear that calling it one alleviates moral responsibility (sin).

Many religious people reject the physical and scientific evidence that addiction is a disease because it doesn't fit in with their theology. They tend to deny reality or change the way they think if it doesn't fit into their box of beliefs. But understanding this concept of addiction as a disease is of key importance because the way you see a problem determines how you will treat it. If addiction is solely a sin, then the cure, of course, is repentance—"Repent and the problem should go away." Unfortunately, we have all experienced times of repentance for our behaviors and attitudes without successful change. I wish it were that simple. I believe the main thing that can hinder hurting people from receiving help is feeling judged. The concept of sin can be fuel for judgment. With that in mind, let's look at this concept both biblically and scientifically, the goal being to help self-destructive people heal more effectively.

Excerpt taken from "Rethinking Addiction's Roots and Its Treatment," by Douglas Quenqua

> "There is an age-old debate over alcoholism: Is the problem in the sufferer's mind—something that can be overcome through willpower, spirituality, or talk therapy, perhaps—or is it a physical

disease of the brain, one that needs continuing treatment in much the same way as, say, diabetes or epilepsy? Increasingly, the medical establishment is putting its weight behind the physical diagnosis. The rethinking of addiction as a medical disease rather than a strictly psychological one began about fifteen years ago, when researchers discovered through high-resonance imaging that drug addiction resulted in actual physical changes to the brain. Armed with that understanding, "the management of folks with addiction becomes very much like the management of other chronic diseases, such as asthma, hypertension, or diabetes," said Dr. Daniel Alford. Equally maligned is the idea that psychiatry or 12-step programs are adequate for curing a disease with physical roots. Many people who abuse substances do not have psychiatric problems. If the idea of addiction as a chronic disease has been slow to take hold in medical circles, it could be because doctors sometimes struggle to grasp brain function. Dr. Volkow said, "It is very simple to understand a disease of the heart. The heart is very simple. It's just a muscle. It's much more complex to understand the brain."[1]

Dr. Daniel Amen[2] is a pioneer in his work on brain imaging and has helped us gain new understanding about the brain, mental illness, and addiction. In his book, *Healing the Hardware of the Soul*, he writes that the brain is the mechanism by which our soul expresses itself. This is a very important idea because it helps to explain the enigma of our inner world. We all know that we have this good person in us that wants to do what's right, be humble, forgiving, and live in a way that our conscience and the Bible teaches us. But when this good part of us tries to express itself, it has to go through our brain—which has become damaged—resulting in a distortion in our thinking and behavior.[3]

Addiction is a chronic relapsing brain disease. Brain imaging shows that addiction severely alters brain areas critical to decision-making, learning, memory, and behavior control, which can help to explain the compulsive and destructive behaviors of addiction.[4] In many ways, we function like a computer. If our hard drive (that is, our brain) has become damaged, it doesn't matter what new programs we put into it—something distorted will come out on the screen. Our self-destructive behaviors work very much the same. No one wants to be addicted to anything. We all want to do things that make us feel good and be in control of how much we do and how long we do it. Most people with addictions hate their addiction and repent; they promise themselves and God on a regular basis they will stop. But when they try, they end up doing the very thing they don't want to do.

> **KEY thought** The limbic system controls our compulsive behavior and is what the Bible calls the "heart."

Addiction is simply defined as a loss of control. I believe all of us have an addiction or destructive coping behavior of some sort. I haven't met anyone that doesn't do something that they know is not good for them. If we know we are doing something that is not good for us then we should stop, so why don't we? In our society, we all know we should eat better, exercise more, not worry so much, be less judgmental, and just take better care of ourselves, but we keep getting worse. Paul wrote about this in Romans 7:19, basically saying, "In my mind I want to follow the Word of God, but in my behavior I do the very thing I do not want to do." So how and why does this happen? Let's look at how James saw this problem (parentheses are mine):

> "Let no one say when he is tempted, 'I am being tempted by God,' for God cannot be tempted by evil, and He Himself does not tempt anyone. But each one is tempted when he is carried away (a bad choice) and enticed by his own lust. Then when lust (desire) has conceived (given in to), it gives birth to sin (bad actions), and when sin is accomplished, it brings forth death (disease)." James 1:13–15

James had insight into the problem of addiction that took science two thousand years to understand. First, he says, "No one is tempted by God, but each one of us is tempted and enticed." I believe the main tool the enemy uses to gain control of us is temptation. Everyone is tempted. We all have something that we struggle with everyday, whether it is morals, food, honesty, money, sex, drugs, anger, work, shopping, TV, computers, judgmental thoughts, negative emotions (like anxiety), pride, gossip, control issues, or codependency. We all try not to give in to our temptations.

"I generally avoid temptation unless I can't resist it."
~ Mae West

"I can resist everything except temptation."
~ Oscar Wilde

> **KEY thought** Temptation is not a sin; neither is having a strong desire a sin.

"Is lust a sin?" I ask this question at most of the *Genesis Process* trainings, and participants usually respond with, "Of course lust is a sin." In actuality, lust is not a sin. Lust is an arousal emotion. Emotions by themselves are not sins. The Greek word for lust is *epithemia*, which means desire. It can be used for both good and bad desires. Lust is simply a strong desire, a great eagerness or enthusiasm for something. I could have a lust for righteousness, a lust for God's will, or even for missions. So what James is saying is that when we become tempted with something that we know is potentially harmful, we need to be careful. If we dwell on the temptation, it can turn into lust, a strong desire (emotion) for what is tempting us.

This is the stage where the battle is won or lost. Dwelling on a temptation is a bad choice, because it will turn into a craving. Eventually that strong desire will begin to take control of us—it wears us down. It compels us to act, and that is when we get into trouble. As desire or arousal increases in our brain, the prefrontal cortex that houses our morals and the ability to reason and consider consequences is diminished and can actually become unavailable. So, when we dwell on (or fantasize about) what is tempting us, it can turn into an overwhelming desire, which can give birth to sin, a bad action. Sin occurs when we act upon or give into a temptation. James says that when sin is conceived, it results in death—which is the disease, the result of sin. Of course not all disease is directly the result of sin, but disease from conscious bad choices is. Philosophically, all disease may be the result of sin, either by bad choices of others or ours.

> *"We gain the strength of the temptation we resist."*
> ~ Ralph Waldo Emerson

> **KEY thought** Addiction is the result of sin—a diseased brain that creates false cravings for non-survival behaviors and substances.

DISEASE IS THE RESULT OF SIN

"Is smoking a sin?" When I ask this question at trainings, I usually get mixed answers. Biblically it is. The Bible tells us, "He who knows the right thing to do and does it not, to him it is sin" (James 4:17). We all know that smoking is wrong. It harms the environment and us, it is costly, and does damage to those around us. But is lung cancer resulting from smoking a sin? As James would say, it's the consequence of the sin of smoking.

Let's look at another example: gluttony. Of course the Bible tells us that gluttony is a sin. But is the diabetes resulting from gluttony a sin? Can you just repent and make the diabetes go away? God gave us free will and there are consequences for our choices. Stay with me; we will get to how all this relates to safe churches in a moment. Understanding this disease concept will lead to grace, which is always the foundation of God's healing power in us.

What we tend to forget is that the brain is also an organ. The word "disease" simply means not to function in a normal, healthy way.

When an organ, such as the brain, doesn't function in a normal way, it is diseased. When our brains don't function normally, the result is that our thoughts, emotions, and actions—and especially reactions—will be distorted. Our brain can become diseased from continuing to make bad choices about things such as drugs, alcohol, sex, food, worry, or relationships. Even emotions, like anxiety, stress, resentment, bitterness, and anger, can cause brain damage, which can result in a loss of control in how we think, act, and feel. We can act and re-act in way that are not like ourselves.

Our brain can begin to associate a substance, behavior, or even an emotion with our ability to cope and survive. When we partake of toxic substances or coping behaviors, the main organ that it affects is the brain. We mostly do these self-destructive things to change the way we feel and function. As the brain begins to associate the coping substance or behavior with survival (real or imagined), the result is that our limbic system (the survival brain) starts to produce a strong survival emotion called a craving. A craving is produced when the brain associates something with survival. For example, if a person uses alcohol or nicotine when they are anxious or stressed, the brain begins to associate alcohol or nicotine with being able to cope and function during those times. So the next time the person feels anxiety or stress, a craving is produced for whatever substance was used previously to feel better. We will look deeper into how all this happens.

ART'S STORY

Dear Michael,

I don't know if you remember me—my name is Art and I talked to you during lunch at your weekend seminar. I have struggled with porn addiction most of my life. Well about a week ago, I was sitting in my living room reading, when out the blue I had an overwhelming urge to go on my computer and look at some porn. It was like you said; it felt like a nail being drawn to a magnet. I resisted it for a while, but in spite of what my mind was telling me, I knew in a deeper place I was going to do it. I relapsed, but for the first time I was able to observe this battle between my two selves. And like Paul, it was like not me doing it. I can see now where a thought or urge becomes a powerful craving that takes me to a place I really don't want to go. One part of me sees the porn as disgusting, but another part is totally excited and filled with pleasure. I never had been aware of this phenomenon before. Even though I gave in that time, I am doing so much better. I realize that my battle is won or lost with that first subtle thought/temptation. Once I dwell on, or what I call "play with the thought," I become powerless. Thanks. I feel I have a tool that I can use to fight this battle.

Art

> **KEY thought** — All mental and emotional illness, including addiction, is driven by brain damage.

> *Remember that your brain is involved in everything you do, every decision you make, every bite of food you take, every cigarette you smoke, every worrisome thought you have, every workout you skip, every alcoholic beverage you drink, and more.*
> ~ Dr. Daniel G. Amen, *Change Your Brain, Change Your Life.* [5]

THE CRAVING BRAIN

The brain is designed to produce natural cravings for the three main areas of survival: food, sex, and safety. So when the brain begins to associate drugs or addictive behaviors, like anger, rage, workaholism, compulsive cleaning, nail biting, pornography, bulimia, or social media addiction with safety (the ability to cope and function), then the brain has become diseased and doesn't function normally. A brain in this state craves things that are actually bad for us. It can also distort natural cravings for things like sex and food to the point of becoming deadly. A diseased and addicted brain can produce distorted thoughts and emotions that are not related to reality and circumstances, causing us to not act like ourselves.

One common example of this is food addiction: Why do we have cravings for food when we're not hungry? The craving feels like hunger, yet we're not low on blood sugar—but we eat anyway. What's happening is that the brain is malfunctioning and compels us to keep eating even when we are full. Food is not just food to us anymore; it has now become a coping substance for altering emotions, just like drugs and alcohol. Cravings are a primal emotion that are connected to real or imagined survival and are very difficult to resist for very long. They wear us down until we give in. The limbic system believes we need it to survive. It takes a power greater than ourselves to overcome destructive cravings.

> *"Imagine trying to live without air.*
> *Now imagine something worse."*
>
> ~ Amy Reed, Author

Dear Michael,

I have been battling compulsions for pornography and sexual fantasy for as long as I can remember. I am forty-four years old now and can't really think of a time when this wasn't a problem. I will be working on the computer or even just trying to take a nap and all of a sudden a craving for porn will be so overwhelming that I give in, despite not really wanting to. I feel like there is something broken in me that causes me to do the thing I hate the most. It is like I switch to autopilot and give up control. I always feel like crap afterwards and sincerely promise myself I won't ever do it again. I went to my church several times, but came away feeling a lot of shame. They have good intentions, but basically said I didn't have enough faith to overcome. I needed to be in the Word and pray more. I have tried that for years and it just didn't work for me. I am in a change group now, and for the first time I have hope, as I am not alone in this battle and I'm beginning to understand the whole brain thing. As we keep each other accountable, my relapses have gone way down and my wife, who was leaving me, now says she will stick it out with me to see what happens. What a battle! I will let you know how it works out.

Jim

> **KEY thought** In the process of recovery, the more you reduce shame the more you increase success.

SHAME VS. GRACE

We have received feedback from thousands of addicts who have gone through the *Genesis Process*. They tell us that learning about the brain has helped them understand the mystery of their self-destructive insanity more than anything else. It helps them comprehend what is broken, reduces shame, and changes their perception that they are just a weak-willed, defective, or a stupid person. By the way, addiction has nothing to do with intelligence—very smart, brilliant people suffer from addictions just as much as everyone else, maybe more.

Shame, however, is an issue in the process of recovery. Most professionals in the counseling field have come to the same conclusion; that shame is what drives our self-destructive behaviors. Of course there is a positive role for shame in our lives that can motivate us to change. It motivates us to conform into a society to better survive. But in recovery, the more you can reduce condemning shame the more you increase recovery. Shame can actually increase the cravings that can lead to relapse. This is such an important point for individuals and churches to grasp as we seek to help the hurting and broken. Understanding the disease model of recovery doesn't alleviate the responsibility for the bad choices made by those with addictions. In fact, it actually helps them to take responsibility for their choices by understanding the consequences. The positive result is that they begin to more fully engage in the process of recovery. I'll show you what I mean.

> *Americans have more food to eat than any other people, and more diets to keep them from eating it."*
> ~ Yogi Berra

Picture a guy who is obese and was warned by his doctor for years to lose weight or suffer the consequences. One day, he goes to the doctor and finds out he has diabetes, which will kill him. What's the first question he will ask the doctor? "What can I do to keep this from killing me?" The doctor gives him a treatment plan that includes major changes in his lifestyle. Most likely he will listen, because the treatment plan can slow or stop the progress of the disease, help him get healthy, and avoid death. It's the same with all addictive behavior. When self-destructive people understand that there are things they can do to keep their disease in remission, and things they can do that will reactivate their disease and the insanity that comes with it, they begin to engage and take responsibility for their recovery plan. They realize, "I really blew it by doing the things I knew I shouldn't do." The resulting thought is, "Now my brain is messed up and I have these cravings for things that are bad for me. If I don't find a way to deal with the problem, it is going to eventually kill me." This is where God and the people He uses come in. The first step to freedom is what we call a "spiritual awakening." Giving up control takes a step of faith by beginning to trust God and the people He works through.

> *"We came to believe that a power greater than ourselves could restore us to sanity."*
>
> *"Made a decision to turn our will and our lives over to the care of God as we understood Him."*
>
> ~ Steps 2 & 3, from the 12 Steps of AA

The question becomes, "How can we help wounded people caught in addiction in a way that models the New Testament's theme of love and grace? Is it a disease of the brain, or merely people choosing to sin over and over again (i.e., they are bad people)?" The answer to this question will define how we minister to broken and hurting people. Many churches inadvertently use shame as a means to motivate people to change behavior, but we know that using shame to change self-destructive behavior is like trying to put out a fire with gasoline. Legalism, the "sin-only" view of addiction, lends itself to judging, and we know that feeling judged is the number one thing that keeps people from seeking help—remember the definition of addiction is that we all do things we know we shouldn't. So, the answer lies in the New Testament's message of acceptance and grace that makes it safe for people with shameful problems to take the risk of trying to change and ask for help. We always seem to end up with *"What would Jesus do?"* How many times should we forgive and try to help a person when they relapse?

Jesus tells us to forgive over and over again (Luke 17:4). Of course, forgiveness doesn't mean there aren't any consequences.

"Or do you think lightly of the riches of His kindness and tolerance and patience, not knowing that the kindness of God leads you to repentance?" Romans 2:4

> *"When you've experienced grace and you feel like you've been forgiven, you're a lot more forgiving of other people. You're a lot more gracious to others."*
> ~ Rick Warren

I know of one particular denomination that is adamantly opposed to the idea of addiction being a disease. Not long ago we were attending one of their services and, with much fervor, the pastor stated, "The whole Christian world is being deceived by the devil in believing that addiction is a disease." He said that those who believe this lie just don't have the faith to trust God. It is "just an excuse to keep sinning." I have had people from that denomination come to me in secret for counseling because, having repented of their sin over and over, their behavior still hasn't changed. They are afraid to go to their leadership for help because they know they will be told that the reason they are still struggling is that they "just don't have enough faith." My secretary, who suffers from a chronic illness, said to me, "Do you know how many times I have heard that same thing?" This same pastor was later caught diverting funds from the church for his own use. He had an expensive problem that no one would talk about—he must not have had enough faith. This is a good example of why people call Christians hypocrites. The real result of this type of hypocrisy is that people needing help probably won't seek it from churches when they hear of this kind of thing happening.

> *"Above all the grace and the gifts that Christ gives to his beloved is that of overcoming self."*
> ~ Saint Francis of Assisi

Religion that operates out of shame always says that the reason a person struggles is because there's something wrong with them—they are weak. God is not blessing them because they aren't doing it right. We use shame-based statements that tell them to do something they don't know how to do like, "You just aren't serious enough," "You just don't have the will or the discipline," or "You don't care enough," or the most popular is, "You just don't have enough faith." Not only does this kind of one-dimensional theology increase shame, but also it increases hopelessness, isolation, which eventually leads to relapse. That is because feelings of hopelessness and shame actually cause the brain to produce more cravings for the very behavior a person is trying to get free from. Sadly, this kind of theology tells others to "Just go out and fix yourself"—"Just go out and get some more faith"—it's setting them up for even more failure and shame. Plus, blanket judgments like these can make it easy for us not to get involved and help. We must try to avoid legalism because it produces condemnation. We will look at the problem of legalism in depth later. Shame doesn't work, but grace and love do. It is grace that brings hope and freedom. God's love leads us to repentance. He usually expresses that love through people. This is the primary message of the New Testament.

> "Let all bitterness and wrath and anger and clamor and slander be put away from you, along with all malice. Be kind to one another, tenderhearted, forgiving each other, just as God in Christ also has forgiven you." Ephesians 4:31–32

KEY thought — Just because you believe something doesn't mean you're right.

Churches and Christians who want to be safe and effective need to allow their ideas about sin and self-destructive behavior to not get in the way of showing love and grace. It is wise to remember that just because you believe something doesn't mean you are right. This humble truth can help free us from hurtful judgments that can make people afraid of us. Only by this kind of honesty can we get the opportunity to help hurting people recover from the consequences of their behaviors. Though legalism might seem easier because it's black and white—"our way only"—we have to resist it. Broken people are looking for acceptance, but they have learned to expect rejection. They need a lot of grace, love, acceptance, and support, especially at first when they are most vulnerable.

Grace is the New Testament's central message and it works. It is love working through grace and the fruits of the Spirit that empowers people to change—not shame and punishment. If punishment worked, our jails would be empty. Our faith needs to be practical and work in the real world. Grace that heals, as it is practically transmitted from one person to another, takes place when you choose to have a relationship with a person's heart instead of their behavior. That's why Jesus was so effective. Even the worst sinners felt safe with him, not judged. Where black-and-white legalism creates walls, grace makes doors for people to be able to trust us. Grace also creates tolerance for what they believe and communicates respect to them just as they are. I will be the first to admit that giving someone grace is not easy, as it is the main focus of my struggle as a recovering Pharisee. Why is extending grace so hard? We will explore the topic of grace in depth in Chapter 8.

I would like to share a personal example of how legalism creates walls and turns people away. My son, Joah, died May 1st, 2013, from cancer. He was thirty-five years old. Joah was born with cerebral palsy; he was a special needs child. He was 6'9", a gentle giant. About six weeks before he died, I went back to visit him in Michigan, where he lived with my first wife on a ranch. We were sitting in the living room talking about some of the things we had done together when he started to cry. I can't ever remember seeing Joah cry. I asked him what was the matter and he said, "You told my mom she was going to hell."

I immediately knew what he was talking about, as my older son, Daylen, and I, had talked about it some time ago. The incident happened about thirty years ago. Daylen was about nine years old at the time and had come home from Sunday school. He came up and asked me, "If my mom doesn't believe in Jesus is she going to hell?" Being a fairly new Christian and a budding Pharisee, I said, "Yes, that is what the Bible says." Well, he went home and told his mom. I guess it still bothered her as she still mentioned it from time to time. There had always been a wall between the kids and me, but I figured it was just from the divorce. I told Joah, "I am sorry, but that was what I had been taught at the time." He said, "I want you to apologize to her," so I called her into the room to apologize and asked her to forgive me. Joah wanted relationship hurts to be resolved before he died.

I learned three major lessons from that experience: 1) Religious judgments (whether they are true or not) hurt others very deeply and create walls; 2) Nothing goes away until it is resolved; and 3) judgments (especially religious ones) are powerful and can create deep heart wounds. How could I have known that for thirty years there had been resentment towards me from a few poorly chosen words that no one ever talked about? I unintentionally created a wall that I don't think anyone really consciously knew was there. Unfortunately, it led to a more superficial relationship with all of them. Seeing the power these past resentments had on my family has helped me to confront and try to resolve other walls that were built by resentments with others. Jesus tells us not to judge and to forgive from our hearts—grace in action. Having an openness to talk about and resolve problems makes it safe for vulnerable people to risk seeking help. I think conflict resolution is becoming a lost art in our society.

> "Grace isn't a little prayer you chant before receiving a meal.
> It's a way to live. The law tells me how crooked I am.
> Grace comes along and straightens me out."
> ~ Dwight Lyman Moody (1837–1899)

KEY thought — Grace that heals is choosing to have a relationship with people's hearts and not their behaviors.

One of the most popular arguments against the disease model of addiction is this: Cancer is a real disease, which you can't choose to stop, but with addiction you can choose to quit. Is it true that addicts can choose to become sober, but they can't choose not to be addicted anymore?

The truth is that they can never go back and drink moderately; their brain is still addicted (diseased), whether they are using alcohol or not. They know they will never be able to drink moderately. It is the same with almost all serious addictions. It will always be there lurking in the shadows.

As people of religion, we tend to make rules for sin that are rigid. It is so easy that way—neat, not messy. But this orientation leads to religious self-righteousness. One rule for sin doesn't fit everyone. This is where the Holy Spirit comes in. It is His job to convict us when we sin (literally, "miss the mark"). Unlike legalism, which condemns us—you broke the rules—conviction comes from a place of love (God). Condemnation comes from the devil and self-righteous people producing guilt and shame, which can create a deeper pit to climb out of.

> "Therefore, to one who knows the right thing to do and does not do it, to him it is sin." James 4:17

KEY thought — The same rules for sin don't fit everyone.

Sin is not a one-size-fits-all notion. For example, if I'm not an alcoholic, it is not a sin to have a glass of wine, but for an alcoholic it is. Many denominations declare that drinking any alcohol is sin. The result of making an absolute rule for everyone is the very definition of legalism and self-righteousness. Of course there are absolutes (Ten Commandments), but I'm talking about denominational rules. Everyday activities, such as eating, shopping, working, using computers, or even housecleaning, can be harmful (sin) in excess. It is the Holy Spirit's job to convict us through our conscience if something is becoming harmful to us. It is not the same for everyone.

I have worked with many sex addicts who can't look at most magazines or watch TV because it can trigger lust (cravings) that they know can cause them to relapse. Remember that dwelling on a temptation can create a craving, resulting in sin—a bad action.

The good news is that the cravings can be kept in remission with competent help and support to a point of real freedom. God usually accomplishes this miracle by working through people by using the kind of love that produces conviction to motivate us to change. The tricky part is that

He uses loving people to convict us much of the time, and when He does, we usually don't realize He's the One doing it.

"All things are lawful for me, but not all things are profitable. All things are lawful for me, but I will not be mastered by anything." 1 Corinthians 6:12

REJECTION AND LOVE: GRACE AT WORK

Dear Mr. Dye,

Thank you letting me share our story. My husband and I were the ideal couple. We married young, but both knew Christ and God blessed our marriage. We had two lovely daughters. I was gifted in pastoral ministry and my husband was very gifted in the area of the sciences and mechanical aptitude. For many years he supported me while I raised our children and worked in various low-paying ministry jobs. We were both active in the church—I, in teaching and preaching, and he in helping ministries, like installing electrical wiring and running sound equipment.

I came home one day to find five police officers searching our house. They told me my husband had solicited illegal pornography online and they had a warrant to search our home. They found locked in his office many computer files filled with the most disgusting forms of pornography. When we were just newlyweds, I discovered my husband had a secret pornography habit—nothing illegal, just the usual Playboy magazines. I was a victim of childhood sexual abuse and told him I would not be with anyone who was involved with any type of pornography or sexually inappropriate activity. It surfaced a few more times in the marriage, always resulting in major drama.

Finally, as I matured in Christ and began working with people in recovery, I realized this was an addiction and he would need outside support to kick it. He was unwilling to go to men's groups or pursue counseling. He was abused by the men in his family and friends of the family, and was afraid of making himself vulnerable to a man or group of men. As the Internet became filled with more and more online pornography, I asked him frequently if he was having difficulty with it. He said, "No," and managed to hide the fact that he had become hopelessly engaged in an ever-expanding search for the most shocking pictures he could find.

While the police were still in my home and we awaited the arrival of my husband from work, I called our pastor. I told him everything and asked him to pray. The police decided not to arrest my husband at that time and left telling us we would be hearing from them. Our pastor came over and talked and prayed with us. My husband was convicted of a misdemeanor charge of possession of child pornography, which he downloaded free from the Internet. He was fired from his federal job. Because he was not deemed a threat to the public, he was given only twenty-eight days in jail and unsupervised probation for two years. He will have to register as a sex offender for the rest of his life for possessing child pornography. At my insistence, we told the board of our church and the church staff. I was asked to resign, which I did. My husband was very open about his sin and was extremely remorseful. We had to tell our daughters and they were extremely supportive. There was some debate among the church leadership over how to handle us. The church board and staff hired an outside pastor as a mediator, and ended up giving him full authority to determine how we would be dealt with. My husband had hidden his addiction because he feared that rather than help, he would just get rejection. He couldn't have been more right.

The hired pastor came to our home and said we were no longer welcome at church. In fact, he didn't want to know any of the details of my husband's sin, but didn't feel he should attend church anywhere. He brought with him $25 to reimburse me for a women's church event I had planned to attend. I was told that since I had chosen to stay with my husband, I was not welcome in the church either. We were shocked and very hurt. We wrote to the board and protested their choice to cast us out rather than walk through the process of repentance and recovery with us. There was no response. We both were unemployed and cast adrift by our church when we needed them the most. If it had not been for the Lord and his faithfulness to us, we would not have recovered. We had Christian friends, who stood by us, and our daughters. My husband enrolled in counseling and eventually we found a recovery church. He was even able to attend a retreat with Christian therapists dealing with sexual addictions. They formed a group and he has attended now for two years.

Through a therapist and the group, he was able to gain a lot of healing and he is still in process. We spent two years in isolation from regular church body fellowship. I took a secular job as a social worker. We attended a huge church where we came every Sunday, but never sat next to the same person twice. We spoke to the pastor about our situation, because we didn't want it to come up later and find we were not welcome. He basically said that he didn't want to know and it was no one's business. He offered no support other than permission to attend. We finally got really tired of being so isolated and took a chance on a small church some friends invited us to visit. We spoke to the pastor and he was very supportive. He invited me to begin teaching again in the church and offered encouragement and support to my husband. One of the board members of the church offered my husband a job, which was very difficult for him to find with a record as a sex offender. We confided in him why my husband was unemployed and how our former church had treated us. The board member not only hired him, but also became his accountability partner. My husband had to work online occasionally for his job. Special software was installed on the computer so that his boss was notified if he strayed where he shouldn't; if he did, they would have a "come to Jesus meeting." This allowed him the opportunity to grow in his recovery and for our marriage to begin to heal.

We have not told anyone else in the church. We still think that is unsafe. We are grateful for the people who have not thrown us away. I am back in full time ministry, working with individuals in recovery from drug and alcohol use and sexual addictions as well. Sexual addiction has become epidemic due to the proliferation of it on the Internet. I think many people could have benefited from walking us through this process instead of rejecting us. Now they certainly will know that they must hide their struggle in this area or face rejection and punishment. What if they could have seen repentance, authentic forgiveness, and healing instead?

Susan

12-STEP PROGRAMS

There is another controversy that I'd like to mention because it is important for helping many addicted people get well. In spite of the evidence of what works, many of the same churches that deny addiction is a disease, also oppose and judge 12-step programs. The reality is that the 12-step program is the most successful program in the world for helping people achieve and maintain sobriety. There are meetings almost everywhere; any time of day that help addicted people avoid relapse when they have cravings. In most cases, rebuilding a broken life is a community project. I have learned by experience that no single agency or person can do it alone. The most effective recovery churches network with outside community resources.

> **KEY thought** Insecurity always manifests itself in control.

"A lack of transparency results in distrust and a deep sense of insecurity."
~ Dalai Lama

Secure churches aren't afraid to expose their membership to the outside world, or to other churches ascribing to different doctrines. They aren't afraid that their people's faith is so fragile that it would become undermined or polluted in some way just by being exposed to other ways of doing things. Many Christians I have met are against 12-step programs because they don't like the idea of the "higher power." This is a typical thought pattern of those who are insecure in their faith. Safe churches are secure enough to allow God to work in someone's life in ways that may be outside their norm. My goal here is to challenge some of your strongly held beliefs, to think about where they came from, and how they may affect someone seeking help. Are they inclusive or exclusive?

God works through many sources, including doctors, social workers, judges, and therapists. *Alcoholics Anonymous (AA)* is not a replacement for church; it is one resource, a part of what works for many. The formation of AA came about during the time of prohibition. In the 1920s, the Woman's Christian Temperance Union was instrumental in getting congress to legislate prohibition. These women had good intentions because they saw how the effects of alcohol were destroying those abusing it and their families. They stated that drinking was a sin and worked to pass a law against alcohol. In those days, the local community (especially the Christian community) would intervene in family problems. Whenever a man was abusing alcohol or drugs, the pastor and elders would go to his home and confront him. They would support him with accountability and biblical truth to help him stop. It broke the power of secrecy and isolation. In many cases, it was very successful. People were getting involved in the lives of others in their community.

However, with the passage of prohibition, many churches began to turn their backs on alcoholics and those with other sinful social problems, declaring the individuals to be unrepentant sinners. Shortly afterwards, while a man named William G. Wilson (a.k.a., Bill W.) was lying in a hospitable bed, God spoke to him and gave him an idea for helping other alcoholics. This turned out to be the beginnings of *Alcoholics Anonymous*.

The 12-step groups originally came out of the Oxford Bible groups in the 1920s.[6] Whenever I hear Christians criticizing the 12-step program, I simply ask them, "Is God in the 12-step program?" Most of them, if they're honest, will admit that He is, which causes them to think that they may be criticizing something God is doing. God honors a step of faith no matter how small—even as small as mustard seed. I have heard many stories from addicts who prayed for God to relieve their cravings and at 12-step meeting, and He did, i.e.—deliverance. Of course they still have free will to make bad choices. If the 12 Step Programs where a religion they would probably exhibit more miracles than any other.

> "Every person is to be in subjection to the governing authorities. For there is no authority except from God, and those which exist are established by God.' Romans 13:1

The 12-step system gets its boundaries of authority from God.[7] The job of the program is to help addicts and alcoholics become sober, and learn how to live a lifestyle that will help them maintain sobriety, which is the first and most essential part of the recovery process. The church, on the other hand, has the authority for salvation and a transformed heart through the indwelling of Christ in the person of the Holy Spirit. Hebrews 11:6 gives us some understanding of how God uses the 12-step programs in His process of drawing hurting people to Himself.

> "And without faith it is impossible to please Him, for he who comes to God must believe that He is and that He is a rewarder of those who seek Him.' Hebrews 11:6

The first three of the 12 Steps exemplify this process:

Step 1: We admitted we were powerless over our addiction—that our lives had become unmanageable.

Step 2: We came to believe that a Power greater than ourselves could restore us to sanity.

Step 3: We made a decision to turn our will and our lives over to the care of God, as we understood Him.

As you can see for most of us, the road to relationship with God occurs in phases. No one makes the transition from atheism to Jesus in one leap. First, we must admit our need for help. Second, we begin to believe there is a God. And third, we come to see that He is a personal God who will help those who seek Him. Then it is possible to understand the role of Christ in God's plan. The 12 Steps can lead broken people through the transition from hopelessness to faith. I know many people who came to Christ through the 12 Steps.

> *"The feeling of having shared in a common peril is one element in the powerful cement which binds us."*
> ~ Alcoholics Anonymous, *Big Book*

Part of why the 12-step program works has been explained through recent brain research through a concept called "herding." Studies have shown that people find the most help from others who have the same problem as they do. When a person or an animal gets into a herd of individuals like themselves, it actually raises serotonin in the brain, which temporarily reduces cravings by making the individual feel safe. As serotonin increases, cravings decrease. That's why addicts say, "I need to get to a meeting," because they are beginning to experiencing cravings for drugs or coping behaviors and they know, almost unconsciously, that if they don't get to a meeting they are at high risk of relapse. The concept of herding also explains why Narcotics Anonymous (NA) people don't go to an AA meeting and vice versa. It doesn't work. It's a different herd and it doesn't reduce the cravings.

Eventually, as Christians increase in grace, acceptance, and especially competency, the "herd" will become the Church. I believe that God intended the two programs to work together. The authority of AA will help people stay sober so they can get into recovery and become the person that God intended them to be in the first place. Remember, the word "recovery" means to return to a former healthy state, the person God intended you to be. You need stay sober to be in the process of recovery.

One of the main principles that we teach in the *Genesis Counselor Trainings* is that individual counseling can give clients insight, understanding, healing, and motivation to be *willing* to change, but it's the support and accountability of the group that makes a person *able* to change. You put the two together and lives change. Churches that are open to God working in ways that may be outside the box can provide the support needed for helping people be successful in the changes they are trying to make. They can see their role and be okay with it.

The self-destructive people that I have worked with tell me that understanding the disease model of addiction has been the most helpful principle in their road to recovery. It explains, "what is broken" and what it will take for them to get better. For churches and Christians it translates into understanding that results in the ability to extend grace. I think the main thing that 12-step programs can teach us is the power of unconditional acceptance. People feel safe to reach out for help because they know they won't be judged no matter how many times they have failed.

THE POWER OF ACCEPTANCE

Dear Mike,

My grandmother took me to church regularly as a child. My parents were both alcoholics and divorced when I was nine years old. I began using drugs and alcohol in my early teens and continued as an active drug addict for over twenty years. I went through several abusive marriages and many other abusive relationships in-between. During my years as an active addict, I lost many things that were precious to me, including my children. I was hospitalized four times for drug overdose and was incarcerated several times. When I finally hit bottom, I was a mess. I went to an AA meeting and realized that God loved me just the way I was. I saw Him in the way they accepted me. He began to fill the void I'd been trying to fill on my own, and I clung to Him for dear life. He had been gently calling me back to Him over the years, and I was willing to go wherever He wanted me. I just didn't know where to start so my 12-step sponsor suggested I return to my roots, church.

* I was a church hopper for a while and had a few bumps and bruises along the way from Christians who just didn't understand where I was coming from. I began to pray and ask God to put me where He wanted me, and within two months He placed me in the most amazing church. There are many people who attend there who are just like me, and many are still active in a 12-step program. We are a motley crew who welcome and love all who walk through the doors.

My pastor welcomed me with open arms and loved me unconditionally the day I walked in. He has a history similar to mine, and although he doesn't live in the past, he uses it help others seeking recovery.

He has taught me to do the same. He reminds the congregation week after week that we are a church that tries not to judge, but gives the water of life without conditions. I've been attending this church for over a decade now and it was the way my pastor welcomed me, accepted me as I was, and took the time to work with me that has made the difference in who I am today. He loves me as Christ does and he leads his sheep to do the same. My pastor is not God, and makes mistakes just like any human does, but I've learned that this is what men and women do. We all make mistakes, but it is never too late to accept God. We just need a safe place to let Him do His work.

Jane

SELF-DISCOVERY QUESTIONS

1. Give some examples of how continuing bad choices can lead to a loss of control (i.e., addiction). Try to think of personal examples.

_____
_____
_____

2. What are some of the areas you are most tempted with? How do you deal with it?

_____
_____
_____
_____

3. Give some examples of when you have experienced both grace and legalism. What was the result?

_____
_____
_____
_____

4. Think of some examples of where you saw God move outside the box.

_____
_____
_____
_____

PRACTICAL APPLICATION

Ask someone you know who has struggled with self-destructive behaviors to tell you what was most and least helpful in their road to recovery. Or, attend an AA or Al-Anon meeting. You won't have to share anything; you can just listen.

CHAPTER FIVE

SECRETS AND FREEDOM

> **KEY thought** — Safe churches and safe people don't have hidden secrets.

Understanding the role of secrets in the process of recovery and preventing relapse is key to being able to help people who want to change be successful. Getting free of current secrets can be one of the most freeing experiences a recovering person can have. Over the years, I have worked with hundreds of broken people who have desperately sought to understand the mystery of their self-destructive behaviors— why they did what they promised themselves they would never do again (i.e., relapse). I believe I have discovered a way to identify the first and most subtle component that begins this insidious relapse pattern. At the heart of the *Genesis Process* is a tool called the *Faster Scale*, which is designed to foresee the unconscious emotions and behaviors that lead to relapse.[2]

The first step on the scale towards relapse is called "Forgetting Priorities," where something or someone has become more important than the goals of recovery. Moving down the scale, the first sign of pre-relapse always seems to begin with a secret. I'm not talking about secrets from the past, like childhood abuse. While at the right time, it can be very freeing to deal with shameful childhood secrets, in this case we are only talking about current ones—things we wouldn't want anyone to know we are doing. In this chapter, we'll explore how secrets not only thwart healing, but can also hinder churches (and ourselves) from becoming safe places for hurting people to seek healing.

> *"The man who can keep a secret may be wise,*
> *but he is not half as wise as the man with no secrets to keep."*
> ~ E. W. Howe

WHAT IS A SECRET?

Very simply, the kind of secret I am talking about is when we are doing something we know we shouldn't be doing and keeping it hidden. It is usually something we are not willing to give up yet, and is usually tied to shame/sin. Secrets are not only a primary indicator of self-destructive behavior, but can also be a powerful tool the enemy uses to isolate us. The New Testament tells us over and over again that both the devil and the deeds of evil men work in darkness and cannot stand the light. In many cases, the Bible talks about secrets in terms of darkness and light.

> "For nothing is hidden, except to be revealed; nor has anything been secret, but that it would come to light." Mark 4:22

> "This is the judgment, that the Light has come into the world, and men loved the darkness rather than the Light, for their deeds were evil." John 3:19

> **KEY thought** — The power of secrets is in isolation.

Secrets drive isolation and isolation drives secrets, which is the most dominant component for continuing self-destructive behavior. In order for a person to relapse, he has to accomplish isolation, which he may go to great lengths to achieve. The deeper a person delves into their destructive behavior, the more isolated they become from both God and people. The simplicity of recovery and preventing relapse is this: *If you prevent isolation, you can prevent relapse.* In other words, accountability and a safe community is an atmosphere to help prevent secrets. It really is that simple. (See the *Faster Scale* in the Notes to understand more about the progression of isolation to the point of relapse.)

MIKE'S STORY

Dear Michael,

I was reading your process on secrets in the group change books and realized how many I grew up with. I think we had an elephant in every room. As a kid I didn't have a clue what was going on, but now I look back and it explains a lot. My step dad thought of himself as a "Playboy" and was having multiple affairs. My mom was a co-dependent enabler who lived in denial. The affect was that my sister and me didn't want to be at home because (I see now) of the vibes. We would get involved with other families until they would kick us out saying, "Don't you have a home?" It also explains why I get into trouble confronting people when we have unspoken issues (bad vibes). People do not like talking about their elephants and don't appreciate others who want to. I hate secrets and the resentments they create. Secrets are the source of superficiality with God and people.

Still trying to get it right,

Mike

> *"If you want to keep a secret, you must also hide it from yourself."*
> ~ George Orwell, *1984*

In the recovery world, secrets in families are described as the "elephant in the room." Imagine a huge, dead, smelly elephant in the room, representing all the secrets and dysfunctions of the family. Family members throw a carpet over it or put a coffee table on it. Everybody kind of knows it is there, but they learn to ignore it. The process of recovery begins with rigorous honesty, but people with secrets can be very defensive toward anyone confronting what they are not ready to deal with. The immediate response is anger, denial, lying, and self-justification—four of the survival brain's primary protective responses to avoid having a secret exposed. Rigorous honesty requires safe relationships, so when safe communities and friendships can't be found, individuals will most likely remain in hiding, unable to think of anyone to tell their secret to. Remember—it takes both grace and competency to make a person or organization safe for people to take the risk of revealing their secrets. The fear of being judged, shamed, and punished is what keeps most people stuck in their isolation.

> *"To be trusted is a greater compliment than being loved."*
> ~ George MacDonald, (1824–1906)

KEY thought — Secrets are addictive.

THE DAMAGE SECRETS DO

In the second chapter on "What's Broken," I said that anything that speeds up the body anesthetizes the awareness of physical and emotional pain. Secrets create both anxiety and drama, both of which speed up the body. Ironically, secrets can become a subconscious addiction as well—a means of producing stress/anxiety, which can be a powerful anesthetic, like cocaine. Anxiety can push back deeper pain—the thoughts, memories, and feelings we don't want to face. Many people live in a constant state of low-level anxiety, never realizing how addictive their anxiety has become, and how anxiety keeps them "safe" from feeling and dealing with deeper issues. It gives them energy. They actually fear slowing down and feeling.

Secrets are usually about a self-destructive coping behavior, something we use to self-medicate and anesthetize our pain and fear and thus be able to function.

The limbic brain sets up powerful defenses against giving up these coping behaviors, which are associated with survival. There are subconscious beliefs like, "If I face the pain, I won't be able to cope," "I need this," and "There is a part of me that fears I will not be able to survive and function." Three of the most common limbic survival responses to avoid giving up a coping behavior are procrastination, confusion, and denial. All three can raise serotonin in the brain, which produces a temporary state of peace by saying, "I don't have to do anything *now*." This whole process of avoidance is mostly subconscious.

Confusion is a good example of a limbic defense mechanism that can become habitual. I have worked with clients who are always confused. They see a truth and get a sense of direction in a session, but come back later confused week after week. What would happen if they gave up confusion? They would have to act, which might result in rejection, making a mistake, looking foolish, or letting go of a coping behavior. As long they stay confused, they don't have to act. Confusion protects them from doing something fearful. It is their self-prescribed Prozac. These types of mental and emotional survival skills can be used to ignore or avoid dealing with a secret, thus temporarily reducing anxiety. The result is a temporary sense of peace, or feeling normal. Let's look at some other types of damage that keeping secrets cause.

> **KEY thought** Secrets produce superficial relationships with God and others.

SECRETS DAMAGE RELATIONSHIPS

I think the most common fear human beings have is taking the risk of trusting God and others—giving up control. Why are secrets so powerful? Because through isolation, they damage the relationships we have with our loved ones and with God. Without close relationships, we have no community or support, and this makes real, personal change practically impossible. Secrets separate us from the people closest to us. We will avoid others, keeping conversations superficial when we have shameful secrets. The "eyes are the windows of the soul," so those who are closest to us will sense there is something wrong when they get too close or try to make eye contact. We may resort to anger or some type of abuse to keep those who care at a distance. It is very difficult to confront angry people, because they communicate that it would be uncomfortable or even dangerous to do so. Confronting people about their secrets can be a very frightening undertaking.

Secrets also cause our relationship with God to suffer. Think about it—if we walked up to Jesus to talk to Him about what is going on in our life, what do you think He'll want to talk about first? The secrets we are keeping. Why? Because He loves us, and our secret is something we are doing that is not good for us. Consequently, if we are not ready to change, we won't want to hear what we know He has to say. We'll avoid personal interaction with Him. Why? Because relationship always requires communication, and communication requires both talking and listening. When we have current shameful secrets, the communication with God becomes one-way. People with secrets pray to God, but really don't want to hear from Him. In practical terms, two-way communication with God is called "relationship"; one-way communication with God is called "religion."

"Nothing weighs on us so heavily as a secret."
~ Jean de La Fontaine, French poet (1621–1695)

SECRETS ARE INFECTIOUS

Secrets are also infectious—like a cold. If you know someone's secrets, they can infect you. Their secret is now your secret and the burden can be heavy. The following story illustrates a common occurrence in residential rehab centers. Judy was one of my clients at the rescue mission. She was doing really well and had been there about a year. She had a job, was going to church, and had a sponsor. She had everything in place for a healthy recovery, but then she relapsed. In our relapse repair counseling session, we were working to identify the unconscious emotions and behaviors that led to her using again. When we got to the area of secrets, the lights started to go on. It turned out that Judy's roommate had been using illegal prescription drugs, and Judy had been keeping it a secret.

Suddenly she had a "change in priorities" (see the Faster Scale in the Notes). She stopped reading her Bible, began skipping church, and hadn't called her 12-step sponsor, which is typical of what we call a "dry relapse pattern" that eventually leads to a "wet relapse" (with substances or behaviors).

Judy unconsciously became more and more isolated, until finally she ended up using drugs herself. During one counseling session, she made a classic statement. I asked her how the secret about her roommate affected her relationship with her accountability partners and staff. She said, "I avoided them as much as possible, because they would get *it* out of me." I asked her, "What about God?" She said, "I just stopped talking to Him." Secrets are infectious. It doesn't even have to be your secret. Just keeping someone else's secret can have the same isolating affect. Secrets in the form of gossip can be just as toxic.

COMBATING SECRETS

Dear Michael,

I attended one of your weekend seminars. When you spoke about how secrets create walls that separate us from God and others, a light went on for my husband and me. My son, Bill, has become more and more distant over the last few years. My husband and I couldn't figure out what was going on. He wouldn't talk to us about anything personal. We talked to his wife (of only a year) and she said he was becoming the same way with her. She tearfully confessed that their love life was almost zero, and they argued more than talked. It seemed like all he wanted to do was play his combat games on the computer. She looked on his computer and found a whole world of porn stuff. Not knowing what to do, she told his dad about it.

My husband took Bill out mountain biking for the day and on the way home said, "Bill, if you don't do something about your gaming and sex addiction, you're going to lose your wife." Bill didn't say anything. About three hours later he broke down and told his dad what was going on and admitted for the first time that he is an addict. Bill's exact words were, "Dad, it's like there is an evil in me that I can't control or say no to." Although Bill has a lot of work to do, it feels like he's back. The power of secrets is broken and we are all able to connect with him again. Also, he is back with the Lord.

It seems so clear now. He had all the symptoms of what you taught us about secrets—isolation, anger, and superficial conversations, but we couldn't see it. We all hate secrets now.

Thank you,
M.C.

> **KEY thought** Secrets can keep us from our destiny and calling.

SECRETS DIMINISH OUR POTENTIAL

The lowest statistics say that at least 50 percent of men in churches and about a third of pastors are struggling with some form of sex addiction, which of course means they have secrets.[3] Think about the devastating effect this has not only on themselves, but also on their families and especially their ministry. I believe everyone has a calling and a ministry, but when we have a secret, the last thing we want to do is to step out into the light of leadership. If our secret is exposed while in leadership, it will result in increased shame and we will have to do something about it. That's why most people with secrets try to stay superficial and in the shadows. Christians with secrets (especially sexual ones) may also feel disqualified to serve. Think what the result would be if 50 percent of the people in churches got free of their secrets! They would be able to respond to their calling and help others who have the same problems. God will make our struggle our ministry. The church would be a force to be reckoned with; its capability to help and reach others would increase. Do you see why it is so important for churches to be safe and open?

> **KEY thought** Safe churches promote openness, honesty, and vulnerability. Safe churches don't have secrets.

Remember, the theme of this book is making churches safe and effective for hurting people, which can only take place if we are open, honest, and transparent. For the last six years, I have mainly devoted myself to working with church people who struggle with various addictions, sins, and secrets. I often ask, "Why haven't you gone to your church for help?" In most cases, they are in a double-bind. A double-bind is a feeling of being "damned if you do, and damned if you don't"—a lose/lose situation.[4] Most say that they are afraid to go to the pastor because by the next day the whole church might know. They are fearful that they could be ask to leave or that the church wouldn't have a clue about how to help them. Even if they feel their pastor has the grace to understand, many don't feel the pastor has the knowledge or the experience to really help them. Some avoid secular counseling because they don't want to be counseled by someone who doesn't share their Christian values. So many of them have just learned to look good and pretend everything is okay. Most have kept up this facade for years. The following story illustrates a common reason why many people haven't asked for help from their church.

STAN'S STORY

Dear Mike,

My name is Stan and a couple of years ago I came to realize that I was a sex addict. I also used marijuana as part of my porn rituals. I was raised Christian and have been a deacon in my church for ten years. Being single, I always felt my sex life was my business and didn't harm anyone else. Eventually, God really began convicting me about my secret life, and I began to become more and more uncomfortable doing it. When I tried to stop (or at least cut down), I couldn't, and realized I was addicted. I had no idea what to do about it.

One Sunday, my pastor preached on sexual sin and gave an invitation for anyone who wanted to meet with him to make an appointment. I was scared, but also sick and tired of the struggle, so I went to see him. He was sympathetic, but didn't really know how to help me, other than pray for me. Well, to make a long story short, he told his wife, and she "lifted me and my problem up" at the women's prayer meeting. By the next Sunday, everyone knew about it. People were standoffish and some gave me shame-laced advice. It was the worst day of my life. I just wanted to run and hide. I never went back and no one ever called me. I eventually did get help when a local "recovery" church had a weekend seminar on sex/porn addiction. I joined one of the groups and have been getting much better, but I am still too afraid to go to the church.

In Him,
Stan

Experiences like these can cause others who are seeking help to isolate themselves even more for fear of this kind of outcome. Shame is the source of some of our deepest heart wounds and one of our most powerful limbic fears.

> *"Jesus teaches us another way: Go out.*
> *Go out and share your testimony, go out and interact with*
> *your brothers, go out and share, go out and ask.*
> *Become the Word in body as well as spirit."*
>
> ~ Pope Francis I

SAFE CHURCH PRACTICES

There are several practices that churches can put into place to help be "safe" and free of secrets. Let's look at some of them.

SHARING TESTIMONIES

Something churches can do on a practical level to be safe and free of secrets is to give people the opportunity to share their stories. I know of one church where the pastor gives someone in the congregation an opportunity to briefly share (about four hundred words) his or her story at most Sunday services. People that we thought were so normal—who look so perfect—stand up before the community and tell stories about abuse, sin, addiction and how it affected them. They also share the wisdom of what helped them get better, giving others hope. This kind of openness makes a church feel safe for others to share their secrets and seek help. When someone tells their story, it can be one of the most freeing experiences they have ever had. It is an opportunity to be totally free of secrets. I've heard people say that when they finally get free of a fear or secret, it feels like someone took a brick out of their backpack that they didn't even know was there. They had been carrying the weight of the secret and shame for so long that they actually felt physically lighter. Secrets literally suck the life out of you and your relationships. The devil loves secrets because secrets give him so much power.

RECOVERY FOCUSED SMALL GROUPS

Recovery-focused small groups are a place where people can be transparent and share their struggles. Of course the group must be safe with structure and confidentiality. When someone shares the story of their struggle, others will identify. Denial is best broken through identification, as opposed to confrontation. Churches that are safe for hurting people realize the destructive power of secrets and have created an open, honest atmosphere for those who want to be free. In most cases, the opportunity to seek help is accomplished in recovery-focused small groups. In *The Genesis Process for Change Groups*, we have rules and standards to insure that the groups are safe. We have found that when it is safe and focused, the heart (limbic system) will begin to reveal its secrets. The average Bible study usually doesn't work because typical Bible study groups are not safe, confidential, nor have the competency to deal with severe problems. We all need a safe and competent place where we can have the opportunity to be real.

> **KEY thought** — Safe churches need safe leaders.

"For no one does anything in secret when he himself seeks to be known publicly. If you do these things, show yourself to the world." John 7:4

LEADER ACCOUNTABILITY

It is even harder for church leaders to find a safe place to deal with their secrets as the people under them have such high expectations of them. So it is harder for them to find a place to be real about their problems, and it is not healthy for them to be accountable to people in their congregation. The best thing for leaders to do is to meet with, and be accountable to, other leaders/pastors. This way, their secrets can be shared and won't affect their ability to be genuine and to hear from God—if they also take action towards recovery with accountability. When a leader's communication with God is diminished because of secrets, their ability to minister to their congregation under God's direction will also be diminished. Healthy churches provide accountability and safeguards to protect their leaders from gossip and slander.

Additionally, secrets (sin) often result in religiosity and legalism. When we lose relationship with God because of secrets/sin, then we must try to earn God's favor by works. Think of the Pharisees. Some have called it the "Jimmy Swaggart Syndrome." This is when a person preaches condemnation of sin (especially sexual), while at the same time, struggles with his own secret sexual sins. We tend to preach about and condemn the things that we personally struggle with the most. Below is a script from a BBC news article in 1988, about the Jimmy Swaggart scandal:

> "Mr. Swaggart's confession of adultery is all the more scandalous since he himself unleashed fire and brimstone against rival TV evangelist Jim Bakker, who a few months earlier committed adultery with his secretary, Jessica Hahn. Reverend Bakker was subsequently defrocked and fired from his multimillion dollar "Praise the Lord" TV station. This time it was Mr. Swaggart's turn to repent, after officials from the Assemblies of God were given photographs showing him taking a prostitute to a Louisiana motel. The photos were handed in by rival TV evangelist Martin Gorman, who was also defrocked after Mr. Swaggart accused him of "immoral dalliances" that took place in 1986."[5]

Sadly, statistics say that approximately one-third (or more) of pastors struggle with pornography or some sort of sex addiction. Unfortunately, we hear these kinds of stories frequently. The press loves them. No wonder so many people say Christians are hypocrites. Secrets are what drive hypocrisy. Recently a local pastor in my area stepped out of ministry. The congregation was told that, "He needed to focus on his family." The real reason was never talked about, so of course all sorts of rumors started floating around. Secrets heaped upon secrets. Speculating about secrets often becomes gossip and slander. What churches often fail to realize is that when a leader falls, it can be an opportunity for others to learn and bring healing to those who struggle with similar issues. Healthy churches, like healthy families, are humble, transparent, and able to talk about anything. We learn more from our mistakes than our successes.

The face is the mirror of the mind, and eyes without speaking confess the secrets of the heart.
~ St. Jerome [6]

COMMUNICATE A SIMPLE, ACCESSIBLE MESSAGE

Healthy churches are led by transparent individuals delivering a simple, *practical* message that is applicable to real life. Secrets are often what differentiates between what is genuine and what is cultish. In both the Old and New Testaments, there are mysteries of God, but not secrets. God never set up an elite priesthood who held the secret teachings only available to a special few. Cults always have secrets—secret teachings, secret symbols, secret meetings, secret handshakes, secret rituals, and especially, super-special, insightful knowledge about God. They also often teach that the way of salvation and truth comes through the leaders (or church's) profound and exclusive knowledge. Can you think of any churches or denominations that are like that?

If exposed to the light, most of this secret knowledge and rituals look ridiculous. Many of the eastern and occult philosophies I was involved in had secret knowledge and power that were only available to the enlightened few who had earned it. Religious pride is driven by the Pharisaical spirit of being "better than" and superior to others, which results in exclusiveness and isolation. Sounds like denominationalism, doesn't it? Pride makes us feel superior, and the enemy takes advantage of it by letting us believe we have a superior corner on the truth than others.

> "We know that 'We all possess knowledge.' But knowledge puffs up while love builds up." 1 Corinthians 8:1 (NIV)

The goal is to do whatever we can to make our churches and ourselves safe and effective to be the answer for those who are praying to God for help and healing. Since He mostly answers prayer though people, we need to do our best to be honest, open, and free from secrets, so that we can be effective in God's work to help those who are hurting. We want to be in a place where it is *OK* to talk about our "elephants."

> "And they overcame him because of the blood of the Lamb and because of the word of their testimony, and they did not love their life even when faced with death." Revelation 12:11

SELF-DISCOVERY QUESTIONS

1. What current secrets do you have? Why?

2. What do you do to keep others from finding out?

3. Can you think of examples of how secrets have affected you, others, or churches in the past?

_____
_____
_____
_____

PRACTICAL APPLICATION

Take a risk by telling someone who is safe about a current secret—breaking its power—and see how you feel afterwards.

SUMMARY OF PART II: WHAT'S BROKEN?

1. Childhood trauma that causes a diminished ability to trust, bond, or attach (attachment disorder) shifts the brain from a normal, explorative, creative state into a survival mode of hyper-alertness or withdrawing and going numb. This part of the brain develops typically in the first eighteen months of life. If the world is perceived as unsafe, the child's brain needs to stay focused or hyper-vigilant. (This raises dopamine through anxiety and suppresses serotonin, which would cause a child to let her guard down.) It is interesting to note that some researchers believe that the amount of serotonin produced in the brain is determined for the rest of our lives during this early period.

2. Feeling alone, unsafe, and unfocused can cause a false (or protective) personality to be formed. If we can't trust and receive gratification from others, we learn to self-gratify. *Addiction is self-gratification.*

3. Anything that makes us feel safe and reduces stress raises neurochemical levels in the limbic system, causing the brain to associate the coping strategy with survival or feeling normal. The limbic system creates a craving (a focus) to repeat the behavior because it is associated with survival. The behavior can become difficult or impossible to say *no* to. The more the behavior is reinforced, the more ingrained it becomes, resulting in a loss of control, and thus an addiction. This is why we do the very thing we don't want to do (Romans 7). The survival brain can equate painful or fearful events and emotions with death creating a focused craving for what we did in the past to survive (what we did to feel normal). Addiction is not about feeling; *it is about not feeling.*

4. The limbic system has a memory system that records experiences having to do with pleasure/reward and fear/pain. Most of our fear and pain comes from being betrayed in relationships. So, the thing we need the most (intimacy) is also the thing we fear the most. It is these fear-driven, reactive systems that drive much of our behavior. The limbic system basically controls everything you can't, especially emotions and reactions. This addictive/reactive memory system is programmed through experiences and needs to be reprogrammed through new and opposite

experiences. It doesn't respond very well to words. This is why effective recovery treatment needs to be experiential and relational. Since people are what messed us up, it will be people that will heal us. The process of recovery is: *learning to trust again.*

5. Secrets drive isolation and are the soil in which self-destruction behaviors and emotion thrive. Secrets also lead to legalism and make us unsafe to help others.

PART III: WHAT WORKS

Introduction to What Works?

Chapter Six: Freedom from Spiritual Stagnation

Chapter Seven: Freedom from the Pharisaical Spirit

Chapter Eight: Extending Grace

Chapter Nine: Restoring Hope

Chapter Ten: Fear

Chapter Eleven: The Pastor's Role

Chapter Twelve: Revival through Unity

Chapter Thirteen: The Joy Center–Healing the Heart

INTRODUCTION TO

WHAT WORKS?

"Preach the Gospel at all times and when necessary use words."
~ Saint Francis of Assisi

We have many options these days to try and help self-destructive people heal. So how can we tell what works? It's very simple—it is anything that helps us become free from sin (destructive behavior) by addressing what drives it in our heart. In other words, we go after the cause, rather than just treating or trying to control the symptoms. Recovery is returning to a former healthy state. In order to achieve recovery, we need to heal the wounds, which have now become intrinsic belief systems driving the coping behaviors.

Destructive behaviors and emotions that emanate from a wounded, distorted heart (limbic system) affect the whole person. In the original *Genesis Relapse Prevention* book, the first thing we address is how a person's problem is affecting him or her in five specific areas. It is a foundational principle of the counseling process for clients to understand how their destructive problems have infected every aspect of their lives. The result of this understanding is that they become willing to participate in a recovery plan that includes all five areas.

For individuals or churches that want to be effective, it is important to understand and include ways to help the whole person in their recovery programs. As you will see, most of the recovery process is just common sense. The five areas that need to be addressed are:

1. Physical
2. Mental
3. Emotional
4. Social
5. Spiritual

Addictions (destructive coping behaviors) are unique. As far as I know, addiction is the only problem or disease that destroys the whole person. Remember, we all do things that we know are not good for us. There are physical diseases that affect the body, like cancer. Mental illness is damage to the brain, appearing as insanity, cognitive problems, or personality disorders. Emotional illnesses cause us to have emotions that don't match our circumstances, like stress, anger, anxiety, and depression. Emotional problems are usually rooted in how we reacted to trauma in the past. Unreliable emotions can also be caused by brain damage or hormonal problems. Social dysfunction can cause us to have unstable relationships, resulting in rejection, shame, isolation, and loneliness. Social troubles are also usually rooted in past interpersonal hurts.

Addictions can destroy our physical, mental, and emotional health, as well as our social life and relationships. Even worse, they can affect us spiritually. Addictions and the secrets they produce can cause us to push God away, which can result in self-righteous defensiveness, legalism, anger, isolation, and an inability to have close relationships with God and others. We saw some ways this can happen in the last chapter on *Secrets*. The self-destructive people that I have worked with say, "I really don't trust God." Unlike the other areas that can be healed by medicines, prescription drugs, counseling, caring people, etc., addictions cannot be healed without trusting God. It is the first three of the twelve steps— you can't skip them. Like I said, addictions can affect us in every part of our being, so every area of our being needs to be treated.

EVANGELISM THROUGH RECOVERY

It is obvious that addiction can be a powerful stronghold of the enemy. He can do so much damage so easily. I recently read that for every drug and alcohol addict, their path of destruction affects about seventy-five people (on average), meaning that family, neighbors, employers, friends, judges, lawyers, social workers, teachers, and doctors are impacted by their destructiveness. At my last seminar, I asked, "How many of you are impacted by someone with an addiction?" Almost every person raised a hand. I commented, "Nowadays, it seems like every family has one." A guy in the front row replied, "You're lucky if you only have *one*." Cathy and I counted all the people in our extended family with addictions, and we were amazed at the fact that just about all the major addictions are represented. It is the new normal.

There is a tremendous opportunity to bring in the Gospel and show God's love and power to places that would normally be closed through effective recovery programs. Addictions are bankrupting medical systems, criminal justice systems, legal systems, social welfare systems, and productivity.[1] Society as a whole is desperate to find anything that is effective in curbing these costs. Secular agencies and governments are even willing to fund faith-based recovery treatment options, if they are effective. There is an open door for spreading the Good News of Christ if we can bring effective recovery through local churches. Remember, the best evangelism is a changed life.

I believe that addiction is second only to "religion" as the most powerful stronghold the enemy uses to destroy individuals, families, communities, countries, and even the next generation (we will delve deeper into the effects of religion in Chapter 7). Both religiosity and addictions can do the same thing—they separate and isolate us from others. When someone with a severe addiction (drugs, alcohol, sex, anger, crime, abuse, gambling, or even religion) gets turned around and becomes part of the solution, rather than the part of the problem, it is possible that seventy-five people are, to some degree, evangelized. The people involved in the changed person's life want to know what happened, what worked? What works is when the whole person is changed, not just the behavior. Believe me, if people are being set free at your church it will grow and be an exciting place to be. Think about if all the people who need to loose weight in your church were being successful, how many new people would come to find out how.

When I was at the Santa Barbara Rescue Mission, the staff and I worked with people who had been through every system available in the community and were known as chronic, hopeless, relapsing, criminal addicts. When they returned to the community clean and sober, employed, and paying off their debts, the first question asked by those who knew them was, "What happened to you?

I didn't even recognize you!" As the recovering addicts and criminals told their stories, real evangelism took place. They were witnesses to the power of God working through people. The rescue mission had doctors, judges, clergy, jail workers, social workers, and other agencies; both locally and from around the world, come to tour and volunteer at the mission to see what we were doing. Wouldn't it be exciting if that was happening at your church?

The Genesis Recovery Process addresses all five areas—the whole person. This section on *What Works* will challenge churches and individuals to consider their activities and belief systems as to what is helping and what is not. Also, the hope is that this section will encourage individuals and churches to experience their full potential as workers for Jesus. We will look at some basic principles that really do work to increase our effectiveness, including: *freedom from spiritual stagnation, freedom from a pharisaical spirit, the power of grace and hope, the role of pastors, understanding the fear of God, the importance of unity in bringing about revival,* and *how joy restores broken people.* When churches can effectively meet the needs for both their own hurting people and those in the community, true change and evangelism will take place. Our goal is to become safe and effective so that we can make a true and lasting difference. You and your church can leave a legacy in your area.

CHAPTER SIX

FREEDOM FROM SPIRITUAL STAGNATION

"Make yourself necessary to somebody."
~ Ralph Waldo Emerson

> **KEY thought** — Healthy churches are others-centered and outward focused.

THE SPIRITUALLY STAGNANT

After many years of trying to avoid it, I finally accepted the task that God assigned to me: to try and make churches and Christians safe and effective for people seeking recovery and healing. At first, I had a rough time deciding where to start; I was out of my comfort zone. After several painful attempts, I realized that I couldn't change the Church by just trying to present my ideas. I'm a prodigal and have to learn everything the hard way—by experiences. I did the only thing I knew how to do, which was to try and design small groups within churches that were safe and effective. The small groups were to be designed with the tools, support, and accountability necessary to help those who wanted to change be able to change.

Many of the people I worked with in the past were not comfortable going to church through the front door (i.e., the regular Sunday service). They felt out of place; they couldn't relate. So I needed to create a back door—develop recovery groups at churches that spoke their recovery language, but operated from a biblical perspective without being religious. To be effective, these groups also had to address the roots of the wounds that drive self-destructive coping behaviors. In other words, groups that brought change through heart healing.

I had all the tools from the previous recovery programs I had designed over the years; I just needed to find a way to apply them to church people in their language. To learn how to approach this new area for me, I did more counseling work with church people, both individually and in groups. I wanted to understand what they were struggling with and learn a language that communicated recovery they could accept. After a few sessions and groups, I was amazed at how people who looked so good on the outside could be so messed up on the inside. The addicts and alcoholics I normally worked with were messed up, but they looked messed up. I discovered that church people had many of the same issues as my recovery clients, but somehow they were still functioning at a socially acceptable level—they had learned to hide their pain and problems very effectively.

I saw the differences between real change and successful coping skills—those who experienced freedom and recovery versus those who created a lifestyle of coping with their self-destructive behaviors. Many of the Christians I worked with over the years tried going to church for help, but couldn't find it. Others went to church leaders, who had empathy for their problem, but no experience or training to help them. Some wouldn't seek secular counsel at all because they wanted to deal with their problems biblically. Others had been in counseling for years, but had not been able to change their behaviors. They felt stuck and they couldn't find effective help for their self-destructive issues. As a result, they had learned various ways to cope. I was amazed by how intensely they were suffering but were somehow still able to function.

Remember that my original goal was to make Christians and churches safe and effective for helping wounded people heal. My primary motivation for wanting to see church people experience real recovery (besides good health in their lives) was my hope that it would inspire them to want to help others. I realized that these Christians had a strength that my people (the addicts) needed. How could I create a bridge between the two groups?

"In everything I showed you that by working hard in this manner you must help the weak and remember the words of the Lord Jesus, that He Himself said, 'It is more blessed to give than to receive.'" Acts 20:35

LAURIE'S STORY

Dear Michael,

My story is probably typical. I survived a horrible childhood, but have continued over many years to try and not let it spoil my life. No matter how hard I try I just can't trust people. I have been to many Christian counselors, who have been helpful, but I was still struggling with my issues. But when I heard you ask the audience, "How many of you have been to counseling?" I was surprised at how many raised their hands. Then you asked, "How many of you no longer struggle with the issues you went to counseling for?" Only a very few raised their hands. You challenged us to seek counseling that actually brought about lasting change. I joined a Genesis Change Group and I have made more real changes in a few months than in all the years of counseling. I think it was the support of others that made the difference. Thank you for steering me in the right direction. As you said, if I was willing to change, then God can use the process and the group to make me able to change.

Moving forward,
Laurie

"It may be hard for an egg to turn into a bird: it would be a jolly sight harder for it to learn to fly while remaining an egg. We are like eggs at present. And you cannot go on indefinitely being just an ordinary, decent egg. We must be hatched or go bad."

~ C. S. Lewis

In order to write the *Genesis Process for Change Groups*, I needed to learn about what church people were struggling with. I organized eight groups with people from several different denominations: six groups with women and two with men. Each group consisted of about eight participants. The issues that most of them were struggling with were the same as my addict clients—depression, anxiety, sex, anger, food, drugs (mostly prescription), alcohol, stress from trying to control relationships (co-dependency), despair, religiosity (and the guilt driven by it), workaholism, being critical, irritability, along with trying to control a variety of coping behaviors and emotions. Even though they were in a church, most were feeling lonely and isolated. Most of them hadn't really told anyone about their struggles, in some cases even their spouses didn't know. But by far, the number one issue underlying all the above symptoms was a feeling of being stuck and unhappy in their relationships. They felt disconnected from people and God. Many said they felt lost and had a deep sense of dissatisfaction, but they didn't know why. For many of them it was also the first time they had shared any of this.

I learned that the main thing that gave them the courage to open up was feeling safe in the group. I already knew that the limbic system (heart) wouldn't reveal its secrets (which are actually belief systems) unless it was safe. I couldn't understand why people who seemed to have pretty good lives were so unhappy. They were smiling and looked good, but on the inside they suffered. I began to realize this was going to be harder than I thought. While praying about how to help them, the thought came to me that their spiritual beliefs and values didn't match their lifestyles—*they were spiritually stagnant.*

> *"No medicine is more valuable, none more efficacious,*
> *none better suited to the cure of all our temporal ills than*
> *a friend to whom we may turn for consolation*
> *in time of trouble, and with whom we may share*
> *our happiness in time of joy."*
> ~ Saint Aelred of Rievaulx [1]

> **KEY thought** — God's universe is always changing. Life is ending and beginning at the same time. It is never stagnant.

MADE FOR A PURPOSE

If there is one thing we know about God from observing what He has created, it is that He is not into stagnation. There is nothing in God's creation that is ever really stagnant. When something dies, it is transformed into something new. The Bible talks about this many times, for example in John 12:24, "Truly, truly, I say to you, unless a grain of wheat falls into the earth and dies, it remains alone; but if it dies, it bears much fruit." It is a principle of nature. So, how much more would He design in us, who are created in His image, a desire to be constantly growing and changing, never stagnant? We are designed for change and growth. Since the opposite of stagnation is change, what do you think God might use to get our attention when we become stagnant? Pain.

> **KEY thought** — Pain is a gift from God that tells us something is wrong so we can respond to it.

> *"God grant me the serenity to accept*
> *the things I cannot change, the courage to change*
> *the things I can, and the wisdom to know the difference."*
> ~ Reinhold Niebuhr, Author of the *Serenity Prayer*

We shouldn't be afraid of pain. In many ways, pain can be God's way of telling us that something is wrong so we can respond to it. It made sense to me that in some cases, God can use symptoms like (depression, compulsive coping behaviors, loneliness, anger, confusion, blaming, anxiety, dissatisfaction in life and relationships) as painful messages to get our attention to encourage change. Unfortunately, as human beings, it can take a lot of pain and discomfort to motivate some of us to change. When we ignore or anesthetize pain through self-destructive coping behaviors, we numb the "need-for-change" message it contains along with the motivation to do anything about it.

> **KEY thought** — We will find ourselves through giving ourselves away.

"For by grace you have been saved through faith; and that not of yourselves, it is the gift of God; not as a result of works, so that no one may boast. For we are His workmanship, created in Christ Jesus for good works, which God prepared beforehand so that we would walk in them." Ephesians 2:8–10

Throughout the New Testament, Jesus tries to communicate our role in God's plan. He says, "Let your light shine before men in such a way that they may see your good works, and glorify your Father who is in heaven" (Matthew 5:16). Part of the evidence of being born again is the desire to glorify God. The Bible tells us that all creation glorifies Him. But what does it mean to glorify God? I think we glorify God when each of us does the part we are called to do by fulfilling the unique purpose for which we were created. We are His body. Just as in nature, where each particular animal or plant has a purpose within the whole ecosystem, each of us has a gift and a calling that works with and benefits the whole of mankind. All creation brings glory to God by working together and benefiting everything else. There is one exception—humans.

Everything in the universe knows its created purpose except us. No matter how hard mankind tries to make things better, we keep making our world worse. Everything in creation seems to know something we don't—it hears something we don't. An ant doesn't have to go to "ant school" to learn to do its job better. It doesn't get depressed because it is a worker ant, when it always wanted to be a soldier ant. Think about how nature's creatures inherently know their job and purpose. No one teaches them. They just live the way they were created to live.

> *"Look deep into nature, and then you will understand everything better."*
> ~ Albert Einstein

Many of the people I've worked with feel lost with no sense of who they are or where they are going. They have said to me that they feel like they are just going through the motions, waiting for something to happen; they are not really alive. One of the main ways the enemy can create this sense of feeling lost is by wounding us in our giftedness. He tries to diminish our sense of purpose, which results in spiritual stagnation. He then uses our empty dissatisfaction to encourage us into destructive ways of coping, thus nullifying our effectiveness in the Kingdom. The result can be devastating to everyone around us, including ourselves.

A good example of this is the epidemic in the U.S. that many men in their forties and fifties that face—the "midlife crisis." These men (women, too) often begin to feel that nothing satisfies them anymore. They feel an emptiness, but don't know why or what's causing it. Their job, wife, home, and sex life aren't satisfying them; even their toys don't do it for them anymore. Something is missing. They feel restless and empty, blaming everything and everybody for their general dissatisfaction. Most of us can think of someone like that.

The most common way men in this situation seek to feel alive is through sex. Many men turn to pornography, have an affair, or get divorced, thinking that a new relationship will fill the void. In fact, the American Academy of Matrimonial Lawyers determined that Internet pornography and sex addiction were significant factors in about two out of three divorces.[2] All of these things may work temporarily to numb the emptiness of the stagnation they feel, but they only lead further away from dealing with the real problem. I have observed that when the men and women that I worked with developed a life with meaning, value, and purpose, including new challenges, their midlife crisis faded away. They felt alive again; the empty feeling of stagnation that was driving their search for vitality was gone.

> **KEY thought** — If you don't know who you are, you will end up somebody else. If you don't know where you are going, you will end up somewhere else.

A COMMON STORY

Jim came to me depressed and addicted to porn, alcohol and marijuana. He thought about suicide a lot. Jim was thirty-six years old and unable to hold on to relationships due to his addictions and anger issues. As we began to explore the origins of his behaviors (symptoms), we came to a memory of when he was six. He and his brother had each drawn a picture of a train for their dad, who was an alcoholic. His dad laughed and ridiculed the pictures. His brother just laughed it off and went out to play (his talent was sports). But Jim was deeply hurt because his talent was art—he was sensitive and creative. His dad said that only "girls and queers" drew pictures. Jim never drew again. Even in school when art was taught, Jim would refuse to participate and acted out; he was labeled a troublemaker.

Jim had totally forgotten these memories. After high school, he became a mechanic like his father. He hated it, but didn't know anything else. What do you think Jim's life was like? He knew something was missing. He said he "just felt empty." He filled the void by coping with drugs, porn, and anger. Through healing the memory, forgiving his father, and enrolling in art school at night, he discovered that he had a natural talent for it. He discovered his true identity and purpose, and even joined a local artist encouragement group. After a time, Jim was able to get free of his addictions. He told me it was the first time he could remember that he felt truly alive. When we live outside of our area of giftedness and purpose, our lives don't make much sense. We can become miserable, discontented, and often rely on self-destructive behaviors to cope.

> **KEY thought** — Each of us has a gift and a calling that God has placed within us to benefit others.

"As for you, the anointing you received from him remains in you, and you do not need anyone to teach you. But as his anointing teaches you about all things and as that anointing is real, not counterfeit—just as it has taught you, remain in him." 1 John 2:27 (NIV)

THE DILEMMA OF FREE WILL

So what went wrong? How did we get so messed up? The Bible tells us that we are unique, created in God's likeness, endowed with the gift of free will. We are the only observable creatures that are capable of making moral choices. We choose right from wrong, humility versus pride, honesty versus lying, grace versus legalism, love versus hate, and forgiveness versus revenge. When we mess up with our free will, however, we tend to blame God. After all, why didn't He step in to rescue us from our choices and those who were hurt as a result? When tragedy happens, I have seen many people lose their faith and become bitter towards God. Why did He let it happen? We love our free will, but we can't have it both ways. He gave us freedom to choose, but there are consequences for our choices.

For example, imagine I got angry and drunk. I drove my car too fast down the street, hitting and killing a child chasing after a ball. Whose fault was this? God's or mine? God could have stopped it, right? Maybe He could have prevented my car from starting or distracted the child into doing something else. Just a few seconds difference and the result would have been a saved life instead of prematurely ended one. As Christians, we might say things like, "Why didn't God prevent it?" "The devil did it." Or, "It must have been God's will." It is probably none of the above. I made the choice to drink, and in my anger, drive. It was the consequence of my own actions that killed the child.

"Jesus said to him, 'Because you have seen Me, have you believed? Blessed are they who did not see, and yet believed.'" John 20:29

Free will . . . this mystery has always bugged me. Why would a loving God give us such a gift, knowing what pain and suffering would come from it? He gave us so many desires and then says to us, "Don't give in to them." An example of this is the struggle men have with sexual thoughts and cravings more times a day than they can count. But if they act on them outside of the rules of God, it is sin. What a struggle! How many times have you heard, "I can't believe in a God who allows so much suffering and evil"? What's the test? What's the game? Why did He allow evil in the first place?

> **KEY thought** — If there was no evil then freewill would be redundant.

From the beginning of history, human beings have had an intense desire to really know Him personally. We have an inherent desire to know what is true, what is real. It drives me nuts. We want to walk and talk with Him on an intimate level. But who has done that? Only one person that I know of—Christ. It took me many years to gain some insight into this frustrating mystery. He gave us this God-like gift of free will, *asking us to love and trust Him enough to give it back to Him—to give Him control.* Without and evil, temptation, and sin there would be no moral choice—no free will. This is the test for our faith—to overcome our fear and the need to be in control and trust Him. "Thy will, not mine." The test is about faith and trust. Jesus is our example of this test. He said, "I don't do anything except what I see my Father doing, and I don't say anything except what I hear from Him" (John 5:19, 30). But even Jesus, who could relate to our struggles, had moments of doubt on the cross. Faith tells me to believe that if I do what's right, somehow, someway, He sees and will bless it. He honors steps of faith. I think the greatest test is to prove that I trust Him enough to give my free will back to Him. It is an ongoing battle and some days are better than others. But out of this test of free will and faith will come an amazing people—a crop of wonderful beings.

> "I have seen the burden God has laid on the human race. He has made everything beautiful in its time. He has also set eternity in the human heart; yet no one can fathom what God has done from beginning to end." Ecclesiastes 3:10–11 (NIV)

> **KEY thought** — Faith in action breaks the power of spiritual stagnation.

BREAKING THE POWER OF SPIRITUAL STAGNATION

When you choose to invest your time, talents, and gifts into the Kingdom of Heaven, you glorify God. It takes faith and courage to invest your life and resources into "that which is unseen" (Heb. 11:1). Think about the *Parable of the Talents* in Matthew 25. How did God feel about the man who hid his talents away rather than investing them? God wants us to step out in faith and take a risk. True faith involves risk and action. When you are glorifying God in this way, the result is faith and peace, but often our wounds and fears can hold us back. For most of us, real faith is a constant battle. But it is faith in action that breaks the power of spiritual stagnation. Remember, change comes from taking risks.

> "But store up for yourselves treasures in heaven, where neither moth nor rust destroys, and where thieves do not break in or steal; for where your treasure is, there your heart will be also. The eye is the lamp of the body; so then if your eye is clear, your whole body will be full of light." Matthew 6:20–22

> **KEY thought** — Glorifying God is investing your talents in what's important to Him.

THE FIFTH GOSPEL

I believe there is a covert message in the New Testament; I call it the "Fifth Gospel." The first four gospels are "the good news," but I call the fifth gospel "the bad news." Jesus conveys this message to those who "have ears to hear." He repeats this message over and over in his teachings, mostly in the form of parables. The message is this: When we have His Spirit in us, we will bear fruit. The majority of His parables and illustrations are about bearing fruit for the kingdom and the consequences we face when we don't. It can be a very uncomfortable message, so I think that is why He communicated it mostly in stories.

> "You are the light of the world. A city set on a hill cannot be hidden; nor does anyone light a lamp and put it under a basket, but on the lamp stand, and it gives light to all who are in the house. Let your light shine before men in such a way that they may see your good works, and glorify your Father who is in heaven." Matthew 5:14–16

For an interesting study, go though the New Testament and just read the parables and allegories of Jesus. Ask yourself, "Who is He talking to? What is the message He is trying to convey?" "How does it relate to me personally?" Look at how many of them are about the same theme. Here are a few parables about bearing fruit you can find in the New Testament (there is a full list of the parables and metaphors of Jesus in the Notes). [3]

- The Talents (Matthew 25:14–30)
- The Goats and the Sheep (Matthew 25:31–46)
- The Unfruitful Fig Tree (Luke 13:6–9)
- The Wheat and the Tares (Matthew 13:24–30)
- The Seed and the Four Types of Soil (Matthew 13:5–8)
- The Mustard Seed (Matthew 13:31–3)
- The Good Samaritan (Luke 10:25–37)
- The Ten Virgins (Matthew 25:1–13)
- The Two Sons (Matthew 21:28–32)
- The Hidden Treasures and the Pearl of Great Price (Matthew 13:44–46)
- The Vine and the Vinedresser (John 15:1–8)

Let's take a look at the last one for further study:

THE VINE AND THE VINEDRESSER

"I am the true vine, and My Father is the vinedresser. Every branch in Me that does not bear fruit, He takes away; and every branch that bears fruit, He prunes it so that it may bear more fruit. You are already clean because of the word, which I have spoken to you. Abide in Me, and I in you. As the branch cannot bear fruit of itself unless it abides in the vine, so neither can you unless you abide in Me. I am the vine, you are the branches; he who abides in Me and I in him, he bears much fruit, for apart from Me you can do nothing. If anyone does not abide in Me, he is thrown away as a branch and dries up; and they gather them, and cast them into the fire and they are burned. If you abide in Me, and My words abide in you, ask whatever you wish, and it will be done for you. My Father is glorified by this, that you bear much fruit, and so prove to be My disciples." (John 15:1–8)

Jesus' message is clear: If He is in us; there will be evidence of it. Fruit bearing in the New Testament comes when God moves through us to change and heal other human beings. The goats and the sheep, and the wheat and the tares are also very clear examples of this same message. God wants to reveal Himself and change the world through us. In other words, we can't bear fruit and be spiritually stagnant at the same time. We have to hear His voice and obey. As in the *Parable of the Talents*, we will have to risk our talents (gifts) to bear fruit. Many people think that when the Bible asks us to be obedient, it means that God wants us to do something, an action; however, in many verses the word obedience in the Greek (*hupakouo*) means "to hear," which requires relationship and intimacy.

This explains why Jesus says so many times, "He who has an ear to hear, let him hear what the Spirit says." He knows our heart, and if we don't have a heart to obey, we won't have an ear to hear what He has to say. It is all about our hearts. This is where religious legalism can sneak in. When we don't have a relationship with God, we try to feel right by obeying all the rules and rituals—the dos and don'ts. Jesus would probably say, "Yeah, that's all good, but where's the fruit?" Neglecting our personal, God-given purpose and gifts can result in Him trying to get our attention through the symptoms of spiritual stagnation—dissatisfaction, suffering, conviction, guilt, isolation, depression, compulsive coping behaviors, loneliness, anger, confusion, blaming, anxiety, relationship issues, etc.

> *Love is a fruit in season at all times,*
> *and within reach of every hand.*
> ~ Mother Teresa

I met a man once who was very religious. I was trying to get him to understand that Christianity is about being able to hear the voice of God personally. He put his hands up and said, "I want none of that. I have children and He will probably tell me to go to Africa where we will all get slaughtered or die of some disease." At least he was honest. I have met many people since who want God, but don't want to give up control. They are not willing to give up their free will and trust Him yet. It is an act of our will and discipline to give up our free will. It begins with enough faith to take a risk, i.e. trust Him. It begins with a decision to move in that direction. As parents, when is it that we experience the most rewarding moments while our children are growing up? For most of us, it is watching them discover and explore their own unique giftedness. Our hearts swell as they discover their natural God-given talents, whether they are athletes, artists, rocket scientists, ballerinas, musicians, good parents, missionaries, engineers, or mechanics. It is one of the most satisfying experiences we have as parents. It is amazing how children with the same genetics growing up in the same environment can be so different, each with unique talents. I believe God feels the same way when He sees us discovering our unique God-given gifts and exploring our potential.

On the other hand, how do we feel as parents when we see our kids just wasting their talents by playing video games all day or not doing anything productive? We turn up the heat; we will do something to try and motivate them to change. God is the same; He tries to get our attention, usually by making us uncomfortable. Change usually begins from being made uncomfortable. We will only discover our true potential through stepping out and risking, which can both fearful and hard work. But to each one of us grace was given according to the measure of Christ's gift. Therefore it says, "When He ascended on high, He led captive a host of captives, and He gave gifts to men" (Ephesians 4:7–9).

Trusting God and taking steps of faith is the hardest part of having a relationship with Him. One idea I've always struggled with is the idea that when we die we are going to be in the heavenly choir for eternity. Somehow that just doesn't compute with how I've seen God work in my own heart and life. I think we are created to be exploring and discovering our potential in Him *forever*. I believe that Heaven will be a continuation of our quest for truth and our real identity. I don't think He wants us to be stagnant and unchanging in Heaven, just like he doesn't want it for us on earth. I could be wrong. Remember, the opposite of stagnation is change. Change usually comes from taking a risk—a step of faith. Looking back, I can't remember God ever asking me to do something that I wanted to do, but His task always resulted in growth and change. It's one way I know that it must be Him doing the asking, otherwise why would I be doing something I don't want to do. Maybe it is just a prodigal thing.

"Change comes from taking risks and the greatest risk is to be honest with yourself and others."
~ Rick Warren, *The Purpose Driven Life*

As I got more involved with the church groups, this idea of spiritual stagnation developed into an action plan that produced real change. I was amazed at how many of the group members struggles began to fade away as they explored their gifts and reached out to others. The group helped each person identify their talents and held them accountable with support to do something with them that benefited others. Many of them got completely off their anxiety and depression medications and became more vibrant and active. The most dramatic result was exhibited in their relationships. Once their lives began to have meaning and purpose, they stopped blaming others for their feelings of emptiness and lack of fulfillment. They realized their problem was internal, not external.

Many of the men with sex addiction began to get better. This concept is not a cure-all for everyone, but it is worth a try. See what happens. What have you got to lose?

RENA'S STORY

Dear Michael,

I have been diagnosed with chronic depression. No one could really figure out why, as my life is pretty good and I don't have any major childhood traumas to explain it. I gave up on counseling, as it didn't help. I just felt down and lethargic most of the time. I have had all sorts of prayer, even deliverance, which didn't help. I felt so guilty for being this way. There must be something I'm not doing right, like trusting God enough? Well, two things happened almost at the same time. First, I read an article on depression that talked about a research project that found that volunteering—helping others—was more effective than medication at alleviating depression. I had also just started the Change Book Process on Spiritual Stagnation, which was saying pretty much the same thing. Well, I felt God was speaking to me. I always thought I was too depressed to have anything to give. My group challenged me to use my gift of mercy by volunteering at a local homeless shelter. The moment I walked in, I began to feel lighter. I can't explain it. It was like "Honey, I'm home." I belong here. I have been helping there along with a women's rehab for a year now and I am so much better. So many Scriptures about loving and giving have really come alive for me. I get much more than I give.

In Him,
Rena

> *"The only thing necessary for the triumph of evil is for good men to do nothing."*
> ~ Edmund Burke (1729–1797)[4]

IMMATURITY VS. MATURITY

There are basically two stages of growth in the life of a human being: immaturity and maturity. In the first part of life, you grow by receiving. Your family and community invest in you for the first twenty years or so (some of us much longer) without expecting much back. Then, as you mature, you're expected to give back by investing in your community and the next generation. Christianity follows the same pattern. At first you are called a "baby Christian," immature in the faith and learning from others how to live as a believer. The church has programs, such as discipleship classes and Bible studies, to help you grow. Again, you're not expected to do much at first, but as you grow, you begin to learn how to serve and give back.

The same is true for the world of recovery. You begin by going to 12-step meetings and getting a sponsor. Your sponsor invests his or her time and energy in guiding you through the steps until you get to Step 12, which says, *Having had a spiritual awakening as the result of these steps, we tried to carry this message to alcoholics, and to practice these principles in all our affairs.* Mature recovering people have learned that their ability to stay sober long-term depends on helping others achieve it too. Giving back what others and God have done for you comes from a grateful heart. It is a *pay it forward* thing.

> "When you cease to make a contribution, you begin to die."
> ~ Eleanor Roosevelt (1884–1962)

KEY thought — If you don't give, you don't grow.

GIVE TO GROW

At some point, we don't grow anymore by only receiving; we only grow by giving. If you don't give, you don't grow. You can go to Bible studies for the rest of your life, memorize the Bible in Greek and Hebrew, and not grow a bit. Growth comes when you try to apply what the Bible says, which takes courage, faith, and good leadership. James 2:14–18 says, "Faith without works is dead." Continual study about God is safe; the knowledge is in your head. However, personal relationship with Him is not safe, because that involves your heart, where you give Him control. It requires maturity in your faith to surrender your heart and will to him. Don't get me wrong—I love the Bible and read it every day. As a recovering Pharisee, I have to guard my heart because knowledge puffs up—knowledge and being right is the "drug of choice" for a Pharisee.

> "You search the Scriptures because you think that in them you have eternal life; it is these that testify about Me; and you are unwilling to come to Me so that you may have life." John 5:39–40

Many of us have been taught that being a good Christian is going to endless Bible studies. When people say they are "in the Word," it usually means they are studying the Bible, but the Bible itself is not the true Word of God; it is a book about the Word of God—God's incarnate Son, Jesus Christ. John 1:1 & 14 says, "In the beginning was the Word, and the Word was with God, and the Word was God. And the Word became flesh, and dwelt among us, and we saw His glory, glory as of the only begotten from the Father, full of grace and truth." The Word of God is a person. The Bible is a book about that person. Many of us have lost sight of this basic truth. We have exchanged a relationship with Jesus for a relationship with a book and a religion. It is easy for us to believe that religion is all there is—study and pray. If we just keep taking in without giving out, we will become spiritually constipated, stagnant. It is a law of nature, much like a dammed up pond with only an inflow and no outflow.

> *Life is like riding a bicycle. To keep your balance,*
> *you must keep moving.*
> ~ Albert Einstein

I think many of us are tired of studying *about* Jesus. Now we want to do something *with* Jesus. Breaking the power of spiritual stagnation and healing our hearts starts with the experience of being "born again," involving a personal relationship with the Creator of the Universe. Because our wounds came from unhealthy experiences in relationship, our healing will come from opposite, healthy experiences. When we are "born again," God starts us on a path of *learning to trust again*. Healing in the Bible always comes through faith, and faith comes from hearing the Word of Christ (Romans 10:17). The Greek term used here for Word is *rhema*, which means, "a spoken, personal word to the hearer." Of course God can speak to us through the Bible, but how long will He if we don't apply it? In my own quest as a recovering Pharisee, there came a point that I simply wanted to know Him, not just study about Him. This is the key step that leads from immaturity to maturity.

> "All praise to the God and Father of our Master, Jesus the Messiah! Father of all mercy! God of all healing counsel! He comes alongside us when we go through hard times, and before you know it, he brings us alongside someone else who is going through hard times so that we can be there for that person just as God was there for us. We have plenty of hard times that come from following the Messiah, but no more so than the good times of his healing comfort—we get a full measure of that, too." 2 Corinthians 1:4 (MSG)

Once again, let's look at the message Jesus is trying to convey in the *Parable of the Talents* in Matthew 25:14–30 and Luke 19:12–27. Jesus tells a story about investing His resources in four different people. Three of them invested well and brought back more than they started with. Jesus tells them, "Now that you have been faithful with the little things, I am going to give you what is important to me, which are cities" (Luke 19:17). What are cities but people? I could never understand Jesus' reaction toward the one poor guy that just went and hid his talent away. He didn't go out and blow it on wine, women, and gambling, and he didn't lie about it. He was just afraid that he would lose it all and the master would be angry, so he hid it away and gave it back to him exactly as he had received it. Jesus continued the story with the master saying, "Throw the worthless slave into the outer darkness; in that place, there will be weeping and gnashing of teeth." I always thought this was a bit harsh. So what's the lesson? The last servant didn't have faith. He didn't risk using the *talents* that God had given him. It says in Hebrews 11:6, "Without faith it is impossible to please God."

Another example is the *Parable of the Two Sons* in Matthew 21:28. The father tells his two sons to go work in the field. One son said he would go and didn't. The other son said he wouldn't go, but later changed his mind and went. Jesus tells us it doesn't matter how we get there, just so we go. I can really relate to the second son because I am basically an "Eeyore," a melancholy pessimist. I eventually do what the Lord tells me to do, but I complain the whole time.

> **KEY thought** Real recovery is to become a human being again.

FEAR KEEPS US STAGNANT

Fear is main thing that prevents us from healing the symptoms that may be caused by spiritual stagnation. You have to take risks with what God has given you. Nothing else will work. It is a risk because it is in giving and being vulnerable with your true talents (identity) that you are most vulnerable and can be most wounded. He tells us all through the Bible, *"Do not fear, for I am with you."* It takes faith to give and you must give to grow. Reaching out to others is something healthy, mature people do willingly and naturally—not because they have to. The desire to give is the main evidence of a mature human being.

As we recover, we return to becoming healthy human beings again. Human beings are designed to feel what other human beings are feeling. It is an emotion called empathy. But when we are immature, struggling with secrets or self-centered fears, Jesus tell us that the "log in our eye" will keep us from being able to see clearly the needs of those around us. The other day I had a frustrated woman ask me, "How can I tell whether a man is healthy or not? I seem to not be able to pick well." I told her, "I think the main sign of a healthy (mature) man is that he is more others-centered than self-centered." I think this same principal applies to churches also. It is not easy to break free of the mindset of the "me" generation.

> *"It is from numberless diverse acts of courage and belief that human history is shaped. Each time a man stands up for an ideal, or acts to improve the lot of others, or strikes out against injustice, he sends forth a tiny ripple of hope, and crossing each other from a million different centers of energy and daring, those ripples build a current that can sweep down the mightiest walls of oppression and resistance."*
> ~ Robert F. Kennedy (1925–1968)

BEWARE OF COMPLACENCY

The following passage about the goats and the sheep tells us by what standard Jesus is going to measure us:

> "Then the King will say to those on his right, 'Enter, you who are blessed by my Father! Take what's coming to you in this kingdom. It's been ready for you since the world's foundation. And here's why: I was hungry and you fed me, I was thirsty and you gave me a drink, I was homeless and you gave me a room, I was shivering and you gave me clothes, I was sick and you stopped to visit, I was in prison and you came to me.' Then those 'sheep' are going to say, 'Master, what are you talking about? When did we ever see you hungry and feed you, thirsty and give you a drink? And when did we ever see you sick or in prison and come to you?' Then the King will say, 'I'm telling the solemn truth: Whenever you did one of these things to someone overlooked or ignored, that was me—you did it to me.'"

He then addresses the goats (who didn't know they were goats):

> "Then he will turn to the 'goats,' the ones on his left, and say, 'Get out, worthless goats! You're good for nothing but the fires of hell. And why? Because—I was hungry and you gave me no meal, I was thirsty and you gave me no drink, I

> was homeless and you gave me no bed, I was shivering and you gave me no clothes, I was sick and in prison, and you never visited.' Then those 'goats' are going to say, 'Master, what are you talking about? When did we ever see you hungry or thirsty or homeless or shivering or sick or in prison and didn't help?' He will answer them, 'I'm telling the solemn truth: Whenever you failed to do one of these things to someone who was being overlooked or ignored, that was me—you failed to do it to me.' Then those 'goats' will be herded to their eternal doom, but the 'sheep' to their eternal reward." Matthew 25:34–36 (MSG)

This is a tough message, but a key thought here is that until Jesus separated them, the goats thought they were sheep. And the sheep weren't consciously aware that they had done anything special. They were just responding to the needs around them. They were not doing good deeds to earn their way into heaven. Many of Christ's parables have the same message. If we are in Him and He is in us, we will be doing some of the things He did, but He says there is a consequence for doing nothing. The good news is that it's never too late to get going, like the workers in the vineyard (Matt 20:1–16). Read John 17 about His prayer for our intimacy with Him. This subject has been probably the most divisive topic in Christianity for hundreds of years: Are we saved by grace or by works? The truth is that no one really knows. If someone says they do, they need to join my recovering Pharisee group.

> "Listen carefully: Unless a grain of wheat is buried in the ground, dead to the world, it is never any more than a grain of wheat. But if it is buried, it sprouts and reproduces itself many times over. In the same way, anyone who holds on to life just as it is destroys that life. But if you let it go, reckless in your love, you'll have it forever, real and eternal. If any of you wants to serve me, then follow me. Then you'll be where I am, ready to serve at a moment's notice. The Father will honor and reward anyone who serves me." John 12:25–26 (MSG)

REDIRECTING PRIORITIES

One of the main strategies of the enemy is to keep us so busy that we feel overwhelmed and don't have time for what is a really important—our relationships. How did we all become so busy? The hardest thing for most of us to give is our time. It is investing time in others that makes them feel valuable and important, which is the most important component in healing broken hearts. Breaking spiritual stagnation is not about doing good deeds or winning souls, it is about a heart change. You won't do anything for very long if your heart is not in it. It is a change in priorities—what is valuable to you.

The Genesis Process is focused on helping people change and heal so that they, in turn, can help others. It is a natural progression a, *pay it forward* thing. For those of you who are already very busy, this may seem stressful—just one more thing to do. But being too busy can prevent you from seeing what is really important. Being busy can become its own coping mechanism or excuse to not have to feel or take a risk. Giving of yourself is a process that will come naturally as you continue to change, heal, and begin to function as a human being again. There are many studies that have shown that one of the most effective treatments for depression and self-destructive behavior is altruism—helping others. I love it when science validates and confirms what the Bible has told us all along. It is more blessed to give than to receive. We always get more than we give when we help others.

The first step to redirecting your priorities is to pray and ask God to share His heart with you about the talents He has given you and the kind of work He has for you to do. You may need to ask the people close to you for what they think. Second, share with others what you believe He is saying to you (this is called accountability). Third, be willing to take a risk in giving of yourself to others. It is most effective if you have the support and accountability of a group. There are such things as good addictions. Once the Holy Spirit moves through you to change a life, you will be spoiled for the ordinary. You will literally come alive.

I don't believe people are looking for the meaning of life as much as they are looking for the experience of being alive.
~ Joseph Campbell, Author

> **KEY thought** — I think in the end what defines us as human beings is the influence we had on others that made them better people.

MORE THAN A PROGRAM

This simple knowledge of getting more when we give brings us to an understanding of how God designed life to work. Wounded people who have become self-destructive—like addicts, alcoholics, prostitutes, and criminals—need the church in order to grow spiritually and not relapse. Not just those outside the church, but the countless numbers of church people who also need help.

Remember—what heals a broken person is when one person invests himself into another. It's interesting how He set this up, because the church (people) needs the broken people to give to in order to grow and prevent the symptoms of spiritual stagnation. The two groups need each other!

Christians can't grow and fulfill their mission for the Kingdom of God without real people to give to. This is a "win-win-win" situation. Christians win when they give of themselves to real people in need—they get out of spiritual stagnation and experience Jesus in a life-changing way. Hurting people win when they experience true change and healing, possibly having God in their lives for the first time. And God wins because He cares more about people than anything else. He gets to see His children reach their true potential and purpose for their lives as He intended. He swells with pride as a father.

*"The purpose of life is not to be happy.
It is to be useful, to be honorable, to be compassionate,
to have it make some difference that you have lived and lived well."*
~ Ralph Waldo Emerson

> **KEY thought** We are the body of Christ; He works through us.

As Christians, many of us have created a safe environment by just ministering to each other over and over again. When Cathy and I were missionaries, we got into this rut many times. It is easy to become self-focused, which isn't scriptural. Healthy people and churches are outward-focused. Within a mile of your church, there are probably a thousand people who have been praying that God would help them with their painful situation. Many of them don't even believe in God, but in the wee hours, when the pain is overwhelming, they cry out to Him for help because they have no other hope. They say, "If you're there, God, give me a sign and send me some help!" When people pray, how does God answer those prayers? Through people! We are the body of Christ; He works through us.

At the end of the gospels, Jesus is taken up into the clouds and He commissions the disciples, essentially saying, "You are my church, you are my body, you are my hands and my feet, my money, my love, and my compassion. When I want to get something done down here, I am going to use you." Between you and me, I don't think it has been a very good system. When I get up there, I'd like to tell Him that He should just take care of things Himself because we are not being very effective down here. He has chosen to answer prayers through us, and it seems sometimes that very few prayers of hurting people are being answered. Perhaps this is because very few of us have "an ear to hear" what God is saying.

Working in the recovery field, one of the hardest lessons that I have had to learn is that programs in of themselves don't work. Change comes through relationships. We need to give in order to grow and others need to receive in order to heal. I believe God always meant it to work this way. Look at nature; everything works together to the benefit of everything else. As we die to ourselves, others are nourished. He is going to change lives through us. I spent years studying and designing programs in hopes of coming up with the perfect strategy that would restore broken lives. I wanted broken people to come through the door and healthy people to exit six months later. If a program existed for healing hurting and addicted people, we would all be doing that program.

> **KEY thought** What works in restoring broken lives is when one person invests himself in another person.

It is safe to say that almost every family has one—someone whose self-destructive behavior or emotion (like anger) affects the whole family. So the question is: How can the church play a major part in helping this overwhelming number of struggling people experience freedom? All this takes us back to the reason for writing this book. If relationships are at the root of our self-destructive behavior, and it takes healthy and healing relationships to produce real recovery, then you can see why it is only the church that has the people resources for this kind of one-on-one investment. Remember what works to heal wounded hearts is when one person invests himself in another. The Bible is full of stories about this principle.

> **KEY thought** We need someone else to complete us.

Wounded people became damaged when they trusted others and consequently were betrayed, abused, abandoned, and neglected—only an opposite experience can heal them. We now understand the logistics of that process by how the limbic system works. Most of my recovery books are based on how these brain/heart wounds drive self-destructive behavior. Healing these heart wounds and real recovery only happens through new positive experiences with healthy relationships. This explains why we have seen such a low percentage of lasting fruit in the recovery ministry. The average recovery rates for most residential Christian agencies are about 10 to 15 percent at best, although I know a few who are doing much better than that.[5] Sex and food addictions have the lowest recovery rates, at about only about 5 percent. It takes more than just a good program—grace and competency invested individually is what makes the true difference. We will look at the power of grace in Chapter 8.

> "In everything I showed you that by working hard in this manner you must help the weak and remember the words of the Lord Jesus, that He Himself said, 'It is more blessed to give than to receive.' When he had said these things, he knelt down and prayed with them all." Acts 20:35-36

God designed it this way from the beginning—those in Christ would need hurting people to minister to in order to exercise their faith, stay healthy, and grow just as much as the hurting people need the church to heal.

It is a partnership. *The best evangelism is a changed life.* In 1 Corinthians 2:1-5, Paul talks about this symbiotic relationship. He says, "And so it was with me, brothers and sisters. When I came to you, I did not come with eloquence or human wisdom as I proclaimed to you the testimony about God. For I resolved to know nothing while I was with you except Jesus Christ and him crucified. I came to you in weakness with great fear and trembling. My message and my preaching were not with wise and persuasive words, but with a demonstration of the Spirit's power, so that your faith might not rest on human wisdom, but on God's power." (NIV)

I think Paul came to the same realization that many of us in the trenches have come to—there is power in simplicity. Actions are more powerful than words. Christ and Him crucified working through His body.

> **KEY thought** — The best evangelism is a changed life.

In our age, what is the demonstration of the Spirit of God that Paul is talking about? For us today, it's not changing water into wine, walking on water, or parting the sea—it's simply a changed life. Someone who used to be part of the problem is now part of the solution. Remember from Chapter 1, the first thing I learned from all those years in eastern religions was that I couldn't change myself. We are made for relationship.

Western culture has become increasingly independent and self-centered. As Christians, we are not immune to society's attitudes. I have had the opportunity to travel quite a bit and observe churches and ministries up close. It seems that many of us believe being a "good Christian" means that we go to church on Sunday, attend a Bible study, go to the retreat every year, be in a small group, and maybe even go on a mission trip and build something. These things are all good, but no wonder we are so stagnant! Most of us are not really involved in the lives of others, especially non-Christians. Jesus tells us that we must lose ourselves in order to find ourselves. We will find the meaning of our lives through giving ourselves away. As we step out in faith and get involved, we end up getting more than we give.

> **KEY thought** For many of us, our lives will never make sense until our pain becomes someone else's gain.

REDEEMING OUR PAIN

We have all wondered at some point why God allows bad things to happen, especially when we are trying to do good. I have seen many workers and leaders who have been hurt, or who have messed up, shrink back from their calling. When we do that, we may never experience the richness of realizing our potential and learn the lesson from the experience. Sometimes we feel completely disqualified from serving God; we fear we have screwed up too badly to be used by Him again. We can be especially confused about why God allowed bad things to happen to us in the first place, especially in our childhood. He could have stopped it or warned us, right? It is one of the oldest theological questions: Why does a loving God allow bad things to happen to good people?

There is a phenomenon I have observed over and over again—for many of us, our lives will never make sense until our pain becomes someone else's gain. I believe God guides us into experiences that can help us make peace with our past and be able to move on with our lives. It is when our pain becomes someone else's gain—our struggle becomes our ministry and our pain is ultimately redeemed for good. It says in Romans 8:28, "And we know that God causes all things to work together for the good to those who love God, to those who are called according to His purpose." God can turn the enemy's plan of destruction into a path of construction. I love it!

Unfortunately, we can be most wounded in our areas of gifting, our true identity. Instinctively, that becomes the area we guard the most. I have trained many missionary teams in these principles and I have worked with wounded people who are trying to sort themselves out in the mission field. Many of them are confused like I was about where they belonged and what they were doing there. Why would God call us into ministry and then let us experience betrayal and more wounds instead of fruit? It doesn't make sense sometimes, and it can be very discouraging. Many are waiting to be healed before they believe God can use them. God honors steps of faith; I have seen many stuck people experience healing by stepping out in faith and doing something for others. God brings healing as they trust Him and begin reaching out to others. If He calls us, He will also equip us.

> *What does love look like? It has the hands to help others.*
> *It has the feet to hasten to the poor and needy.*
> *It has eyes to see misery and want.*
> *It has the ears to hear the sighs and sorrows of men.*
> *That is what love looks like.*
>
> ~ Saint Augustine

What I try to do is to put stuck people in a situation where the Holy Spirit will move through their experiences and giftedness to change another life. At that moment, many have a flash of clarity that I believe no other experience can produce. It is a moment where confusion is replaced with peace. I think that's the way God always meant it to work—our struggle becomes our ministry. Many of the stories in this book are about people's struggles becoming their gift to others. Many of my addicts have become very effective addiction counselors. He begins by doing more in us than through us because it is out of who we are that He will give us something meaningful to do.

My wife and I spent the first fifteen years in ministry bearing little lasting fruit while He worked on our (mostly my) character flaws. I don't think there will be a point where He is done with me. Prodigals learn everything the hard way. He says He will prune and discipline those He loves, so some of us seemed to be loved more than others. Looking back, it was all worth it—seeing our pain become someone else's gain. It is all about faith; our pain redeemed.

"My son, do not make light of the Lord's discipline, and do not lose heart when he rebukes you, because the Lord disciplines the one he loves, and he chastens everyone he accepts as his son. Endure hardship as discipline; God is treating you as his children. For what children are not disciplined by their father? If you are not disciplined—and everyone undergoes discipline—then you are not legitimate, not true sons and daughters at all. Moreover, we have all had human fathers who disciplined us and we respected them for it. How much more should we submit to the Father of spirits and live! They disciplined us for a little while as they thought best; but God disciplines us for our good, in order that we may share in his holiness. No discipline seems pleasant at the time, but painful. Later on, however, it produces a harvest of righteousness and peace for those who have been trained by it." Hebrews 10:6–11

GAIN FROM PAIN

Dear Mike,

I have a long history of abuse and making bad choices. I was abused by most of the men in my family. Starting at about eleven years old, I became promiscuous and started using drugs. My drug use increased to the point where I found myself prostituting for drugs and drug money. I became a compulsive thief and liar. By the time I was eighteen, I think I was spending as much time in jail as out. I felt I had no value and really didn't care what happened to me. A judge ordered me to either go to treatment or go to prison. Even though I was angry and hated him, as he seemed hard and cold at the time, he probably saved my life. The only program I could afford (which was free) was a local Christian rehab. I was very resistant because I hated God for my life and Christians who I judged as hypocrites. Many of my sex customers were supposedly Christian, some ministers. Well to make a long story short, Jesus visited me one night and I gave my life to Him. I told Him I was mad at Him for allowing so many bad things to happen to me. He just said, "Trust me." That was three years ago. I am now going back into the jail teaching the Bible and the Genesis Process. They listen to me because I have been there. I also do a group with teen girls at church who are cutting themselves. They know I understand their pain and don't judge them. I now look at my past and don't resent it anymore because I am seeing so many lives changed. My past has become my bridge to helping others. He has given me a reason to live and stay clean. I could never have imagined my life could count for something.

Viv

> "No one is useless in this world who lightens
> the burdens of another."
> ~ Charles Dickens

Paul's life is a great example of someone who experienced the redemption of his pain, in his case, his self-righteous pride. His struggle was with being a judgmental, legalistic Pharisee. Instead, he became the New Testament author of grace. But God gave him a thorn in the flesh (pain) with a specific purpose—to keep him humble. He prayed three times that God would take it away and God said, "No. My grace is sufficient for you" (2 Corinthians 12:6–8). So think about your life and all the thorns in your flesh and heart, most of which are from people. Why do you think he allowed those thorns, especially from other Christians? Ask yourself, "How can the struggles I have gone through benefit others?"

SUMMARY

There is a danger in remaining spiritually stagnant. Until you do something good with your pain by helping others, you cannot break the power of spiritual stagnation and you will not grow. Worse, your pain may never make sense. When you don't see the gain from your pain, then you will most likely focus only on the pain, which can result in anger, bitterness, depression—or worse a self-destructive coping behavior. Most of us know someone who seems stuck like this. Their pain has become their identity. Paul tells us in Hebrews, "Pursue peace with all men, and the sanctification without which no one will see the Lord. See to it that no one comes short of the grace of God; that no root of bitterness springing up causes trouble, and by it many be defiled" (Hebrews 12:14–15).

We can generate an atmosphere in which our bitterness and stagnation affects those around us. It doesn't have to be that way! Our joy, peace, and faith will also affect others. In the 60s we called it our "vibes." The best cure for bitterness and unforgiveness (bad vibes) is to see ourselves, our circumstances and people through God's eyes. It can be hard to accept the life He has given us, but the fruit of reaching out in a step of faith will be to experience spiritual renewal, freedom from (or acceptance of) our pain, and the joy, peace, and faith that comes along with it.

I think the hardest part of recovery is to accept our limitations, our thorns, but it can be done. All of this may feel a bit overwhelming, but I hope you can hear the goal of my heart is to:

- Make individuals and churches safe and effective to help hurting people.
- See God glorified through the church, which happens when one person invests himself in another.
- See Christians changing and becoming excited about what God is doing in them and through them.

You have to break the power of spiritual stagnation to do that. You have to give to grow, and change is exciting. That is true evangelism.

FREEDOM FROM SPIRITUAL STAGNATION

I have included a basic format in the notes for a *Change Group* for those who wanted to try something different. It is designed to encourage *Christian Spirituality* and personal growth.[6]

SELF-DISCOVERY QUESTIONS

1. Does your church give opportunities and encouragement for stepping out and finding your potential?

2. What, if any, symptoms of spiritual stagnation do you identify with?

3. If you had no fear, money was not a problem, and you could go anywhere to help a particular group of people, what or who would it be? Who do you have a heart for?

PRACTICAL APPLICATION

Take a risk—a step of faith—by reaching out to someone, or some group, and give of your area of talent. How did you feel? What was different?

CHAPTER SEVEN

FREEDOM FROM THE PHARISAICAL SPIRIT

> **KEY thought** — In a safe church, people are more important than rules.

"Do not judge so that you will not be judged. For in the way you judge, you will be judged; and by your standard of measure, it will be measured to you. Why do you look at the speck that is in your brother's eye, but do not notice the log that is in your own eye? Or how can you say to your brother, 'Let me take the speck out of your eye,' and behold, the log is in your own eye? You hypocrite, first take the log out of your own eye, and then you will see clearly to take the speck out of your brother's eye." Matthew 7:1–5

DEFINING THE PHARISAICAL SPIRIT

When talking about what works to help the hurting heal, we also need to look at what hinders. Understanding the significance of *Pharisaical* and its implications in effective ministry is of primary importance. A Pharisee is defined as one who is "self-righteously obsessed with rules; one acting with hypocrisy, self-righteousness, or obsessiveness with regard to the strict adherence to rules and formalities."[1] Overcoming the Pharisee in me has been my biggest personal struggle since becoming a Christian. I've learned over the years (the hard way) that this spirit (attitude) is the most common hindrance to helping seekers be able or willing to receive help. It is insidious and very hard for Christians to see because it can be so self-justified. The Pharisaical Spirit is the spirit of religious legalism and most of us have it to some degree.

> *"The devil loves nothing better than
> the intolerance of reformers."*
> ~ James Russell Lowell [2]

> *"Forbear to judge, for we are sinners all."*
> ~ William Shakespeare

I have a friend named Ted who owns a gas station in a small town. He is very evangelistic, especially on tow truck calls. He has seen many come to the Lord through his words and acts of kindness. He told me a story about a lonely man who lived by himself out of town. He was an alcoholic and a very angry person. Ted had been trying for several years to get him to ask Christ into his life and come to church. Finally, one day the man hit bottom and asked Ted to pray with him. He had a genuine experience and wanted to change his life. The man began going to Ted's church and had stopped drinking. He went forward during an altar call and wanted to be baptized. The pastor found out that he was aqua-phobic—he couldn't put his head under water. The pastors and elders had very heated meetings for several weeks about what to do. They finally decided that the man could not be baptized because they believed the "Greek" word for baptism (*baptizo*) means *full immersion*. If he couldn't put his fear aside to be baptized biblically, he wasn't really serious. The man went back to his old lifestyle and wouldn't have anything to do with Ted or the church.

Another friend of mine, who read this story, wrote: "The same thing happened in our church growing up, except the woman agreed to be immersed. I remember the service. She came up sobbing and clinging to the pastor, who told the congregation what an amazing lady she was to be so obedient, because there was no other way one could be baptized." What would Jesus have done?

In the first chapter, I talked about my struggle as a recovering Pharisee and how much I was like Paul when he was still Saul. Paul was the "Pharisee of Pharisees." He struggled with religiosity, legalism, self-righteousness, being judgmental, independence, pride, and the violence and anger that stem from these. After Paul's life-changing encounter on the road to Damascus, he had to wait about twelve years before Barnabas came to get him in Tarsus. For twelve years, life must have been pretty frustrating for Paul. He experienced many visions and insights and had a very clear call on his life to reach the nations outside Israel with the gospel. But during that time, he didn't establish any churches or accomplish very much. It took twelve years for God to deal with Paul's heart of pride and self-righteous legalism before He could use him. It took me sixteen years—I must be a harder case than Paul.

Eventually Paul understood that this trial was part of God's plan to make him the New Testament author of grace. What a turnaround! God turned Paul's greatest struggle and character flaw into his area of ministry from a self-righteous Pharisee to the New Testament's primary author of grace.

How do you know if you're a Pharisee or not? There are several indicators to consider.

PHARISEES DON'T BEAR FRUIT

Since Paul and I share many of those same character faults and struggles, it was no surprise that my early efforts to help people weren't bearing much fruit. Like Paul, I also believed I could do it on my own and didn't need other people. My core belief was, "Other people need me, but I don't need them." At the same time, I was frustrated with God because I wasn't seeing fruit in my missionary work. I eventually learned that it was my pharisaical nature that kept me from bearing fruit in the ministry God had for me. In those days, I proudly wore a t-shirt that summed up my black and white theology. It simply said, "Turn or Burn." I also blamed everything and everyone else for my problems, especially the devil. That is always an easy explanation. It really didn't occur to me that I was the problem. I was frustrated, unsafe, and unfruitful. Like Paul, I had insights and gifts that I knew could help people change. The problem was that no one wanted what I had to offer. It took many years to find out that the real source of my frustrations was me.

Trying to identify and remove what was "religious" in me was difficult and frightening, as I became unsure of what I really believed. I found that so much of what I believed was based in doctrinal religiosity and it really didn't work in the real world. I had to become an empty new wineskin. Recovering from sex, drugs, and rock 'n' roll was easy compared to being a recovering Pharisee. Trying to not be judgmental is the most difficult part—I only relapse about sixty or seventy times a day! It's a humbling exercise to try counting how many times a day you are critical or judgmental. Since feeling judged is the foremost fear that will drive people away, I had a lot of work to do.

> *"I don't want expensive gifts; I don't want to be bought. I have everything I want. I just want someone to be there for me, to make me feel safe and secure."*
>
> ~ Princess Diana

PHARISEES AREN'T SAFE

My conscious recovery as a Pharisee began when we were running our own residential recovery program in Santa Barbara and struggling to see the fruit of our labors. The Lord spoke to me one day and said, "Michael, if you create a safe atmosphere, I will heal people." I began creating a safe program using acceptance, communication, and conflict resolution techniques expecting things to change. But they didn't. I asked God what I was doing wrong, and he told me something that changed my life. He said, "The safe atmosphere is not a program or a place, it is a person." I was the safe atmosphere He was talking about me, not the program. Bummer!

This is when my recovery as a Pharisee really began. God showed me that it was my religiosity, self-righteousness, doctrinal rigidity, and my critical and judgmental spirit (in short, my pride) that made me unsafe for helping hurting people. My recovery as a Pharisee went to a new level, as I realized that both biblically and neurochemically, it takes safe, healing relationships to help wounded (addicted) people seeking help to be able to receive it. The limbic system (heart) won't reveal its secrets unless it is safe. God was inviting me to become the "safe place" He could use to bring healing to others.

One morning, while I was walking, I felt led to pray for God to help me love the things He loves and hate the things He hates. I really didn't want to pray that prayer... I knew I was going to be in for it. Over the next few months, I began to develop a real disdain for religion, both in me and outside of me. It was like looking for yellow Volkswagens—I began to see Pharisees and legalism everywhere. As I read through the New Testament looking for insight, I realized that Jesus had compassion, empathy, and kind words for everyone he met, even those who were most hated by the Jews—like prostitutes, tax collectors, and even Roman soldiers. Jesus demonstrated patience and kindness, blessing them with wisdom, healing, and deliverance. Jesus was safe; He didn't judge them. He spoke love to their hearts.

> **KEY thought** Religion is about what you have to "do" to be right with God and earn His blessings.

"Anyone who thinks sitting in church can make you a Christian must also think that sitting in a garage can make you a car."
~ Garrison Keillor [3]

PHARISEES ARE PERFORMANCE DRIVEN

The one group that Jesus had no patience for was the Pharisees and other religious people of the day. He called them a "brood of vipers," "hypocrites," "sons of the devil," and assigned to them all the "woes" in Matthew 23. Pretty serious stuff! They were practicing a religion mostly made up of a lot of rules, rituals, and behaviors that you had to perform in order to earn God's love and salvation. It was all about doing it *right* so God would bless them and judging everyone who wasn't. Why do you think Jesus was so angry and intolerant with these religious leaders? They were the only group He talked to this way.

I believe it was because they invalidated the message that the Father sent Jesus to communicate: God's love, blessing, and salvation were gifts by grace; they weren't given to us because of our own acts of righteousness.

We can't earn His grace or love. Fear and guilt are the fruits of religiosity. We can't earn our salvation, but if we have His spirit in us, we will bear fruit through having His heart. Religion is like the picture of a donkey with a carrot on a stick just beyond his reach. No matter how fast he runs, he will never quite reach it.

> *"If you feel that you can follow a few little rules or some clever gimmicks to make you a mature Christian, then you have fallen into a subtle trap of legalism."*
> ~ J. Vernon McGee (1904–1988)

The Old Testament is based on religion—rules and punishments—while the New Testament is based on relationship, choices, opportunities, and grace. God gave us the incredible gift of free will. We have the ability to not only choose Him on an eternal basis, but to also give Him control of our lives on a daily basis. Our choices—both good and bad—have consequences, but they do not change His love for us. That is unconditional grace. The Pharisaical Spirit is a religious spirit—a spirit of legalism, all religions have it. It says, "If you're not doing it our way, then you are not doing it right." Tim's story is an example of this:

TIM'S STORY

Dear Michael,

You asked us to write about our experiences asking for help from the church for serious problems. I have struggled with sex addiction and anger for many years. I have gone to my leaders for help several times in three different churches. Even though they had good intentions I always came away wiped out. Pretty much they said that if I just stayed in the Word and believed, then I wouldn't keep relapsing. I just didn't have enough faith. I tried and tried but would still relapse. I felt horrible. I just wasn't doing something right. I am doing much better now that I am involved in a recovery support group. But part of my recovery is recovering from the condemnation I felt from not being good enough for God to deliver me.

Tim

I can't tell you how many times I've heard the same story. Even as a recovering Pharisee, I still think about what I am not doing right as the reason why God doesn't answer my prayers. What's the formula?

> **KEY thought** — The Pharisaical Spirit is a spirit of religion. All religions have it.

"I like your Christ, but I do not like your Christians. Your Christians are so unlike your Christ."
~ Mahatma Gandhi

PHARISEES ARE HYPOCRITICAL

Change usually begins with the courage and openness to ask the right questions. For example: Why do Christians struggle with certain self-destructive, addictive behaviors as much, if not more than non-Christians? As much as we try not to be hypocritical Pharisees, we fall into religious hypocrisy when we profess our faith as Christians, but don't appear to be different than the secular world. I get embarrassed as a Christian when I hear some of the statistics about Christian lifestyles compared to the secular world. For example, many statistics say there is a higher rate of divorces with Christian couples than in the secular world. George Barna, President and Founder of The Barna Research Group, commented: "Divorce rates among conservative Christians were significantly higher than for other faith groups, and much higher than atheists and agnostics experience. While it may be alarming to discover that born again Christians are more likely than others to experience a divorce, that pattern has been in place for quite some time. Even more disturbing, perhaps, is that when those individuals experience a divorce, many of them feel their community of faith provides rejection rather than support and healing. But the research also raises questions regarding the effectiveness of how churches minister to families. While the ultimate responsibility for a marriage belongs to the husband and wife, the high incidence of divorce within the Christian community challenges the idea that churches provide truly practical and life-changing support for marriages."[4]

Statistics like these can be controversial, but also helpful to get us to look at the kind of ongoing resources our churches have to help troubled marriages and whether they are they effective or not. I can't tell you how many stories I have heard about how some churches have turned their backs on people when they have gotten divorced. I have also heard many stories about how some churches have really helped people heal from the heart wounds divorce causes. It's the same religion, but vastly different experiences and responses to the same problem.

Why are there more failed marriages in Christian families? I believe one answer lies in the epidemic of sex addiction—especially among Christians. The American Academy of Matrimonial Lawyers determined that Internet pornography and sex addiction were significant factors in two out of three divorces and is one of the most pervasive areas that Christians struggle with.[5]

I know quite a few people who are working in the field of Christian ministry with sex addicts. The *Genesis Process for Change Groups* was not designed specifically for sex addictions, but about half of the groups are focused on this problem. They all tell me that the problem of sex addiction in the Church is overwhelming. The statistics run from a low of about 50 percent up to about 75 percent of Christian men struggling with some form of sex addiction.[6] Sex addiction is not just about infidelity and pornography; it can include fantasizing and chronic masturbation. Some of the best statistics we have are from the Promise Keepers stadium events where 53 percent of the men surveyed said they had viewed some form of pornography within seven days prior to the event. And these men were probably more committed to their faith than the average Christian because they were attending this kind of event. Keep in mind this was ten-plus years ago when pornography was not nearly as widespread and available as it is now.

So what do you think the average for your Church might be? The best statistic I could find is that the national average for men with sex addictions is about 8 to 19 percent.[7] So, why do Christians have a three to four times higher rate of sex addiction than the national average? Good question, huh? You might be interested to know that while facilitating the first *Genesis Change Groups* with women in the church, I was surprised at how many of them also struggled with fantasy, porn and masturbation. Self-gratifying problems with sex is not limited only to men. Here are some of the effects of sex addiction that can be very uncomfortable for most churches to talk about. If we can't talk about these things in church, then where can those struggling to find help—especially young people.

- Porn is one of the main causes of erectile dysfunction.
- The earlier the porn experiences, the more ingrained it becomes. The average age of first porn contact is 11 years old. Some surveys say 8 years old.
- Porn tends to objectify women, making sex something you do to women, rather than with them in relationship.
- 60 percent of divorces have porn as a major factor.
- Porn is the main cause of both men and women's dissatisfaction and shame with the appearance of their genitals.
- Porn can make permanent changes to the brain that can distort normal sex for life.

Reliable statistics can be hard to come by on the issue of sex addiction because many churches don't believe, or want to believe, there is even a problem, or that it is so widespread. Do a Google search on "statistics sex addictions among Christians" and you will find an overwhelming body of information. It is a problem, a huge problem—an epidemic that needs to be addressed. Recently, I wrote to Ted Roberts, retired pastor of Easthill Church in Gresham, Oregon, to inquire about the pervasiveness of sex addiction in the Church. Ted is the President of Pure Desire Ministries International and the author of the *Pure Desire* workbooks on sex addiction. He wrote back, "I have spoken at a number of large churches and

Christian men's conferences and the lowest percentage of men that admitted they were losing the battle with porn was 60 percent; the average is about 75 percent. That is why I am devoting the next twenty years of my life to equip the Church to fight this battle and WIN. We will never have revival until we do."

My heart really goes out the young kids who are being exposed and infected with porn at such an early age. Porn can corrupt the adolescent brain/heart that can create a lifetime of struggle. If I had had the kind of porn that is so readily available now, I don't know how I would not have become addicted. How many churches do you know of that are intentional and safe about helping kids with the bombardment of sexual pressure they are exposed to on a daily bases.

"The sting of death is sin, and the power of sin is the law."
I Corinthians 15:56

> **KEY thought**   The law excites sin.

"The Law came in so that the transgression would increase; but where sin increased, grace abounded all the more."
Romans 5:20

So why are Christians struggling so much with "doing the very thing they don't want to do," seemingly more in many areas than secular people? It's a mystery. Mysteries have always bugged me, but this is one I have been trying to solve for a long time. As an addiction counselor, I know that faith in God working through people is the most vital component in the recovery process. Yet, I needed to identify the part of Christianity that not only sabotages recovery, but also actually increases the potential for self-destructive behavior. Why is there more sex addiction, divorce, and self-harm in Christians than in the secular world? Statistics say that food addictions (obesity) are also higher among Christians. I found the answer in Romans 7.

"What shall we say, then? Is the law sinful? Certainly not! Nevertheless, I would not have known what sin was had it not been for the law. For I would not have known what coveting really was if the law had not said, "You shall not covet." But sin, seizing the opportunity afforded by the commandment, produced in me every kind of coveting. For apart from the law, sin was dead. Once I was alive apart from the law; but when the commandment came, sin sprang to life and I died. I found that the very commandment that was intended to bring life actually brought death." Romans 7:7–10 (NIV)

In the beginning of Romans 7, Paul describes how before the law came he didn't have a problem with coveting. But as soon as the law said, "Thou shall not covet," he coveted everything. Paul basically states, "The law took advantage of me and increased sin in me." The reason that Christians struggle so much with sin is that "the law excites sin." The more wrong something is, the more exciting it is, and thus the more the limbic system attaches to it. The more exciting something is (the more of a rush) the more the limbic system says, "that felt good", and produces a do it again craving. For example, pornography and casual sex are legal and acceptable in the minds of the secular world. But for Christians it is iniquitous, making it more enticing. Christians will get a bigger rush in the pleasure/reward/excitement system in our brain. The more intense the experience, the more the limbic system creates a "do it again" craving.

> *"There is a charm about the forbidden that makes it unspeakably desirable."*
> *~ Mark Twain*

FORBIDDEN FRUIT

Dear Michael,

My husband is supposedly a very "good Christian." He constantly points out my sin whenever I make a mistake and do something that is counter to the Bible. But he is also a sex addict himself.

And you know the strange thing? He only cheats on me when I'm nearby. He has gone to bed with women in our own bedroom when he knows I'm coming home and about to walk in the door. Once at an office party, he was caught having sex with a lady in a hallway closet, while I was sitting at the dinner table close by. He made a point to tell me beforehand, "I'm going to the restroom. You just sit right here." This pattern happened over and over. I didn't get it. Why would he cheat on me so close by, when I might catch him? Then one day my Genesis counselor pointed out that he was getting a bigger rush from it with me nearby. My presence made it more risky, and thus more exciting. It wasn't as intense without the risk of getting caught.

A.R.

Let me give you another real world example. My wife and I have been helping a mission to start a Genesis outpatient recovery program in Nagaland, India. As a whole, India is only 2.3 percent Christian, as opposed to 80.5 percent Hindu and 13.4 percent Muslim. Nagaland, however, is 87.5 percent Christian and suffers from the highest heroin addiction and crime rate, by far, in all of India. I don't know about you, but to me this is embarrassing. Genesis is also supporting a recovery ministry near Delhi, India. The missionaries there went to the local City Council to get a permit to open a rehabilitation center and the Council refused them, saying, "We don't want Christianity here. Look at Nagaland."

There is an aspect of the dynamics of religion that excites sin. Proverbs summarizes it well: "Stolen water is sweet; and bread eaten in secret is pleasant" (Proverbs 9:17). For example, imagine I bake a batch of cookies and divide them into two plates. I tell you that you can have a cookie from the first plate, but not from the second plate, because those cookies are very special. Then I leave the room. What are you going to do? Researchers have shown that the cookies on the "forbidden" plate will actually taste better than the ordinary ones.

FREEDOM FROM THE PHARISAICAL SPIRIT

> *"Most dangerous is that temptation that doth goad us on to sin in loving virtue."*
> ~ William Shakespeare

My native missionary friend in Nagaland said, "This makes a lot of sense, because in my country, the average church here is very legalistic. The only way they know how to deal with sin is punishment and rejection." The more legalistic the church, the more secrets and self-destructive behaviors flourish. In other words, religious legalism creates isolation and fear. Another example is Islam, which is probably the most legalistic religion in the world. Do an Internet search about the sexual abuses in Islamic countries, especially the rules for women and girls. They also have some of the highest and most bizarre porn search rates. South Korea is another example; they spend by far the most money per capita on pornography than any country in the world. [8] I have worked with many Korean missionaries who tell how legalistic their churches are.

This issue seems so clear when you read the New Testament—Jesus and Paul tell us over and over that it is grace that gives us power over sin, not the law. Yet, it is so hard to find genuine grace in action. Grace takes the power out of sin. It is love that leads us to repentance, not judgments and punishment. Grace simply is what works.

> For the law was given through Moses; grace and truth came through Jesus Christ. John 1:17

A STRUGGLE WITH PORNOGRAPHY

Dear Michael,

I am writing you my story with the hope that it can help others who have had a similar experience. I am thirty-seven years old and have been addicted to porn since I was about nine. I am a pastor's kid and grew up feeling ignored and unimportant. My dad was on a mission for God so I felt guilty taking away from that with my own needs. Somehow porn made me feel connected. At first it was magazines and voyeurism. But when the Internet hit, I became hopelessly addicted. I felt like a slave. Going to church the whole time made it worse. My secrets and dual personality became part of the rush.

In my mid-twenties, I finally went to biblical counseling. The counselor read me the scriptures about being married and "staying in your own cistern." So I decided to go ahead and get married, thinking the porn and masturbation would go away once I had the real thing. To my surprise it made it worse. In my men's group I found this misconception common. I was able to hide my problem for about eight years; when she found out I almost lost my marriage. Like most sex addicts, I was very good at hiding it. I had done it all my life. It forced me to try and find some real help. I came to one of your weekend seminars and when you taught that legalism makes the sin we are struggling with worse, it explained my whole life. You said it is like putting out a fire with gasoline. You said grace is what works and it comes through safe people who know what they are doing. I signed up that weekend for a Change Group and found a safe place without judgments and men who supported me step by step. I have a year of clean time now and am leading new groups. I can't say I don't ever struggle, but for the first time, my life is going in the right direction. I can't tell you how good it feels to be free of guilt.

In Him,
R. C.

> **KEY thought** — Church wounds can create deep heart/limbic scars.

"Legalism says God will love us if we change. The gospel says God will change us because He loves us."
~ Tullian Tchividjian [9]

PHARISEES CREATE WOUNDS WITH GUILT AND SHAME

I have been counseling wounded people for many years and for some reason it seems church wounds can go deeper and be harder to get over than even our childhood wounds. Most church wounds come from some form of legalism—trusting followed by judgment and betrayal. Most of the perpetrators seemed to have had good intentions, but have wounded others through applying the "Word" in a legalistic manner. The "Word" is a two-edged sword, capable of healing as well as wounding. Jesus lamented many times about religious leaders perverting his Father's love with rules and punishment.

SENDING THE WRONG MESSAGE

Dear Michael,

Once I brought a vanload of eight men from our residential recovery program to my church. We got there a few minutes early and the men stopped outside and had a smoke. One of the church leaders approached the men smoking and asked them why they were smoking on church property. We entered the church and people were looking at us in a way that made us all uncomfortable. After we sat down, people around us started to get up and move away. I was so ashamed. I don't remember what the sermon was about, but I do remember that I expected Christian men and women to sit down and be polite to these newcomers. What message were they giving these men? The message the men received from this church was that they were not welcome and please go away. The next week we went to a different church and they welcomed us with open arms. We have been attending that church now as a mission for seven years.

G.S.

My wife and I were missionaries for ten years and have been in full-time ministry for over thirty-two years. We have experienced the same pervasive problem over and over again. The number one reason we see people leave the ministry, and especially the mission field, is not because the work is too hard or because of discouragement, illness, or lack of funds. They leave because they were wounded by other Christians. The Pharisaical Spirit always seems to be the driving force behind the wounding. I am involved with training and helping Christian agencies, churches, and missionaries all over the world, who are trying to help some of the most difficult people—addicts, prostitutes, criminals, and the severely wounded. Most of the workers say that working with the clients is hard and sometimes heartbreaking, but it is also a joy. They say the hardest part is working with Christian colleagues, especially leaders and boards. It shouldn't be that way. We should be the ones building each other up, especially when we mess up. Can you think of someone who left the ministry? What happened to them and how did others react?

> *"Encouragement to others is something everyone can give.*
> *Somebody needs what you have to give.*
> *It may not be your money; it may be your time. It may be*
> *your listening ear. It may be your arms to encourage.*
> *It may be your smile to uplift. Who knows?"*
>
> ~ Joel Osteen

The Church in general can be very resistant to change. When someone goes outside the box to bring in change, they tend to get nailed by those inside the box. It is consistent throughout the Bible and political history. Jesus is the perfect example. He threatened the control of the religious leaders. The prophets and apostles were change agents, all of whom were martyred by the people they were trying to help. These rebellious change agents, when later proven right, are then called heroes and prophets. Human nature seems to react to the fear of losing control by responding with anger, rage, slander, and violence. We see examples of this kind of reactive violence all throughout history.

"One of the religion scholars spoke up: "Teacher, do you realize that in saying these things you're insulting us?" He said, "Yes, and I can be even more explicit. You're hopeless, you religion scholars! You load people down with rules and regulations, nearly breaking their backs, but never lift even a finger to help. You're hopeless! You build tombs for the prophets your ancestors killed. The tombs you build are monuments to your murdering ancestors more than to the murdered prophets. That accounts for God's wisdom saying, 'I will send them prophets and apostles, but they'll kill them and run them off.' What it means is that every drop of righteous blood ever spilled from the time earth began until now, from the blood of Abel to the blood of Zechariah, who was struck down between altar and sanctuary, is on your heads. Yes, it's on the bill of this generation and this generation will pay. You're hopeless, you religion scholars! You took the key of knowledge, but instead of unlocking doors, you locked them. You won't go in yourself, and won't let anyone else in either." As soon as Jesus left the table, the religion scholars and Pharisees went into a rage. They went over and over everything he said, plotting how they could trap him in something from his own mouth." Luke 11:45–54 (The Message)

> **KEY thought** Religious legalism is driven by fear and guilt.

OVERCOMING SHAME

Dear Michael,

My husband and I were new Christians coming out of a partying lifestyle. After seven years of marriage we hit bottom with sex, drugs, and alcohol. We just got tired of it all. I think it was God. We had been going to church for about six months and trying to figure out what was okay and what wasn't. My husband and I liked watching porn on occasion to add variety and fun to our sex life. We thought we should ask our pastor about it because we wanted to know if it was all right. Big mistake. He told us that it was sin and the fact that we still did it meant we had probably never really been saved. He went on and on about how real Christians turn away from the past and "were new creatures in Christ, the old things passing away."

It wasn't so much what he said, but the way he said it that wiped us out. We felt so much shame and confusion. He came down on us so hard, so judgmental. It felt so black and white, like all or nothing. We felt like we were no longer acceptable there and went about a year without going to church out of fear. Then we came to one of your Weekend Personal Change Seminars and understood how change is a process and a healing journey. We got into a Change Group at that church and have slowly found acceptance and a safe place to grow. God tells us what is all right and what is not. As you said, change comes from the inside out. We now lead groups for other couples and are doing well, as the Holy Spirit shows us the next thing He wants us to deal with. As you said, it is not the same for everyone. By the way, we heard later that our first pastor had to step down for reasons of sexual impropriety.

L.H.

"But He said, "Woe to you lawyers as well! For you weigh men down with burdens hard to bear, while you yourselves will not even touch the burdens with one of your fingers." Luke 11:46

A PASTOR'S STORY

Dear Michael,

I became aware of a woman who had attended a strict church as a young adult. She found out she was pregnant. The church also found out that she was pregnant. The pastor told her she was going to have to go in front of the entire congregation and tell them the story of how she got pregnant and ask the congregation's forgiveness in order to remain a part of the church. She never went back and, to the best of my knowledge, she has never entered the doors of a church again. She married the man and they have two great children who are now around nine and six years of age. Her grandfather sent me to see them and they were very guarded while talking with me. I tried to convince them that all churches are not that judgmental and I even told her about my daughter who had become pregnant before marrying my son-in-law and how the church handled that situation with love, compassion, and grace. They were so deeply wounded that they were not yet willing to risk getting hurt again. They still haven't come anywhere near our church or any other one in town, to the best of my knowledge. I hoped I could develop a relationship with the family and the wounds could be healed, but that chance may not come about. What a shame.

Pastor James

I think most of us have some Pharisee in us. But we also are in conflict with our Pharisee to be like Jesus. As you read through these stories, ask yourself—what would Jesus have done? How would He have handled it? It is such a simple question; it is amazing how often we forget to ask it.

STEPS TOWARD CHANGE

The good news is that we don't have to be an active Pharisee anymore. We can change. Even Paul recovered from this struggle and was used in a powerful way by preaching the gospel to non-Jewish nations in the past he was so judgmental towards. He probably never saw that coming! There are practical things we can do to change from a pharisaical spirit to one of grace. The main thing is to want to change—to recognize that you probably have some pharisaical tendencies that need to go. Who or what are you most judgmental about? Like Paul, God can turn your main struggle into a ministry for Him, if you are willing to let go of the pharisaical spirit, i.e. the need to be right. Ask Him to show you how He sees situations and people. Seeing life through His eyes frees you from the "log in your eye." Since I've been through this struggle myself, let me suggest to you a few steps to take to begin the process of overcoming the Pharisaical Spirit.

> *"You can fool some of the people all of the time,*
> *and all of the people some of the time,*
> *but you cannot fool all the people all the time."*
> ~ Abraham Lincoln

DEFEAT DENIAL

The first step in the process of change is telling our selves the truth and asking the right questions. We have to be willing to look at this problem of religiosity in the light of our own hearts by applying the "golden rule." When you are down and full of shame, how would you like to be treated? What do you need? The answer is always the same—grace, understanding, guidance, and acceptance. What is it that keeps us from giving these healing helps?

There is a filtering process we use to avoid problems that we are afraid to look at—it's called "denial." It has taken me several years to begin to understand the mystery of why Christianity, (statistically) as a religion, doesn't seem to be working very well on a practical level. How is the church ever going to be safe and able to help hurting people if it stays in denial about the problem of legalism? The first step is telling our selves the truth. Being honest about your own tendency toward legalism (i.e., being rules, punishment, or performance driven) takes courage and faith. Ask yourself, "How do I think about or judge those who mess up? What do they deserve?" Changing the standards that you measure others with can be frightening. Why? Because legalism and judgments can be addictions—give them up and you will experience withdrawal. It takes being willing to not have to be right.

> *"Saving faith is an immediate relation to Christ,*
> *accepting, receiving, resting upon Him alone, for justification,*
> *sanctification, and eternal life by virtue of God's grace."*
> ~ Charles Spurgeon

> **KEY thought** — The Holy Spirit convicts us with love. Religion condemns us with guilt and fear.

"Therefore, to one who knows the right thing to do and does not do it, to him it is sin." James 4:17

ONE SIN DOESN'T FIT ALL

Another step toward freedom from religion involves understanding the role of the Holy Spirit. The most difficult part of the message that Jesus brought was that of grace—giving us His spirit to guide our lives, showing us what is right and wrong from the inside out. He does this through what is called "conviction." What is a sin to you may not be to me. Religion can be black and white and attempts to make rules that apply to everyone. I may be able to watch an R-rated movie that has sex scenes and you may not. I can have a glass of wine and you may not. I can have a piece of chocolate cake and you may not. It is the Holy Spirit's job to convict us personally of what is okay and what is not. Marijuana is now legal in many states. So is it a sin to use it? It leads to an interesting theological question—what is sin? As James tells us above, it can be different for each person.

Sometimes He uses people to convict us. But that's where it can get tricky. It can be hard to tell the difference between religious guilt and heart conviction.

Heart conviction comes from love, whereas legalistic guilt comes from condemnation. Change comes from the inside out. Unfortunately, the rules we create in religion can replace the relationship with His spirit and we can get to a place where we can't tell the difference anymore. What are the rules with grace?

The new Pope, Francis I, has stirred up a theological hornet's nest in the Catholic Church with his belief that basically says, "People are more important than church doctrine." He asks Catholics to reach out and accept people, like homosexuals and atheists, rather than reject and judge them. He even included Protestants. Recently he said this:

"Since many of you do not belong to the Catholic Church and others are non-believers, from the bottom of my heart I give this silent blessing to each and every one of you, respecting the conscience of each one of you but knowing that each one of you is a child of God."

> *"We judge ourselves by what we feel capable of doing, while others judge us by what we have already done."*
> ~ Henry Wadsworth Longfellow

AVOID THE TRAP OF JUDGING OTHERS

People who are judgmental are not safe. Why? Because judgments create heart wounds (Matthew 7). The enemy uses the Pharisaical, religious, judgmental spirit to hinder each other's work—it's a trap we must avoid. Judgments don't merely criticize or attack our behavior; they attack the kind of person we are—our core identity. Judgments go beyond a person's actions, striking deep at his very heart and motives. When we think we know why a person did or said something, then we are judging them. For example, if I say, "John really doesn't care who He hurts," the conclusion I made about his caring is a judgment; or "John is a jerk." Jerk is judgment. The problem is that our hearts and its motives are things that only God can see. When Samuel was trying to find the king and looking at David and his brothers, God tells him: "Man judges the outer appearance, but only God can see the heart." So when we judge a person's heart and their motives, we are acting as if we can see what only the Holy Spirit can see. These kinds of judgments can create deep and lasting heart wounds.

Remember, the main attribute of people who are safe for helping hurting people is that of acceptance, not judgment. Twelve-step meetings like AA are safe because no matter what you've done or how many times you've relapsed, you are welcome without judgment. The only requirement is the desire to be sober. It's one sinner helping another. Many of my clients have said that they sense the Spirit of God more at their 12-step meetings than they do at church. My main struggle as a recovering Pharisee is to try to be free of my judgments. In order to judge someone, you have to believe you are superior to him or her. When I function in humility, I am able to suspend my judgments making me more effective in just about every area of my life, especially my internal world. Humble people are transparent and vulnerable.

> "For I say, through the grace given unto me, to every man that is among you, not to think of himself more highly than he ought to think; but to think soberly, according as God hath dealt to every man the measure of faith." Romans 12:3 (KJV)

During a one-day follow up seminar in England, I did an exercise to illustrate who is a safe person and who is not. The point of the exercise was to expose the fact that we really can't see ourselves as to whether we are a safe person or not. But others can sense what is in our hearts through our body language and "vibes." At this seminar, there were several leaders, pastors, Christian radio personalities, and counselors from large churches and ministries. Most of them were recovery focused. There were also some rehab workers that had been to the last *Genesis Relapse Prevention Counselor Training*, some of whom were not far removed from their addiction. I asked, "If you had gone out last night and relapsed into your most shameful behavior and were feeling convicted and full of guilt and shame, who in this room would you feel the most and least comfortable sharing your shame with?"

This exercise was a good reality check, because I asked them to pick someone they didn't know just by looking at them. I have since done this same exercise many times and it is amazing how we can intuit if someone is safe or not just by the "vibe" they emanate. Eighty percent of what we communicate is non-verbal, so our body language, tone, and especially facial expressions, give us away. Our vibes expose what is in our hearts, and we can't really hide it very well even if we try to. We think no one notices our bad attitude, discomfort, or judgmental thoughts because no one ever confronts us on how we come across. Of course no one confronts us because we are not safe. We have learned to be superficial by ignoring what we really feel and see. Our recovery mostly involves learning how to be real with our selves and others, which takes tremendous courage and support.

During the exercise, there was one man who was uncomfortable with how personal this was; even though I didn't have the group share their observations. He raised his hand and challenged me: "Okay Michael, who would you pick to be that vulnerable with?" I looked around and saw a woman named Rachel, a rehab worker in her early twenties. Rachel had a lot of tattoos, piercings, and multi-colored hair. She had shared with me that morning that she had relapsed with a man and had used, lied about it, and was working hard to get it back together. I said Rachel would be the one I would share with. With all the leaders and their degrees and experience, this young addict would be the safest person. Why? Because I knew she wouldn't judge me. Being a recovering Pharisee, I can usually spot another Pharisee. We do some of the same things the original Pharisees did. Instead of listening to a speaker, we— like lawyers—try to find a flaw in what they are saying. And when we ask questions they are not really questions, they are challenges.

> **KEY thought** Being real and honest is risky and takes tremendous courage.

Unsafe people are not usually open to criticism. Like the religious leaders in Jesus' day, they couldn't hear His message. In their fear-driven hearts, they were trying to find a flaw in what He was saying because they were threatened by the simple truth of what He said. Insecurity always manifests itself in control. Their questions were always traps that ended up exposing the motives of their hearts. We Pharisees are basically insecure in our beliefs (even though we appear just the opposite) and are looking for ways to feel in control by judging others and proving them wrong. Remember most wars are fought over conflicting belief systems. Politics and religion seem to be able to bring out the best and worst in us.

> "The scribes and the Pharisees were watching Him closely to see if He healed on the Sabbath, so that they might find reason to accuse Him." Luke 6:7

"Why do you not understand what I am saying? It is because you cannot hear My word." John 8:43

Let's look at some of the ways the enemy uses legalism to hinder the work of God. The word "devil" in the Greek translates *diabolos*, which means *slanderer/accuser*. The word "Satan" translates as "adversary." Our adversary is a slanderer, a liar, and the father of lies. The truth is not in him. In 1 Timothy 3:11, the word "gossips" is used as a noun, translated "slanderers," where the reference is to those who are given to finding fault with the demeanor and conduct of others and spreading their innuendos and criticisms in the church. *Slander doesn't have to be a lie.* So when we judge others and speak those judgments (usually in the form of critical gossip), we are of the same spirit as the devil. He uses us in likeness to his own original sin—pride. This can cause a lot of damage, including division, lost relationships, or worse, turning someone away from God completely. As I said above, judgments are so powerful because they create heart wounds.

> **KEY thought** — Just because you believe something, it doesn't mean you're right.

LET GO OF HAVING TO BE RIGHT

Recovering from the need to be right is the main principle I have found in those who God can use to help the wounded and vulnerable heal. This powerful concept has been the most helpful in me getting free as a recovering Pharisee and originally came from an experience at my dentist's office, of all places. I was getting all the mercury fillings in my mouth removed because I thought they were part of my struggle with chronic fatigue. The dentist and I were arguing, as he believed that silver fillings are completely safe. I told him about all the research I had done and that even a small amount of mercury could be the cause of my symptoms. He dug in and said that I had been misled. I responded, "Just because you believe that, doesn't mean you're right." It got very quiet; the nurses couldn't believe I said that. No one had a reply.

That truth stuck with me like glue. It has taken the power out of my self-righteousness. I began to see that what I believe could be (and probably is) wrong or at least only partially true. We all can't be right, especially about God. We all *"see through a glass dimly."* No one really knows what He is going to do or how He is going to do it. He is a mystery. Think about all the different religions and factions (denominations) within them and how they argue about who is right. If everyone believes they're right, then probably no one is. Thinking that what I believe is right can make me intolerant of what others believe. Most of what we get upset and argue about as Christians is the controversial things like the gifts of the Spirit, the rapture etc. We mostly agree about the basics, like who Christ is. Paul came to the point where he came to say. "For I determined to know nothing among you except Jesus Christ, and Him crucified."(1 Corinthians 2:2) Grace heals and and results in heart change. Not having to be right can result in peace and peace is what will draw people to you.

> "We don't yet see things clearly. We're squinting in a fog, peering through a mist. But it won't be long before the weather clears and the sun shines bright! We'll see it all then, see it all as clearly as God sees us, knowing him directly just as he knows us!" 1 Corinthians 13:12 (The Message)

KEY thought The roots of religious legalism are fear and pride.

"Humble yourselves in the presence of the Lord, and He will exalt you." James 4:10

The pharisaical, religious spirit is a spirit of judgment and pride. It is a spirit of superiority and self-righteousness. In order to judge someone, you have to believe you are superior. The way religious people feel superior is through knowledge. The Bible tells us that knowledge puffs up and the root of legalism is fear. Those with insecurity (fear) always need to try and be in control to not feel threatened, especially in what they believe.

FREEDOM FROM THE PHARISAICAL SPIRIT

Historically, religion controls with fear and guilt. The most prevailing religious fear, of course, is going to hell.

> *"Often the people most concerned about others going to hell when they die seem less concerned with the hells on earth right now, while the people most concerned with the hells on earth seem the least concerned about hell after death."*
> ~ Rob Bell, *Love Wins* [10]

I think a good example of how "the need to be right" is legalistic and fear driven is by what happened when the book, *Love Wins*, by Rob Bell, was published. The theme of his book was that hell might not be eternal. He gave a lot of good scriptural examples to support his *theory*. I found it interesting and thought provoking. Well, the religious keepers of the correct doctrine (the Pharisees of our day) went nuts. They attacked him on every level; one leader even ex-communicated him. They tagged him with the worst label they could come up with—they called him a "universalist." I'm not sure what that means, but it can't be good. Why do you think they got so venomously upset when the truth is that no one really *knows* how God is going to judge us? We really don't know who is saved and who is not; it depends on which scripture you read. Remember the parables of Jesus?

> **KEY thought** The more we admit we don't know, the more we have to live by faith vs. knowledge.

Why can't we have differences in our beliefs and not attack each other? What is so threatening? Cultish churches or denominations use this kind of self-righteous exclusivity by communicating that their church's rules or leader defines salvation, rather than God. Which boils down to—your salvation is in the church.

This kind of pride says, "I'm right and you're not," which is the main "bad vibe" that makes us unsafe for others to seek help from. It says, "It is not okay for you to believe different from me. I have the real keys to the kingdom. If you do everything like me, you will make it to heaven." This may sound extreme, but many people see Christians this way. I was talking with an older pastor of a large church who also taught in seminary. I was telling him that I had a heart to reach out to un-churched Christians who had been wounded. He told me very matter-of-factly that if they didn't go to church, then they weren't really Christians and not saved. He really believed that.

> *"I don't like to commit myself about heaven and hell—you see, I have friends in both places."*
> ~ Mark Twain

"For it is not an enemy who reproaches me, then I could bear it; nor is it one who hates me who has exalted himself against me, then I could hide myself from him. But it is you, a man my equal, my companion and my familiar friend; we who had sweet fellowship together walked in the house of God in the throng." Psalm 55:12–14

> **KEY thought**   It is easier to learn than to unlearn.

The root of the Pharisaical Spirit is pride and seems to be part of our human DNA, especially for men. The question is: What can we do about it so that the enemy can't use us to help him impede the work of others? The main struggle I have as a recovering Pharisee is to separate in myself what is "religion" versus what is "true spirituality" with God. It's not easy. I have been working at it for over fifteen years now and I'm still confusing the two. I have found it is much easier to learn than to unlearn. Beliefs don't change easily, especially spiritual ones. Beliefs can be a deep part of the limbic survival system and resistant to change in spite of contradictory data. Beliefs have to do with our identity, which can be associated with our worth. So contrary beliefs can threaten our sense of value, thus we come defensive. All of this may feel like an overwhelmingly negative view of religion, but change begins by looking at what is not working and why. It is really not about religious beliefs; it is about what it is in us that causes such strife, including wars. If we simply believe everything is fine, then we don't need to change anything. Remember, change begins from being made to feel uncomfortable.

For us to be safe and effective at healing, we have to be aware of the wounding presence of the Pharisaical Spirit and be in active recovery from it. The opposite spirit is the Spirit of Grace. The New Testament is dedicated to this subject. When we look at some of the statistics on sex addiction, divorce, and other maladies, we have to ask a hard question: How is Christianity *as a religion* working? Is it practical and relevant to the needs of our society? As I have traveled, I have sensed a growing unrest in Christians. They are tired of religion. Many say they are weary of studying about God—they just want to know God and work with Him. They know there must be something more, but they don't know what it is, or even where to look. Grace is a struggle for us all. We will look at how grace works in the next chapter.

MARY'S STORY

Dear Michael Dye,

Because of my rough home life growing up, I wasn't much on reaching out and trusting people, especially the ones in the church I grew up in. Everyone in that church seemed to have it all together and I absolutely did not; and if they didn't, they didn't talk about it. The message I received was, "If you finally get it together, then you can join our clique." I don't really know how true that was, but that's how I felt. It wasn't okay to have any real problems.

After running from God for many years, He led me through a series of personal crises, cancer being one of them. He also led me to a loving church and family that taught me how to grow and trust. Through the teaching and the humility of the pastor, along with their grace in accepting me with all my sin, anger, and doubts, I began to heal. They invited me to their small groups and made me feel a part of the "family." God began to heal me. It was a partnership. I began to take responsibility for the lies I believed, and replaced them with His truth. I began to feel more alive, empowered in who I was as His daughter, missionary, and friend. The process is still going on to this day. I thank Him for the healing place that He sent me to. It began in one church and now missions have taken me around the world to receive and share that same love and acceptance. I now counsel, teach, lead, and love the unlovable (smile) that were just like I used to be. Grace is contagious.

Mary

Not letting pride take advantage of us through our beliefs is not easy, but it is a journey towards being like Him. I know I will always be a work in progress.

SELF-DISCOVERY QUESTIONS

1. What examples from your own life can you think of where Christians have hurt each other? Describe what they did and the affect it had on you.

   _____
   _____
   _____
   _____

2. Why do Christians have more divorces, food, and sex addictions than the secular world?

   _____
   _____
   _____
   _____

3. How legalistic are you? Think of the last religious (or political) argument you got into. What was it about? What was the result?

   _____
   _____
   _____
   _____

4. How legalistic is your church? How do they handle sin? How is grace applied in a practical way?

_____
_____
_____
_____

PRACTICAL APPLICATION

Write down and share with someone some of the religious beliefs you have, and how they have resulted in being inclusive vs. exclusive.

CHAPTER EIGHT

EXTENDING GRACE

"Grace (Gk. Charis): Favor on the part of the bestower; the friendly disposition from which the kindly act proceeds; graciousness, loving-kindness, goodwill generally."
~ Vine's Expository Dictionary of New Testament Words

Over the last thirty years, I have had the opportunity to help people in many different cultures who want to change their self-destructive behaviors. Like all of us, they are trying to find some meaning and peace in their lives. Many of them, like me, have tried just about every approach possible to find this elusive place of peace and happiness. The conscious movement to find inner peace and meaning started back in the 1960s and continues even now. Those of us on this existential quest have gone through many stages, including Eastern religions, drugs, psychology, hedonism, self-help, work, materialism, relationship experimentation, adrenalin activities, religion, and last, but not least, pharmaceuticals. Like me, I think most have found that these pursuits didn't work for very long; they just temporally covered up the pain—the "empty place. "So, what is left? Many have run out of hope and are unable to think of what else to try. We have become the Prozac generation—a drug to fix every problem and emotion. Experts say most of those prescriptions are unnecessary. The United States makes up only 4.6 percent of the world's population, but consumes 80 percent of its opioids and 99 percent of the world's hydrocodone, the opiate that is in Vicodin. (ABC News) Why? I think it is because we are also the most isolated people—once again it is about trying to anesthetize the awareness of the empty place.

Many prodigals of all ages are coming full circle and returning to where they started, searching for spiritual answers. They are looking to God and religion for answers that the world and their own efforts have not been able to provide. They have explored many counterfeits and want the genuine. How is the church going to respond to these seekers who are looking for real answers to real problems? It will require a practical and effective Christianity that addresses their felt needs and makes sense.

> **KEY thought** A safe grace-based church is where real change is happening.

TWO ESSENTIALS: GRACE AND COMPETENCY

There are two things that make a church or person safe for hurting people to seek change: grace and competency. Both are essential elements that must be present for people to share their secrets and struggles. Why? Because when those two things are present, seekers won't be afraid of being judged or rejected. Think about why Jesus was so effective—He saw people through the lens of grace and He was competent (able) to help them in a meaningful way.

In a practical sense, grace is seeing people's hearts, rather than just their behaviors. It is unmerited favor—loving and helping people when they don't deserve it. Competency is the "know-how" element. For someone to be willing to take the risk of exposing their problem (sin) they have to believe the person or agency has the experience, understanding, confidentiality, and program to help them change. When they see a church or person that is successfully helping others with their type of problem, they will believe that it is safe for them to take a risk and trust. Competency produces hope and hope gives us the willingness to take risks. It is not easy to find churches or people with both grace and competency.

> *"Competence: The ability to do something well, measured against a standard, especially the ability acquired through experience or training."*
> ~ Encarta Dictionary

I believe God is calling more churches to focus their resources toward understanding and helping hurting people heal. Everywhere I go I meet pastors who say God has been leading them to reach out to the broken and the lost. They are waiting for Him to show them how to do it. Remember, the main reason I wrote the *Genesis Change Group Books* to provide a tool to make individuals and churches safe and effective for helping hurting people—to help those who want to change be able to change. Most churches can't do this alone; they will need to call on those in the Para-church helping ministries (like the Rescue Missions, counselors, 12-step programs, and rehab centers) to be proactive in sharing their knowledge, experience, and resources to help create safe churches—places where struggling people can find long-term support and healing. Their expertise can be part of the answer to show the church the "how." I have worked extensively with these kinds of ministries and have devoted years learning how to help churches and community resources work together.

> "Most people already know what they're doing wrong. When I get them to church I want to tell them that you can change."
> ~ Joel Osteen

Some churches I have visited exercise a lot of grace. People can come every week and be prayed for without being judged or preached at. Others have good programs, but when you mess up they come down hard. Churches that practice grace in a practical way and also demonstrate facilitating successful change, will become popular and experience growth. People will respond to their authenticity. Many churches are doing an excellent job of using a multi-faceted approach to help people change. The ones that are most effective are willing to go outside the box to find programs that work, even if the programs may be outside their theological comfort zone. These healing churches don't just create a lifestyle of abstinence; they also help people grow into healthy social and spiritual human beings. A church where people are changing is an exciting place to be. People will naturally be drawn to it.

> **KEY thought** Practically, healing grace is manifested when you have a relationship with a person's heart instead of his or her behaviors.

"I do not nullify the grace of God, for if righteousness comes through the Law, then Christ died needlessly." Galatians 2:21

WHAT IS AUTHENTIC GRACE?

In order to change what you do, you have to change who you are. Our self-destructive behaviors are not the problem; they are symptoms of the problem. So how do we change who we are? Real change requires a heart change, which begins by understanding and experiencing true grace. The heart won't take risk unless it is safe. There are many things that grace is and many things it is not. Let's take a look at these things so we can better understand it.

"And you know, when you've experienced grace and you feel like you've been forgiven, you're a lot more forgiving of other people. You're a lot more gracious to others."
~ Rick Warren

> **KEY thought** Humility can ask for help, while pride says, "I can do it myself."

"But He gives a greater grace. Therefore it says, 'God is opposed to the proud, but gives grace to the humble.'" James 4:6

GRACE IS HUMBLE, NOT PROUD

God gives His grace to those who are humble. It usually flows through people and is received by those who are willing to humble themselves enough to receive it. True heart change begins with humility—the ability to ask for help from God and people. It's important to recognize that when we receive the help we've asked for, it is undeserved (unmerited favor); it is given to us regardless of our actions. It is being shown that we have worth and extending acceptance even though our actions stink. This is grace. Those who need it the most are those who deserve it the least.

In practical terms, humility gives us the ability to ask for help, while pride says, "I can do it myself." Even though God pours out grace unconditionally, it still must be received. Pride blocks our ability to receive it. We have free will and God says, "Go for it. Try to control it yourself. I'll see you when you are willing to let me help you." He's patient; He'll wait. We all know people who are destructive and won't admit they have a problem or ask for help. It is always someone else's fault. They are still stuck in their self-justifications. They have not yet hit bottom. They still want to be in control. The pain and consequences of their behaviors hasn't been enough to motivate them to change.

> **KEY thought** — Pride blocks the ability to receive grace.

> *"Humility is not thinking less of yourself,*
> *it's thinking of yourself less."*
> ~ C. S. Lewis

In my experience, seekers who have experienced hitting their bottom have a genuine attitude of humility. Humble people are willing to look for spiritual answers for changing their lives. They have come to the end of themselves saying, "I give up" and realize that their own thinking has taken them to a place they never wanted to go. They know they need a miracle and feel very vulnerable. It is a huge risk for them to ask for help. Remember, recovery is a process of *learning to trust again*.

That's where safe people and churches can make an impact. Safe churches are places where people who are humble can come to ask for help without fear of judgment. When people are first seeking help, they are extremely exposed and any kind of feeling of judgment can cause them to flee. They need to be met with a response of grace and compassion, rather than haughtiness, criticism, or disdain. Even advice can feel hurtful in the beginning. Think about what it feels like when someone humbly asks you for help. There is something disarming about humility that can cover a multitude of sins and invoke grace in us. Asking for help is the easiest way to begin to heal a broken relationship.

> *"After crosses and losses, men grow humbler and wiser."*
> ~ Benjamin Franklin

The thing I hate most about being humbled is that it is usually so humiliating. Being a visionary type of person, I have always struggled with pride, which I like to call self-confidence. I would try to be humble, but couldn't really feel it. Once, after being humiliated by a pastor in front of 500 people, I felt so bad the next day that I thought this must be what real humility feels like. Then I realized how proud I felt about being so humble and it ruined the whole experience. I'm not sure if we can humble ourselves without being proud of it. I think true humility is a mystery.

"Pride goes before destruction and a haughty spirit before stumbling." Proverbs 16:18

> **KEY thought** — The opposite of legalism is grace.

> *"What gives me the most hope every day is God's grace; knowing that his grace is going to give me the strength for whatever I face, knowing that nothing is a surprise to God."*
> ~ Rick Warren

GRACE IS UNCONDITIONAL

God pours out the free gift of healing (recovery) to all those who ask. It is unconditional. When He does, He gives us a supernatural strength to overcome our self-destructive cravings. He's not discriminatory, either; He rains on the just and unjust alike. He doesn't give it or withhold it based on whether you've earned it or deserve it; that would be religious legalism. Religion says, "God will bless you when you do everything right." But God and His love never change; what changes is our ability to receive it. Grace comes through an attitude of gratitude. Unconditional grace and love give us a new hope and strength, whether it comes from God or people. *It is having a relationship with people's hearts, even when we disapprove of their behaviors.*

There is a very large group of what I call "un-churched" Christians, where this kind of unconditional love and grace can be especially effective. Most of these are people who have responded to a call to step out into ministry, but either experienced some deep hurts from the leaders or fell out of ministry because of sin or and couldn't find restoration. Many suffer from feelings of rejection, disqualification, and the fear they can't be useful again. Sometimes it seems like "one strike and you're out." I think that this is the reason why many Christians opt to stay in the pews because they aren't as likely to get hurt—they are not as exposed. Making a safe place for wounded workers to find restoration can be very powerful because many have a gift and a vision that can benefit many people. They also are usually very humble and can extend grace to others who are struggling.

One thing I know for sure is that all hurting people have one thing in common—they are vulnerable to rejection. They need a safe, nonjudgmental environment in order to heal and learn to trust again. As I have previously mentioned, the church can be a powerful place for restoration and healing, a place that demonstrates Gods love in practical ways. But it has to be consciously safe and effective, a place of *grace and competency*. The church has the resources and structure for the kind of one-on-one investment that it takes to help wounded people heal. When one person invests himself or herself into another, it produces a sense of self-worth, which is the foundation on which to build a new life.

> *"Nothing humbles and breaks the heart of a sinner like mercy and love. Souls that converse much with sin and wrath, may be much terrified; but souls that converse much with grace and mercy, will be much humbled."*
> ~ Thomas Brooks [1]

> **KEY thought** — Grace and truth come from seeing others and myself as He does.

> *"It was pride that changed angels into devils; it is humility that makes men as angels."*
>
> ~ Saint Augustine

GRACE SEES THE HEART

A personal breakthrough for me in the area of grace came when I was sitting in church one Sunday feeling sorry for myself. Things at the Rescue Mission were not going well and I had upset some of the people working for me. I made a vow several years before that if I was ever a leader, I was not going to hurt those under me like I had seen leaders hurt others and myself. Well, Jesus tells us not to make vows, and now I understood why. I ended up treating those under (and over) me the same way I had been treated in the past.

I was whining to God as usual, telling Him about all the things He wasn't doing right, when I felt Him speak to me. He said, *"Michael, you see yourself by the ups and downs of your successes and failures. When you are doing well, you feel good about yourself. When you are doing poorly, you feel bad about yourself. But I don't see you that way. I see you by the momentum of the direction of your heart."* It was one of the most life changing things He ever said to me. It explains why He doesn't see our sin anymore. He looks at our heart, not our behaviors.

So now when I mess up, I don't beat myself up *as much*. And even though I may have messed up and sinned, I ask myself, "Has the direction of my heart changed? Have I turned away from Him, given up?" I want to see others and myself through His eyes. He doesn't see my behaviors (sins); He sees Christ in me, and the ongoing work He is doing—not the ups and downs along the way. This truth has become one of the foundational premises of my work with hurting and addicted people. I want to have a relationship with people's hearts and not their behaviors. The truth—the victory— that can set us free is when we *see others and ourselves as God does*.

> **KEY thought** Pain is a message from God to tell us that something is wrong so we will respond to it.

"Or do you show contempt for the riches of his kindness, forbearance and patience, not realizing that God's kindness is intended to lead you to repentance?" Romans 2:4 (NIV)

GRACE IS ACCEPTANCE, NOT ENABLING

We know from previous chapters that bad behaviors and destructive emotions are symptoms of heart (limbic) wounds. Seeing and treating others as He does is grace applied. This sounds so simple, but it is not easy. Wounded and addicted people can be very hard to love. Their anger, defensiveness, and tendency to blame everything and everybody for their problems can be very frustrating. Al-Anon, a program for those impacted by the destructive behavior of others, teaches acceptance of people for who they are, rather than who we want them to be, and to do this without enabling.[2] It can be hard to know when our efforts to help others are helping and when they are hurting. Enabling (co-dependent rescuing) ends up hurting more than helping. Enabling is when someone, such as a spouse, friend, or family member, takes responsibility, blame, or makes accommodations for a person's bad behaviors. They usually have good intentions, but their helping actually does more harm than good, because it minimizes the natural consequence of the person's behavior. It can actually shield the person from realizing that they have a problem and, thus, reduces their motivation to change. One of the things I teach Genesis Counselors is to understand the difference between consequences and punishment. Understanding this concept can be a key to working with teens.

It is pain that motivates us to change, so enablers minimize the consequences of the person's choices, taking away their motivation to change. Co-dependent helping always causes harm because you are doing something for others that they should be doing for themselves. Examples of this could be calling in sick to work for an alcoholic and making excuses so they won't be held accountable for their choices, or think about how we sometimes protect our teenagers from the consequences of their choices. Saving the prodigals from the pigs. Are we helping or hurting them? Grace is not enabling—it leaves room for the consequences for our choices.

> *"Your pain is the breaking of the shell*
> *that encloses your understanding."*
> ~Khalil Gibran [3]

KEY thought: It is God's job to make people willing to change, and it is our job to make them able to change.

Grace works because it allows the natural consequences for the choices we make to take place without condemnation. God uses and sometimes orchestrates those painful consequences to motivate us to change. Unfortunately, as human beings, most often it is only pain that motivates change. Of course love is an equally powerful motivator for change. It is God's job to make people willing to change, and it is our job to make them able to change.

It is His grace and competency flowing through others that makes us able to change by love and effective helping. It is a partnership. I learned this principal at the rescue mission. People came asking for help because the pain of their addictions had become intolerable. Life and God had made them *willing* to change. They came to me to make them *able* to change. So when they relapsed, I felt I had not done my part, making them able, which motivated me to seek new and better ways of preventing relapse. Our goal is to trust that God can give us this strength and ability beyond our human capacity to love those who are the hardest to love—to give them grace, yet allow them to experience the pain that will motivate them to change. Our job is to always be looking for better tools to make them successful.

Pain is actually our greatest humbler. We cry out to God for help when our pain gets great enough. C.S. Lewis said, "Pain is God's megaphone to a deaf world." When the pain of doing a behavior becomes greater than the pain of giving up the behavior, then and only then, will we be willing to change. It's called "hitting bottom." Be aware that some people have greater pain thresholds than others. Some can ignore pain for a long time. Unfortunately, some of the people I have worked with didn't seem to have a bottom; their bottom was death. Pain ultimately brings us to humility to ask for help, but when things start going well again, we may start to take back control and say, "I can handle this myself; it really wasn't so bad." This is a sign of both pride and denial.

People are very vulnerable when the pain and shame from their behaviors humbles them to a place to cry out for help. They need acceptance, grace, and hope extended to them to be able to trust and receive help. One word or even a look of judgment can cause them to flee back to where they came from. People will trust you if they believe you genuinely care about them and will stick with them.

> "Brethren, even if anyone is caught in any trespass, you who are spiritual, restore such a one in a spirit of gentleness; each one looking to yourself, so that you too will not be tempted. Bear one another's burdens, and thereby fulfill the law of Christ. For if anyone thinks he is something when he is nothing, he deceives himself. But each one must examine his own work, and then he will have reason for boasting in regard to himself alone, and not in regard to another. For each one will bear his own load." Galatians 6:1–5

> **KEY thought** Safe churches and people see themselves and others through the eyes of the Holy Spirit, as opposed to religious doctrine.

"Above all the grace and the gifts that Christ gives to his beloved is that of overcoming self."
~ Francis of Assisi

GRACE IS SPIRIT DRIVEN, NOT LAW DRIVEN

Once again, we need to go back to Romans 7. Paul keeps doing the same sinful thing he promised himself he wouldn't do. He writes, "I find then the principle that evil is present in me, the one who wants to do good. For I joyfully concur with the law of God in the inner man, but I see a different law in the members of my body, waging war against the law of my mind and making me a prisoner of the law of sin which is in my members. Wretched man that I am! Who will set me free from the body of this death? Thanks be to God through Jesus Christ our Lord! So then, on the one hand I myself with my mind am serving the law of God, but on the other, with my flesh the law of sin" (Romans 7:21–25).

Then Paul tells us what has set him free from the condemnation of his struggle with sin: "Therefore there is now no condemnation for those who are in Christ Jesus. For the law of the Spirit of life in Christ Jesus has set you free from the law of sin and of death" (Romans 8:1–2).

> **KEY thought** Grace and the law are always in opposition to each other.

Paul, a recovering Pharisee, must have been very frustrated by not being able to overcome his problem of sin (addiction) on his own. This may have been the thorn in the flesh he talks about in 2 Corinthians 12:6–9. He struggled with something from God that was meant to keep him humble, so that he could identify with the rest of us. It helped him to be less self-righteous. God saw his heart through the Spirit, and did not see his behavior through the condemnation of the law. He used a thorn to help him become the man he was designed to be. Safe churches and people see themselves and others through the Spirit, which is simply seeing what is true. They don't use the lens of the law, which judges others by ever-changing religious rules. *When we can see what God is doing in someone's life and participate with it, this is real grace that heals.*

Seeing others through the eyes of the Spirit is the main attribute that makes us safe for God to trust us with hurting people. Grace makes us able to see behaviors as symptoms of deeper issues, resulting in compassion. Of course, this is how we would like others to see us (the Golden Rule.) When we don't have the lens of the Spirit, we end up applying the law, judging behaviors, instead of ministering to the heart. The Law (and the doctrines that come out of it), as we know, can have many interpretations. Many "helping" programs I have visited are "rules and punishment" driven. They preach the New Testament, but run an Old Testament program.

> *"Power is of two kinds. One is obtained by the fear of punishment and the other by acts of love. Power based on love is a thousand times more effective and permanent than the one derived from fear of punishment."*
> ~ Mahatma Gandhi

KEY thought — If we don't have the tools and skill to help someone learn and heal from their mistakes, then all we have left is punishment.

One of my biggest challenges has been to come up with practical ways to implement this knowledge about grace. In the *Genesis Processes*, we have worked hard to develop practical tools and exercises to use every behavior, including relapses, as opportunities for growth and healing. If churches and people don't have the skill to do this, all that is usually left is shame and punishment to try and get people to change. I tried shame and punishment to motivate self-destructive people to change. Not only did it not work, it made those I was trying to help worse. One of my main goals is training others to see human beings differently. As counselors, the goal is to see negative behaviors and emotions (like anger and anxiety) as symptoms, and go after the cause—the root cause. I am a "what works" guy, and this is what works. This is the way Jesus saw people. Their behavior was a manifestation of a malfunctioning heart (limbic system).

One of the best stories of the transforming power of grace comes from Victor Hugo's *Les Miserables*. The main character, Jean Valjean, spends nineteen years in prison for the crime of stealing a loaf of bread for his sister's starving children. During his prison time, he was hounded by a cruel guard, which added to his bitter sense of injustice. After leaving prison, Valjean finds that life is hard, and is cheated out of his honest wages. With every injustice, he grows more bitter, his heart harder. Finally, after being released, he is taken in by a kindly and humble bishop, and given bread and wine. That night, against the warnings of his housekeeper and sister, the bishop gives Valjean a bed to sleep in and treats him with kindness. Valjean, for the first time, does something truly evil—he steals the silverware from the cupboard and flees. He is quickly caught, which sets up the experience of grace that the rest of the story is based on. The bishop tells the police to let Valjean go because he gave him the silver as a gift. The bishop insists on giving Valjean the silver candlesticks as well, with this privately spoken blessing: "Jean Valjean, my brother, you no longer belong to evil, but to good. It is your soul I buy from you; I withdraw it from black thoughts and the spirit of perdition and I give it to God."

This unexpected mercy triggers a profound spiritual crisis in Valjean, who responds by becoming a believer. From that one moment of grace, Valjean's life is transformed. Assuming a new identity, he establishes himself in a town. He breathes new life into the town's trade and he rises to become the owner of a factory and finally mayor. He uses his position and wealth to build schools, improve hospitals, and give shelter to the poor. The rest of the story is about more tests of injustice and cruelty to which he continues to respond with kindness, mercy, and grace, which in the end changes the life of the one who hated him the most. Grace received, always encourages us to *pay it forward*.

> *"I have always found that mercy bears*
> *richer fruits than strict justice."*
>
> ~ Abraham Lincoln

> **KEY thought** — A mature person is more others centered than self centered.

"'But if your enemy is hungry, feed him, and if he is thirsty, give him a drink; for in so doing you will heap burning coals on his head.' Do not be overcome by evil, but overcome evil with good." Romans 12:19–21

"And whoever wants to be first must be slave of all. For even the Son of Man did not come to be served, but to serve, and to give his life as a ransom for many." Mark 10:44–45

GRACE IS SACRIFICIAL AND OTHERS-CENTERED

Most of the fruits and gifts of the Spirit are others-centered. The fruits of the Spirit make us safe and the gifts make us effective. As James says, true religion is serving widows and orphans (James 4:12), and faith without action is dead faith (James 2:14–26). It is altruistic, sacrificial faith in action that separates religion from true relationship with God.

It is how God always designed our relationship with Him to be a—partnership. Remember back from Chapter 6, to break the power of spiritual stagnation, you have to give to grow. It really is more blessed to give than receive. And when we do, we actually end up getting more than we give. But the glitch is that giving is a heart issue. We can't give expecting to get. It's the real step of faith.

God has given people the ultimate gift—free will. He will let us take control so we can see for ourselves if we can succeed without Him. Then, when we come to the end of ourselves, by doing the very thing we said we wouldn't do, we pray for His help. He responds with grace and mercy. He doesn't say, "I told you so. I'm going to let you suffer awhile." Instead, He gives us His love and grace according to our ability to receive it, which is mainly determined by our humility. It doesn't mean, however, that He takes away the consequences of our bad choices— He is not an enabler.

I had a good friend who was an alcoholic. He died while waiting for over twenty years for God to deliver him from his addiction. He was too proud to go to a 12-step meeting and receive help (grace) from other alcoholics. I think he used religion as an excuse to keep drinking. As the director of rehabs, I've heard story after story from addicts who would wake up in a dumpster covered in filth and shame for what they had done the night before. They would cry out, "Oh God, help me." They knew they had done awful things to themselves and others and deserved punishment and death. But down the street there was a rescue mission where they could receive free room, board, and a recovery program for a year—they only needed to ask.

> **KEY thought** — Giving grace is its own reward.

God usually answers prayers through people. If people don't step up and get involved, or if the hurting don't humble themselves and seek help, then real healing can't take place. Helping people is sacrificial and grace is motivated by His love in us. Think about how He has answered your prayers in the past. It costs about $12,000 to help an addict in a mission-type recovery program for a year. Prison costs about $30,000 plus. What a miracle it is that people who don't know this criminal/addict, and normally would not want to be involved with him, could give money and volunteer their time to support a recovery ministry where he has a chance to get well. That is practical grace that heals—sacrificial, pure spirituality. Grace is giving to those who don't deserve it without expecting anything in return.

> "The Spirit of the Lord is upon Me, Because He anointed Me to preach the gospel to the poor. He has sent Me to proclaim release to the captives, And recovery of sight to the blind, To set free those who are oppressed,[19] To proclaim the favorable year of the Lord." Luke 4:18–19 (NIV)

One reason I love working with rescue missions is that they are one of the few places where I see all of the ministries of the Holy Spirit from Luke 4:18–19 happening in one place. Where His Spirit is, we should see at least one of the five ministries above in action. Our spirit will feel some of what is on His heart and respond. Remember—a sign of a mature person (or church) is when they become more others-centered than self-centered. Religion, in and of itself, is self-entered. Giving is its own reward.

> "For while we were still helpless, at the right time Christ died for the ungodly. For one will hardly die for a righteous man; though perhaps for the good man someone would dare even to die. But God demonstrates His own love toward us, in that

while we were yet sinners, Christ died for us... but the free gift is not like the transgression. For if by the transgression of the one the many died, much more did the grace of God and the gift by the grace of the one Man, Jesus Christ, abound to the many." Romans 5:6–8; 15

> **KEY thought** — When you see people investing their lives and resources into people that don't deserve it, that's the genuine—that's grace.

"The first question which the priest and the Levite asked was:
'If I stop to help this man, what will happen to me?'
But the Good Samaritan reversed the question:
'If I do not stop to help this man, what will happen to him?'"
~ Martin Luther King, Jr.

GRACE IS AN ACTION, NOT A THEOLOGICAL CONCEPT

God wants to partner with us in answering prayers. That's the relationship. We are the body of Christ and when He wants to get something done down here, He uses us. As a recovering Pharisee, my biggest struggle is trying to separate (especially with my motives) what is "religion" in me from what is *truth and genuine relationship with Him*. The goal for me is not to view God through theology, but to simply see through Him as to what is true and important. The real faith that moves a mountain—which really doesn't take much faith—is seeing what God is doing and participating with it. It is not my desire here to get you to believe my point of view theologically, but for you to examine what you believe and how it is making you into a more mature Christian—one who is progressively becoming more others-centered.

Grace that heals is practical, not a theological concept. Jesus teaches us over and over again about how His spirit will look in believers. It is the real evidence of His spirit that makes a person or a church safe for wounded people. You can't fake it. Before I became a Christian, I spent thirteen years exploring eastern religions, the occult, metaphysics, and just about everything the 60s and 70s had to offer. I had no church background. One of the first things I noticed when I became a Christian was that a lot of the signs and wonders I saw in the church, I had also seen in the eastern religions. All of the gifts (and most of the fruits) of the Spirit have a likeness in other religions and spiritual practices. Almost anything in Christianity can be duplicate in the occult and other religions. In fact, members of many other religions appear to be much better at living New Testament principals than Christians are. When I was practicing Hinduism and Buddhism, I saw and experienced much more spiritual discipline, as far as meditation, prayer, study, self-sacrifice, and fasting, than I have ever seen in Christianity.

So, how can we tell what is real and genuine from the counterfeit? What is real relationship spirituality versus just religious practices? I have sought the answer to this question for many years. What I found seemed almost too simple. There is one thing that shows the genuine heart of God, the Creator of the universe, that can't be successfully counterfeited, at least not for long. *It is the phenomenon of seeing people invest their lives and resources into others that don't deserve it.* When the Creator of the universe lives inside of our hearts, which are being born again and filled with the His Spirit, we will naturally have a burden for the things and people that He cares about. Jesus loved and invested Himself in some of the most despised people of His time, because they needed grace and they received it with humility. If you took Christianity and all the big and small things that Christians do to help others in this country (and around the world) away, our society would collapse fairly quickly.

How many other religions can you think of that are invested in helping the poor, needy, sick, imprisoned, and addicted around the world? Religion in and of itself is self-centered; God is others-centered.

> *"What does love look like? It has the hands to help others. It has the feet to hasten to the poor and needy. It has eyes to see misery and want. It has the ears to hear the sighs and sorrows of men. That is what love looks like."*
> ~ Saint Augustine

> **KEY thought** — Is what I believe inclusive or exclusive?

GRACE IS TOLERANCE

In order to be safe people or organizations, we also need to look at how we present Christianity. Basically, the world views Christians as conveying, "We are all going to heaven and you're lost and going to hell no matter what kind of person you are." Think about how someone like that would affect you. We want our Christianity to be a door, rather than a wall. As we love and accept people, it is His job to draw their heart to Him. For example, think about how we view others who don't believe the same way we do? Say you have a Catholic priest or a Peace Corps person who has spent their life helping lepers in South America. One prays to Mary, the other to nature. Then you have a church person who believes *right*, but never really went out of his way to help others. According to the Parables, who is saved? One is saved purely by what they believe, the other by what they do. So who is right, who is going to heaven? It's an interesting theological dilemma and can produce very heated discussions. It is natural for us to want the perks of Christ without the burdens.

The truth is no one really knows exactly how God is going to judge us, do they? If God gave us a formula, we would make a religious imperative out of it. This argument has been going on for centuries. I am not trying to create a theological argument; just a look at how what we believe affects others who may be seeking help. Living in a way that admits to not having all the answers makes room in our heart for God to use us to help anyone—even if they don't believe "right." Live knowing that God is a mystery—His thoughts and ways our not like ours. Just because you believe something doesn't mean you are 100 percent right. No one is. But I think we can all agree that the Bible tells us that if He is in us, there will be fruit, evidence. We will have His heart and actions. In the end is it better believe in Jesus or act like Him—I think the answer of course is both.

"Therefore Jesus answered and was saying to them, "Truly, truly, I say to you, the Son can do nothing of Himself, unless it is something He sees the Father doing; for whatever the Father does, these things the Son also does in like manner." John 5:19

"At times our own light goes out and is rekindled by a spark from another person. Each of us has cause to think with deep gratitude of those who have lighted the flame within us."
~ Albert Schweitzer

GRATITUDE

The result of humility and receiving undeserved grace should always be gratitude. Since we are all in the process of recovering (returning to a former healthy state), gratitude should be universal. Receiving a life-giving gift we don't deserve is the central theme of the New Testament. The process of recovery usually begins with a spiritual awakening. We start by believing that there is a power outside of ourselves that can give us the strength and ability to overcome the destructive behaviors we can't overcome on our own. The addict's prayer is, *"God save me from myself."* When that happens, we will naturally be grateful. But when we start to grumble and complain that life, people, and God aren't treating us right, our ability to receive His grace through humility is diminished.

God gives grace to the humble and opposes the proud. We can measure whether or not we are in recovery by simply checking our level of gratitude. An attitude of gratitude and humility is the key to receiving God's restoring power. Of course, His grace usually comes through those who invest themselves in us when we don't deserve it. They see something valuable in us, which is how He sees us. Faith, humility, and gratitude are a daily battle. Gratitude is simply realizing who is really in control. Your goal as a human being should be to be the kind of person that when the people that you have met "hit their bottom", you will be the first person they think of to ask for help—a person of *grace and competency*.

> **KEY thought** — Grace is simply walking in reality.

"And He has said to me, 'My grace is sufficient for you, for power is perfected in weakness. Most gladly, therefore, I will rather boast about my weaknesses, so that the power of Christ may dwell in me." 2 Corinthians 12:9

I learned this lesson like I learn everything, the hard way—the prodigal way. I have had Lyme's Disease for the last eight years, which has profoundly restricted my ability to continue my work, or do much of anything, especially travel. My wife has had chronic migraine headaches for over twenty-five years. I prayed daily that He would heal us. I would say, "You need to heal us so we can serve you." I would also remind Him about all the good things I could do for Him if He would just give me those lottery numbers. I would try all sorts of ways to bargain or make Him feel guilty about how hard we have worked and why we don't deserve to be sick. Mostly, He would answer the same way, quoting from 2 Corinthians 12:9, *"My grace is sufficient for you."* I hate it when He says that. This was God's answer to Paul when he asked God to remove the "thorn in his flesh." I would get angry, saying, "What kind of answer is that? I don't even know what that means." I really couldn't come to a place like Paul to "delight in my weakness."

One day I asked Him to show me what grace He was talking about. He simply said, "Michael look around." A light went on. His grace is *life and life abundant*—the air, the food, the beauty, the opportunities, even the struggles and the ability to overcome and grow—life given freely without me having done anything to deserve it. His grace (what He has already done) is sufficient; it is enough. My lack of acceptance and complaining kept me from not only receiving it, but from even seeing it. I was telling Him that what He had given was not enough, and I deserved better. Like so many, my strength is also my weakness. My never being satisfied and always trying to improve everything and everybody drove me to create *The Genesis Process*, which is helping thousands of people recover from their hurts and addictions. But, in a way, it also makes me ungrateful—it's never enough. I still struggle, but at least I have this truth (reality) to return to. Like with so many of my weaknesses, God is gracious and His power is being perfected through them.

A STORY OF GRACE IN ACTION

Dear Mike,

I am responding to your email about good and bad church recovery stories. Mine is a good story and I'm happy to share it. I had been in prison for five years when you came to speak and start the Genesis Change Groups. At first I thought, "What does this guy know? He's not one of us." But then you said something that messed with my head. You said recovery, especially for prison people, is becoming a human being again. You also said that if you want to be a healthy person you have to hang out with healthy people. You can't learn to be healthy from other addicts and convicts. You said that is a problem because we convicts are very afraid of "normies" and avoid them when we get out. I have been in and out of jail and prison all my life and realized I never hung out with any regular people. I realized I was afraid of them. They would judge me.

Well I did the Change Books and when I got out I went into a Genesis-based rehab program. It was one of the hardest things I have ever done. I am used to rules and punishment—do the crime and then the time. This program was what they called "grace-based." When we messed up, those who really wanted help got more chances and those who didn't had to leave. Well, I relapsed and expected to go back to prison. The staff said they saw something in me worth working with. They used some of the process tools to help me see what went wrong and a way to prevent it from happening again. They actually helped me more when I screwed up, I learned a lot from it. It was a life changing experience. I am now on the road to becoming an addiction counselor.

I want to help other convicts to have the same experience of how grace is so life changing.

Thanks,
R.S.

IMPORTANCE OF MODELING GRACE

Safe people and churches have this attitude of gratitude that flows from staying in touch with reality—the grace we have received. Gratitude and the humility it produces can keep us from being judgmental and acting superior. When we model grace, people respond in kind with grace. The grace I receive, I also want to give. When I see grace, I want to participate with it. Likewise, if what I experience is legalism, I will want to participate with it also. It's all about what is modeled to us. Since heart change involves changing people's perceptions, we need to make sure that our faith is proven genuine by the grace we pay forward. I think the first step towards becoming a person of grace is to ask Him to change your heart. The second would be to have others hold you accountable for how you react to people and situations that can be opportunities to extend grace. Third would be to gain some practical skills to extend grace in a useful way. We'll know whether it's authentic or not when we are:

- Humble (not proud)
- Unconditionally accepting (not legalistic)
- Seeking to look at the heart of people (not the behavior)
- Helpful, but not enabling
- Spirit driven (not law driven)
- Others-centered (not self-centered)
- Actively loving others (not merely talking about it)

SELF-DISCOVERY QUESTIONS

1. In what areas of your life do you feel you need the most grace?

2. In the area you struggle with the most, how painful would it need to get to motivate you to change?

3. Ask God to show you through His eyes the person you have the least grace for and why. Share what you saw.

4. Which of the actions of the Spirit from Luke 4:18–19 do you see being practiced in your church or community?

PRACTICAL APPLICATION

Reach out to the person God showed you in question 3 above with an act of acceptance and kindness.

CHAPTER NINE

RESTORING HOPE

"Hope is the thing with feathers that perches in the soul and sings the tunes without the words and never stops at all."
~ Emily Dickinson

"And not only this, but we also exult in our tribulations, knowing that tribulation brings about perseverance; and perseverance, proven character; and proven character, hope; and hope does not disappoint, because the love of God has been poured out within our hearts through the Holy Spirit who was given to us." Romans 5:3–5

THE POWER OF HOPE

Hope plays a big part of *what works* to help struggling people not give up. Hopelessness can keep them from even trying. I have had the opportunity over the last thirty years to study hundreds of people who had relapsed into their destructive behaviors. I noticed a key difference between those who relapsed and those who didn't. Both groups had gone through a similar, difficult experience, but one relapsed and the other didn't. As I looked for the reason behind this mystery, I discovered that *hope* was a key component.

"We must accept finite disappointment, but never lose infinite hope."
~ Martin Luther King, Jr.

There are basically two kinds of hope. One is based on a desire or longing, as in, I hope everything is going to be okay. *I hope bad things never happen. I hope it doesn't rain this week (or that it does).* The other kind of hope is based on reality—what is actually taking place in a person's life. For recovery purposes, which is a process we are all engaged in, hope is not a verb—it is a noun. It is something you either have or you don't. When you project your current situation into the future, either hope or hopelessness looks back at you.

For example, if you are stagnant and stuck in your painful emotions and destructive coping behaviors (basically stuck in life), how will you see your life six months into the future? What looks back at you? Will you perceive that things are going to be worse or better? In other words, if the pattern you are in right now continues and nothing changes, where will you be six months from now—probably worse? It is likely you will feel a sense of despair and hopelessness. This is dangerous, because depression and suicidal thoughts often stem from feelings of hopelessness and despair—the perception that the pain or circumstances you are in now is never going to get any better. Depression, and the neurochemical changes it produces, is the number one cause of suicide. It's like the chicken or the egg—do brain changes create depression or does depression create brain changes? I think it can be either way. You can have thoughts like, *"If the way I feel now is never going to get any better, why live? I don't want to be here anymore."* [1]

On the other hand, let's say you are experiencing real change. You are exhibiting signs of progress toward positive change—your life is improving because you are taking risks and working to resolve your problems and fears (especially in relationships). You are taking steps to obtain your goals and dreams. Will your perception of life in six months be better or worse? In this case, it is likely you will see good things ahead and feel positive and optimistic. This is an example of real hope.

Hope is a very powerful and important element in our ability to recover and change. When you possess hope, it gives you the ability to get through a bad day (today), because you are able to put things into perspective. If you are stagnant and have a bad day, you won't be able to think of a single reason *not to give in* to your compulsions to coping behaviors, i.e. relapse.

But if you have hope and are able to see that your life is going in the right direction (and that this was just a bad day), you will be able to think of many reasons *not* to relapse. In other words, you will act according to the hope you have.

> *"Optimism is the faith that leads to achievement.*
> *Nothing can be done without hope and confidence."*
> ~ Helen Keller

THE HOPE FORMULA

The Hope Formula is one of the Genesis Process tools created as a simple way to see where a person is in the process of change (recovery). It involves four components: Hope, Change, Risk, and Faith. Each element is dependent on the others for success. It begins with hope, which comes from the progress made in change. Change usually comes from taking a risk, which requires an act of faith. You have to believe that if you take a risk towards change, you will benefit from it because God blesses steps of faith. By taking this step of faith, you gain more hope, which helps you to take more risks to change. It's like a circle, each part of the formula energizing the next. Being active in this formula can get recovering people through a bad day.

Remember that the limbic system is programmed to avoid fear. It tries to get us to avoid risk since taking risks always involves some fear and can result in pain. Limbicly, it is not safe to take risk alone. Of course our greatest risk involves trusting and giving up control. Support and accountability gives you the *ability* to take risks. A safe church that is challenging and supporting its members to change is a "what works" church. When people begin to change, others see those changes, which can give them encouragement and the power of hope.

THE HOPE FORMULA[2]

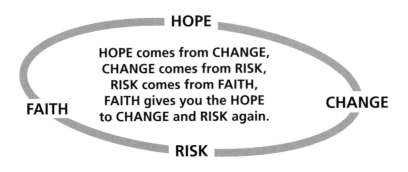

HOPE

HOPE comes from CHANGE,
CHANGE comes from RISK,
RISK comes from FAITH,
FAITH gives you the HOPE
to CHANGE and RISK again.

FAITH   CHANGE

RISK

"Why not go out on a limb? That's where the fruit is."
~ Will Rogers

ISABEL'S STORY

Dear Michael,

I was doing the process on hope in my change group and it spoke so much as to what I had been through. So, I wanted to write you about my story. I grew up in a home where my mom had many boyfriends. Some of them took advantage of me. In my teens and 20s I got into one bad relationship after another. As you say my "picker" was broken. At 28, I made a decision to never get into a relationship again; to me, all men were dogs. I had lost hope about ever finding love and trust. Well a friend with a similar story to mine got into a group of women who supported her to take a risk with an online dating service. She found a good guy and got married. It gave me hope. If she could do it, maybe I could.

I joined a group at her church doing your process. I found I could take a risk like she did because I didn't have to trust my broken picker. The ladies in my group checked out my thinking and helped me to go slow and not make a bad choice. Well, to make a long story short, I also met a good guy and got married. It was like a fairy tale. It was hope that made me able to take a risk, which produced real change. I could have never done it without the group. My change is bringing hope to others; I think hope is contagious.

Isabel

> **KEY thought** If you want to change behaviors, you have to change your heart.

"Guard your heart above all else, for it determines the course of your life." Proverbs 4:23 (NLT)

WHAT WORKS? HEART CHANGE

One of the fundamental rules of recovery is that if you don't heal the pain that drives the craving for the anesthetizing coping behavior, you just end up trading one addiction for another. In other words, if the underlying issue hasn't changed, a new way to cope will be found. A heart (limbic) change is the only way to get at the root issues that the behavior was there for.

In the "*What's Broken*" chapter, we looked at how experiences from relationship wounds set up the limbic system to create cognitive, emotional, and behavioral ways to avoid the pain and fear of being hurt again. That's why addictions are so insidious. Even Paul declares, "I do the very thing I do not want to do. It's not me doing it—it's sin in me" (Romans 7:20). He is saying that there is something stronger within us than the person we are aware of causing us to do things we don't want to do. Psychology talks about this as the *subconscious*.

Studying the brain has helped me to understand the mysteries of the Bible and how to apply it to help people more than all the Bible studies and schools I've gone to. I find it exciting when science validates what the Bible has been telling us for two thousand years. The problem is the same now as it was then—how do we change our heart? I have found that the basic formula for healing and changing heart (limbic) issues involves changing our false and destructive beliefs that drive our self-sabotaging behaviors. In order to do that, we need to understand the differences between thoughts and beliefs and how they work.

> **KEY thought**: Thoughts and beliefs create emotions that drive behaviors.

UNDERSTANDING THOUGHTS AND BELIEFS

For the church to create programs that work, it is essential to understand the differences between thoughts and beliefs and the power they have in affecting behaviors. Biblically, the heart is the center of one's self. It is where your emotions, your will, and especially your beliefs reside, whether they are true or false, positive or negative. Thoughts stem from what you have consciously learned and are aware of in life. They are fairly easy to verbalize and identify, and are more at the surface of our thinking patterns. It is also fairly easy to change our thinking by assimilating new information.

> "For the word of God is living and active and sharper than any two-edged sword, and piercing as far as the division of soul and spirit, of both joints and marrow, and able to judge the thoughts and intentions of the heart." Hebrews 4:12

Beliefs are different and more powerful than thoughts and are found in the subconscious—they are the deeper perceptions of life about truth, people, values, self, and reality. Your beliefs are at the core of your self-worth and identity. They are mostly subconscious perceptions that are formed from your experiences. These deep beliefs reside in your heart, which is why they can be such a mystery—they aren't easy to identify or uncover. They have a biological, emotional, and spiritual foundation. People will argue about their thoughts, but they will die for their beliefs.

Our belief systems are extremely powerful in driving emotions and reactions. According to the key thought I described above, if you want to change your destructive behaviors, you have to first identify the emotions that the coping behaviors are anesthetizing, and then the belief systems that are driving those emotions. Most of exercises in the *The Genesis Process Workbooks* are based on this principle. Let's use anxiety and stress as examples of this concept. We know that anxiety and stress are other words for fear, and worry is the primary way we create anxiety. During my seminars, I ask the ladies, "What do women worry about?" They answer "everything." I explain to them that worry creates anxiety and stress, which have similar neurochemical effects on the brain as cocaine. After a while, worry can be addictive because you get energy from the emotions created by it—anxiety and stress (fear) can become subconscious and habitual.[3]

How does anxiety relate to belief systems? In order for anxiety to be created, you have to *believe* something bad is going to happen. The actual belief is mostly subconscious and you need help to name it. The belief is expressed in the emotion. For example, if you are anxious or stressed, you might ask yourself, "What am I afraid of?" Try this and see what happens to the emotion. The answer is found in the form of a belief system (i.e., what you believe, or fear, is going to happen). That's where groups and counseling help affect change. Counselors or group members ask targeted self-discovery questions to bring these destructive beliefs into the light where they can then be dealt with. We call it "Name the Sucker," the belief that is driving the behavior or emotion.

> "My Father is glorified by this, that you bear much fruit, and so prove to be My disciples." John 15:8

We know that the number one thing that glorifies God is a changed life and a changed life is the result of a heart change. *What works* in achieving lasting change is helping people replace their false beliefs (limbic lies) with *the truth*. It seems simple, but it is not easy because it must be safe for this process to happen. The heart will begin to reveal its secrets when it feels safe. We tend to focus on filling people's heads with information to help them change—that's easy. But what is necessary is targeting their heart, which doesn't really respond very well to words. It is changed through experiences. What is effective in achieving real change is healing the distorted beliefs that originate from hurtful experiences mostly from relationships. This is why safe groups can be so powerful. We will hit what we are aiming at, and what we want to hit is hearts, not heads. Jesus is a heart experience.

" . . . For with the heart a person believes, resulting in righteousness, and with the mouth he confesses, resulting in salvation. For the Scripture says, 'Whoever believes in Him will not be disappointed.'" Romans 10:10–11

"Prayer is not asking. It is a longing of the soul. It is daily admission of one's weakness. It is better in prayer to have a heart without words than words without a heart."
~ Mahatma Gandhi

> **KEY thought** — It is heart change that creates the "Power of Hope."

OUR ROLE IN HEART CHANGE

Paul states that it's with our hearts we believe and these beliefs result in our righteousness (Romans 10:10). What is righteousness?[4] It's basically having God's influence in us in such a way that it affects our behaviors—the way we act. This explains why we ask Jesus into our hearts. That never made sense to me before. It seemed to me we should ask Him into our mind, our soul, or our spirit. It's funny how we have talked about the heart in so many different ways for so many thousands of years, and we really haven't had a clue what we are talking about.

Remember, this *heart* is the center of ourselves that seems to control who we are (our worth), what we feel, and how we act and re-act. It also controls how we do relationships. Have you ever heard the expression, "He had a change of heart"? We're not talking about the actual muscle that beats in our chest, so where is this heart? As humans, we have always known that we need a deep heart change to heal our wounds and hurtful behaviors.

It is what we seek and pray for. "Oh God, change my heart." *What works* is when we understand our role in the process.

"If you talk to a man in a language he understands, that goes to his head. If you talk to him in his internal language, that goes to his heart."
~ Nelson Mandela

> **KEY thought** — Jesus is Hope.

WE ASK JESUS TO FILL OUR HEARTS

So how does the heart get broken and how does it get healed? The answer is in the reason why we ask Jesus into our hearts in the first place because, again, the heart is the center of our beliefs and emotions. We know it is the source of our pain. When Jesus comes into our hearts, He changes our beliefs, which in turn changes the way we feel, resulting in changes in how we act. When we come to Jesus, it is usually because of the pain that our behaviors have caused others and ourselves. We say something like, "Jesus, I hate myself. Please come into my heart and set me free from these painful, destructive emotions and behaviors." Christ came to reveal to us how the Father sees us and wants to be apart of our lives. He was so safe and effective because He instantly connected with people's hearts and pretty much ignored their behavior. This was good for most, but not for the Pharisees because their hearts were evil. That is our goal—to be like Him. Jesus is hope.

Let's review a little about how all this heart change happens. Hope lies in the difference between the Old Testament and New Testament.

The difference is having the law in our minds, versus His Spirit in our hearts. In fact, the word *heart* is a central theme of the Bible, appearing 830 times (KJV). The Old Testament (and religion in general) is about trying to control our destructive nature through religious disciplines by obeying the rules. The New Testament is about an empowering personal relationship with the Creator of the Universe without having to earn it. The life of David is a good example. David loved and wanted to serve God, but he couldn't overcome his lust. He sinned over and over. Yet God called him *a man after His own heart*, because David was a humble man of great faith, who trusted God and gave Him control in all his trials. God saw David's heart as who he really was, more than just his behaviors. Nevertheless, God did not take away the consequences for David's choices.

> "For You do not delight in sacrifice, otherwise I would give it; The sacrifices of God are a broken spirit; A broken and a contrite heart, O God, You will not despise." Psalm 51:16–18

> **KEY thought**   Grace brings Hope.

FOSTER A PERSONAL RELATIONSHIP

In the Old Testament, God created a system of sacrifices in which something innocent had to pay the price for the guilty, thus the reason for animal sacrifice. These sacrifices didn't help change the sinner's nature. It was an analogy and a foreshadowing of what was to come (Hebrews 10:1–7).5 In those days, humans were trying to be acceptable and holy before God by their own human efforts by not breaking any of the rules. But in the New Covenant, God said, "I am going to take the law which I wrote on stone (the Ten Commandments) and write it on your heart" (Hebrews 8:10). This was so that we would be able to overcome our destructive desires and behaviors through a relationship instead of a religion. *What works* is building and fostering a personal relationship with the Creator of the Universe so He can give us power to overcome sin from the inside out. People will be drawn to Him by experiencing His changes in us—our role in changing hearts.

So, why the law? The law with grace is about love. God is basically saying; keep to the rules and limitations I have set for you and all will go well for you. They are just the natural laws built into nature the way I have created you. We all struggle with trying to overcome temptation and do what is right, yet we are defined by what we overcome. People who have been through much and have overcome much have a depth of character. Not just sin, but the also the trials of life and how we respond and either grow or shrink. Out of this basic struggle of overcoming our destructive desires, God is producing amazing god like creatures that even the angels envy. We will reach our potential as human beings by what we overcome. Like the old analogy of refining gold.

> *"The Bible is not a history book. It is the manual for life. When you study the Word of God, you develop a personal relationship with the Father. Then, you begin to gain understanding on how to mirror Him. When you imitate the Father, like Jesus, you will make a mark in the lives of others that can never be erased!"*
> ~ Creflo Dollar [6]

COOPERATE WITH THE HOLY SPIRIT

The Holy Spirit is given to us when we ask Jesus into our heart. He helps us want to change and be able to change. A good example of this principle can be seen in marriage. If we were to be completely honest with ourselves, most of us (especially men) would like to commit adultery or have casual affairs. The idea of having sex with someone new is exciting and fun. Sociologists tell us that human men are not designed to be monogamous. We have sexual cravings constantly. At my seminars, I ask the men how many sexual thoughts they have a day. The response is always, "We couldn't possibly count them all." But what stops us from acting on these cravings is the knowledge that infidelity would result in a loss of relationship. We would betray a commitment and create a heart wound in someone we love.

> "He restores my soul; He guides me in the paths of righteousness For His name's sake." Psalm 23:2

It is the same with God. The Bible calls us the *bride of Christ*. We have a love/trust relationship with Him that we don't want to betray by sinning because it would result (at least temporarily) in a loss of relationship. It's not that He rejects us, but our sin puts up a wall between us. Remember the chapter on *Secrets*? We learned that He calls us back to relationship with Himself through a feeling of what we call being convicted, which comes through love. Love relationships give us the power to say *no* from the place we used to say *yes*. Even when we fall, God will work in our heart and conscience to convict us to do what is right. It is healthy guilt.

Of course, we still have free will and can block off His voice when we don't want to change. When God and life circumstances bring us to a place of repentance (wanting to change), we are very vulnerable and need grace and love from others. *What works* is allowing the Holy Spirit to work in us from the inside out—participating in what He is doing in our lives and the lives of others. Like Jesus, we want to participate with what we see the Father doing (John 5:19).

> "I will put My Spirit within you and cause you to walk in My statutes..." Ezekiel 36:27

A TRUE STORY OF WHAT HURTS AND WHAT HELPS

Dear Michael,

After college I married a young pastor. Although he and I held the same degree from the same Bible College, as a pastor's wife I was not allowed to be a part of the paid staff. So I pursued my passion for ministry by helping him and volunteering my time in Women's Ministry and the Worship Department. Our church had about 1,200 active members and we had two small children, so I kept busy enough. Our marriage was based on our working together in ministry, but we had no real intimacy. I was very lonely. I became friends with David, who was married and served as an elder in the church. He was very easy to talk to and genuinely interested in what I had to say. Over the course of about three years, we fell into an affair of the heart, which eventually led to a physical affair.

God's conviction was so strong that I finally confessed to my husband. I also wrote a letter to the church elders, confessed the affair, and took full responsibility. The church asked me not to return and told area churches not to accept me into fellowship.

The congregation was instructed (with our children present) not to have fellowship with David and me. Within a week, I lost my church family, my physical family, my job (at a Christian school), my home, and all my friends. David and I both asked our spouses to forgive us and take us back. Neither wanted to. So, we both divorced. We tried to stay apart, but without any support system we finally decided we should just get married and try to start over.

We slinked into the back row at a large church and cried our hearts out during worship for the first year. I can't describe the emotional and physical pain I experienced over disappointing God in such a dramatic way. We knew that even if God didn't strike us dead, he surely could never use either of us in ministry again. We had done something unforgivable. But we didn't really know God back then. We only knew religion, performance, and punishment. As we sat under the new pastor's teaching and attended healing from divorce classes, we slowly began to believe the truth about God and His forgiveness and passionate love.

Within two years, I was active in women's ministries, while also serving on the worship team. After five years, we fulfilled my lifelong dream to serve in missions, and began to travel to Northern Ireland to minister. Now, twelve years later, I'm on staff and David serves on the Missions board. We have had many opportunities to serve and share from the experience of our healed wounds. The hardest part is trying to explain to people how much grace God showered on us. It doesn't make sense. Not only did he forgive me, a pastor's wife, for having an affair with a church elder (unforgivable sin, right?), He let me marry my best friend, who loves me more passionately now than twelve years ago. God's love is so outrageously passionate and gracious! I don't deserve it and I'll spend the rest of my life trying to understand it and express my gratitude for it. I teach others that with God, no mistake is final. Those who are forgiven much love much.

Serving Him,
T.C.

WHAT CAN SAFE AND EFFECTIVE CHURCHES DO TO RESTORE HOPE?

We know hope is a primary motivator and reward for healthy change, so how do we help recovering people get there? In other words, how do we help them get to the place where they can experience true change that will allow them to have hope and further recovery? There are several things that safe churches and people can do. It comes back to giving grace, love, acceptance, and support by investing in others and restoring their self-worth.

Safe churches are ones that realize that their religious structure is there to *support and encourage* one's personal relationship with God through Christ and *not replace it*. It is the Holy Spirit's job to convict people. It is our job to restore them. There are natural consequences to sin; our self-righteous judgments should not be one of them. As in the above story, those who are truly repentant should receive forgiveness and grace. Grace in action is when we are given another chance.

Change comes from the inside with the help of the Holy Spirit guiding and convicting us. Some times He uses people to do that, but it is done in love and concern. God does not need our help in this process by punishing and shaming people to get them to change. Otherwise prison would work (approximately 67 percent reoffend).[7] God usually answers prayer through people to heal people. He says His Spirit will come upon us and we will do the same things that He did— bring healing and hope (Luke 4:18–19).

> **KEY thought**
> Religion is about control.
> Relationship is about value.

VALUE THE PERSON MORE THAN THE RULES

This is the problem: In order to replace religion with relationship, we have to give up control. We have to value the person more than the rules. This is the message the new Pope, Francis, is trying to convey, and it is causing a lot of division and heated emotions within the Catholic Church. When the God begins to move in a person's life, many times it's in ways that don't fit in our theological box. We all have a box we look at self, life, events and circumstances through. We interrupt just about everything through that box it is our worldview. We try to fit everything in that box and we can be uncomfortable with anything outside of it; our box also contains our identity, values and self-worth.

We have to keep our minds open and not hold on to our old ways, like the Pharisees. We need to be open to expanding our box. As we talked about earlier, our belief systems are very resistant to change, especially religious ones. It is much easier to learn than to unlearn. We need to be receptive and open to new ways God might want to move. Jesus conveys this principle when he teaches about trying to put new wine in old wine skins (Matt. 9:17). How old is your wine skin? Grace in action is about giving up control; there are no rules with grace. Without rules, we have no power and control. It comes down once again to faith and trusting enough to give Him control—simple, but not easy.

> **KEY thought** — Rebellion is the fear of being controlled.

"The world as we have created it is a process of our thinking. It cannot be changed without changing our thinking."
~ Albert Einstein

Throughout history, the people and churches that give God this kind of control have been the most effective at pioneering positive change. These "change agents" followed God outside the box. As we accept ourselves through the eyes of God, we will also extend acceptance to others. But we have to get free of our judgments to do it, which is a lifetime discipline. It comes back to practicing the *Golden Rule* and considering What *Would Jesus Do?* Personally, my forty-plus years of struggle with following God have been one of building a bigger box for Him. Just as soon as I think I have it figured out, He does something totally outside of how I thought He was supposed to and then I have to build a bigger box! Of course, my goal as a recovering Pharisee would be to not have a box at all. But I don't think I will achieve that in this lifetime. Churches that have an *ear to hear* and a *heart to obey* what God is doing in people's lives have to be secure enough to trust Him by giving up control. Trusting God puts the sense of adventure back into our faith as He can be full of surprises.

> *"So few want to be rebels anymore.*
> *And out of those few, most, like myself, scare easily."*
> ~ Ray Bradbury [8]

Insecurity manifests itself in control. I think this principle is most vividly demonstrated throughout history in both political and religious revolutions. In fact, it seems to me that the people who are the most insecure in what they believe are the most defensive and even violent in defending it. The people I have met who seem most secure in their beliefs are the most peaceful in discussing them. They are not threatened by what others believe. Many of the non-churched Christians I have encountered were wounded because they were stepping out in ministry and doing something outside the box. The leadership tried to control them to bring them back inside the leadership's comfort box, which resulted in rebellion, conflict, disrespect, and hurt. The Bible is full of stories about "rebellious people" doing something new for God and the price they paid. I hate absolutes. For twenty years, I have tried to find an exception to the precept "all contention cometh by pride." I haven't found one yet.

> "Only by pride cometh contention, but with the well advised is wisdom." Proverbs 13:10 (KJV)

I received this email from a couple that pioneered a drop-in recovery program in inner city London. I get these kinds of messages regularly.

OUTSIDE THE BOX

Dear Mike,

John and I have decided after much prayer to find another church. My ministry was once again attacked by people in the body who feel the best way to treat people with addictions is only through prayer and contention for the miraculous. Those of us on the frontlines see how both miraculous transformation and a recovery process fit together. People in my recovery program were told by my church not to do the program anymore. One guy who was interested in the counselor training became confused and discouraged, so he stopped his involvement with us altogether.

An elder approached me recently and told me that I don't do things the way Jesus did! So, it's time to move on and we're very sad. We are getting excited about our new journey and have some good friends behind us who will provide support and accountability through this transition. We are seeing lives changed and are willing to do what is needed to continue being a part of what God is doing with us and through us.

Dawn

Sadly, many people we know have had to leave their church to continue doing their recovery work. I have had many experiences that are similar to this story; the people (like the elder) who are most critical of recovery programs are usually people who never been in the trenches with real addicts themselves, it is all theology.

OFFER ACCEPTANCE AND SUPPORT

Throughout history, those who think and operate "outside the box" get labeled as unsubmissive and rebellious. Later on, once they are successful, they are called prophets, pioneers, reformers, and visionaries. I call them "change agents." The leaders of their time were resistant to change and tried to control them, but exerting control resulted in rebellion. I am one of these, so I understand how leaders react to change where they are not in control. Change agents also make a lot of mistakes along the way, but this is the way we learn. Parents and teenagers do this dance a lot. By nature, teens try to be independent to explore their identity. Parents are afraid (insecure) about their teens making mistakes and bad choices, so they try to control them. Parents may be concerned about their safety, or oftentimes, about how their kid's behavior will reflect on them. The more the parent tries to control, the more the teen rebels, and around and around it goes.

Churches can be the same way. *What works* in healing wounded people is supporting them in their calling and helping them when they make mistakes. Remember prodigals learn from experience, especially mistakes. Prodigals can be very difficult because they don't just accept the way things are—they are always asking "Why?" and "How do you know that is true?" Leaders and teachers usually try to discourage prodigals by making us think something is wrong with us. We often get labeled as "rebellious"—especially if we should dare to questions the Bible. I have been told many times that my nonconformity was demonically driven or that I have probably never been born again and thus not saved. I don't know; is blind faith the best kind of faith?

IN A SAFE CHURCH IT IS OK TO QUESTION

I learned from having spent so many years in eastern religions and cuts that it is important to ask questions. Most religions don't encourage asking questions or voicing doubts—don't ask, don't think, just believe. I believe that truth is something that reality should bear witness to. I remember when I first became a Christian I had a hard time with the whole trinity thing. It just didn't make sense to me. I ask a lot of questions about it and was told that I just needed to accept it because it was in the Bible. Not a good thing to tell a sixties prodigal. Well I really struggled with it until one morning I ask God to show me what was true. He simply said, " you are made in my image." I realized that I was three separate beings, yet one. I am physical and my body has its own needs and wants and communicates them to me and others. I am a mental/social/emotional being who has a life and needs of his own, like when I am dreaming, and get bored or lonely. I am also a spiritual being who has needs that are usually *too deep for words*, especially to seek truth and be connected to the Divine. Three separate beings, yet one. Now it made sense and I could move on. It is OK to question, God can handle it, some people can't.

ACCEPTANCE CAN BE HARD

Accepting people with all of their idiosyncrasies and crazy beliefs can be a challenge and a growth opportunity for everyone involved. But safe people and churches are consciously working on it. Acceptance doesn't mean minimizing consequences or cosigning bad behavior, because there are natural consequences for our behaviors and choices. Granted there are people who do not want to change (repent) and who can be toxic to the whole. They may need to be let loose for a while until they come to a place of humility. Paul talks about how pain results in change in 1 Corinthians 5:4–6 and Galatians 6:1.9 But like so many stories in this book, when someone looked past sinful behaviors and ministered to the person's heart, change and healing began. Sometimes this can be a hard call, but if it is done in love, it is probably the right one. *The right thing to do is usually the hard thing to do.* Ask what Jesus would do? Remember—the people who are the hardest to love are the ones who probably need it the most.

A WHAT WORKS STORY

Dear Michael,

My wife and I adopted three of my grandchildren from a previous marriage. We quickly became a "blended family" in every aspect. I am African American and she is Caucasian with a German background. The children we adopted were like wild things "from another planet." They were raised in a drug and gang environment. One child has fetal alcohol syndrome, one has attachment disorder, and the oldest of the three assumed the role of the mother for the other two children. She had a son out of wedlock years before we met. One child was five years old and suffered from ADHD. Another was eleven and then we had our own daughter. It was a mess.

We soon discovered that we disagreed on child-rearing issues, discipline strategy, correction, and consequences. We disagreed on visitation issues revolving around their birth parents. We even disagreed on how much money to spend on them for Christmas.

These kids pushed every button we had. It got to the point where we became verbally and emotionally abusive to one another.

We went to the church for help and were told that we needed to step down from all ministries to focus on our personal problems. I was on the church council, worship team, and urban missions. My wife was on the women's dance team and prayer ministry. We both were also leading Genesis groups. We decided that we would try to apply the Genesis processes in our own lives to address the hurts and pain of our own past. It was the first time we agreed on anything for quite some time.

We decided to show grace for our children and allow them to make mistakes as we came alongside them, but we didn't rescue them from the consequences. At your seminar, you said that teens are rebellious because they don't want to be controlled. You said rebellion is the fear of being controlled and to not give them anything to rebel against. You recommended treating them with respect by giving them choices and consequences. We used the Double Bind Worksheet a lot.[10]

It took all our faith to give up control, but as we began to treat them equally and with respect, real change and healing began to happen. It was amazing to find out my control was the primary problem, not their behavior. Now the girls are teenagers and our son is a Marine, who just returned from Iraq. Our marriage is better than ever and we are back in full-time ministry at our church. Now we have some real tools and experiences to help other parents. We didn't run away from the church. We stayed and led by example.

L.C.

> **KEY thought** — Healing the heart heals the whole person. It's miraculous.

INVESTING TIME IS WHAT HEALS

When one person invests into another, it restores the sense of worth and hope that was taken away by someone else. In my experience, this is *what works* in restoring a broken life. *Self-worth* is different than our modern concept of self-esteem, which is not really a biblical concept. The Bible does not tell us to esteem ourselves, it tells us to die to ourselves. But self-worth is one of the most important themes in the Bible. It tells us that we are of such worth that Christ died for us. If something has little value to you, you will most likely treat it poorly. But you will guard something that has great value to you; you protect and make sacrifices for it.

When we are abused, betrayed, shamed, rejected, or abandoned, it creates a belief system that says, "There must be something wrong with me. I'm not good enough; I must deserve to be treated badly, nobody really cares about me." People with these kinds of wounds and the self-beliefs they create are looking for and expecting rejection. Recovery is a process of *learning to trust again. What works* to heal wounded people and their coping behaviors is a changed heart/limbic belief system that restores their joyful identity. The most common subconscious protective belief is, "If I am vulnerable and trust people, they will hurt me—I deserve rejection. There is something wrong with me" It will take an opposite experience to change that belief.

> **KEY thought** What heals a broken heart is when one person invests himself into another.

> *"I suppose that since most of our hurts come through relationships so will our healing, and I know that grace rarely makes sense for those looking in from the outside."*
> ~ Wm. Paul Young, *The Shack*

The only thing I know that will heal these kinds of self-worth distortions is when someone invests their time in us. *We need another person to complete us.* You can give someone money, advice, and provide programs, but what really gives them feelings of worthiness is your time—it produces hope.

It shows that they are valuable and gives them hope and the ability to take risk. Upon that foundation they can begin to build a new life. People with low self-worth will begin to value themselves by what you see in them, by your words, and by your actions—especially keeping your word and being committed to them.

Remember the story of "The Good Samaritan" (Luke 10:25–37)? The Samaritan had mercy on the man he didn't know and invested time and money in him—we can assume this resulted in a changed life. The church is the only place that has the resources for that kind of one-on-one investment. Safe people in safe churches working in competent programs will change lives—they will heal broken hearts (limbic systems). But you can't fake it—you have to have His heart for the lost and broken.

"Never believe that a few caring people can't change the world. For, indeed, that's all who ever have."
~ Margaret Mead

"For it is in giving that we receive."
~ St. Francis of Assisi

PARTNER WITH GOD

God designed His church to function with Him in a symbiotic relationship. As we discussed in the chapter on *Spiritual Stagnation*, you have to give to grow. Church people need hurting people as much as the hurting people need the church. God wants to partner with us. When He wants to get something done down here and answer prayers, He uses us—His body. When we do our part, He will do His part. Working in this partnership is one of the main things I teach in the *Genesis Counselor Trainings*. For example, it is the counselor's job to identify the wound, the coping behavior, and the belief system that drives a client's self-destructive behaviors. But it is God's job to heal the heart by changing the belief system, replacing limbic lies with *the truth*. This is what works, it always has.

Remember, it is not so much the trauma that happened that still affects us today. It is the survival lies entrenched in our beliefs that are the driving forces behind destructive emotions and behaviors. The truth sets us free. I have learned a simple principle over the years; the simpler you make something, the more powerful it is. It is the simplicity of the Gospel that is the most powerful. When you experience God moving through you to change someone's life, it "spoils" you for the ordinary. You will never be the same. You will get much more back than you give. Without a doubt, I have learned more from helping people than they have learned from me.

APPLYING WHAT WORKS

Let's look at how all this information can be applied in practical terms. We know that programs and organizations by themselves don't work. *What works* is investing time and energy into people's lives. When we provide them with experiences opposite of the painful ones that wounded them, they will heal.

Churches that want to be safe and effective for the wounded people God brings them will have certain elements, such as:

1. **People with a heart for the broken who are willing to get involved and be trained and supervised.**
2. **Backing from the pulpit.** In my experience, if the pastor doesn't promote a ministry or program it won't last very long. The pastor has to have a heart for recovery and healing. He doesn't have to head the recovery ministry up, but needs to show support and oversee it.
3. **Openness in Sunday services that makes it safe for people to seek help.** This means making room for testimonies that allows a person to tell what happened to them, how it affected them (usually resulting in a destructive coping behavior), and what worked for them to get better. Also, a pastor who is open about his/her own problems makes it safe for others to seek help.
4. **Relevant sermons about issues the congregation and community are struggling with.** I think the best sermons I have heard have been

ones that not only talk about what we should be (like Christ), but also provide practical information on how to do it. For example: If I am speaking on forgiveness or sexual problems, do I also have a program and support network in place for those whom the sermon impacts?

5. **Groups with trained leaders who use effective materials that focus on helping people make successful changes.** This would include home Bible study groups focused on building relationships that encourage and support one another in realizing each other's potential. Remember it takes grace and competency to make it safe for people to take the risk of being vulnerable. When group leaders are trained to facilitate, there will also be confidentiality, which is the main thing many churches, or groups, lack.

6. **Lay people trained to come alongside special populations needing help and extra support** (e.g., young married couples, teens, those impacted by divorce, family members of the mentally ill, single moms, the elderly, employment help, those addicted, and so on). A practical example of this is a church that assigns an older couple to a newlywed couple for a year in a mentor-type of relationship.

7. **Trained (or by referral) one-on-one counselors that help the people with more severe issues beyond the scope of the groups or church's abilities.**

8. **A grace-based community. Grace is foundational for success.** Like so many of the stories in this book, people will watch very closely how your church handles those who have messed up.

9. **A transparent, welcoming community that doesn't keep undercurrents of secrets or excludes others who are different.** I have been in churches where there is the *in crowd* or *inner circle* that is hard to break into. It can feel like an "us and them" atmosphere. It is important to welcome all who want to serve.

PRACTICAL EXAMPLES

When a church has some of the above components, people seeking help will have hope—which I believe is the key for taking the risk of asking of help. The seekers will be attracted to churches they perceive to be competent, safe, and effective, i.e. a practical Christianity. Here are a couple of examples of what I am talking about.

STRESS: A RELEVANT TOPIC FOR MANY PEOPLE TODAY

The number one problem that people in our society struggle with is stress. Remember that stress (anxiety, worry) is another word for fear. As we talked about earlier, it is the number one issue behind most of our problems—physical, emotional, social, addiction, and relational. One reason so many people are turning to eastern religions and philosophies is because they are focused on relieving stress through practical disciplines and exercises. What is the church and Christianity in general doing to help people overcome stress in a practical way? We might have to look outside the box for things that will work.

One idea is to have meditation, yoga, breathing exercises, biofeedback, and exercise classes, like Pilates, even dance classes like Zumba, all in a Christian context. I still use many of the breathing and meditation techniques I learned forty years ago in my hippie days. They are tools that help me deal with life and the stress it creates. I think people would respond enthusiastically to this kind of practical Christianity. Remember change comes from asking the right questions. Why doesn't Christianity as a rule have these kinds of practical and *fun* groups? I have included a mediation in the notes that I developed that is proving very beneficial to not only relieve stress, but also to also help reprogram many of our self-sabotaging negative belief systems. Try it for thirty days—it works.[11] You can also print it out on my web site (genesisprocess.org) under, *handouts*.

ENCOURAGE FUN

I don't know about you, but I haven't experienced very many Christian activities whose sole purpose was to just have fun. I remember times growing up when my parents had a group of friends that would get together once a month to have a party. They would eat, drink, dance, laugh, and play cards. It has been a long time since I can remember being invited to a party with my Christian friends without any agenda.

I think one of the things that make people back away from Christianity is that we don't seem to have much fun. We are not sure what kind of fun we can even have! Is it sin? Because most sin—if not all sin—is fun, or at least pleasurable. Otherwise it wouldn't be attractive. Hosting events or gatherings that are designed just to provide fun is good for everyone. I think it is easy for us to take ourselves too seriously. We may need to simply lighten up a bit.

"Few things are more infectious than a godly lifestyle. The people you rub shoulders with everyday need that kind of challenge. Not prudish. Not preachy. Just Cracker Jack clean living. Just honest to goodness, bone-deep, non-hypocritical integrity."
~ Chuck Swindoll

EDUCATE ON THE IMPORTANCE OF INTEGRITY

Integrity, in practical terms, simply means *to keep your word*—do what you say you are going to do, when you say you are going to do it. I read an article a while back about a survey regarding employers. The number one thing that the participants said they were looking for was an employee with integrity. This means not only keeping their word, but what their actions are when no one is looking. They stated that over the years, this problem has gotten much worse.

I don't know about you, but I have people say they are going to do something or call me at a certain time, and don't—on a regular basis. Christians seem to have a particularly bad reputation in this area. Just the other day a neighbor said to me, "If I see a fish on someone's business card, I won't deal with them. I have had so many bad experiences with Christians." I have heard this over and over again. I had to agree with him, as I have had some of the same experiences.

It may be one of the reasons why when people think of Christians, the first word that comes to mind is "hypocrite." I think this is an area that we can work on. If people are going to be attracted to Christianity and trust Christians—especially hurting individuals who have been betrayed repeatedly—they have to see that we have better integrity than the world. This is definitely *what works*.

ANOTHER "WHAT WORKS" STORY

Dear Michael,

I have been struggling with sex addiction since my early teens and have been in active recovery for about six years. I was working hard to gain some long-term momentum and sobriety while volunteering in the church, trying to appear strong and having it all together. In February of 2010, I hit a low point and after being confronted by close friends who knew my real story, I realized I needed a significant disruption in my life and was encouraged to look into an inpatient recovery program. It was full-on rehab. I hated the idea of it. I hated that my life had come to a point where this wasn't just a good idea, it was necessary. I couldn't continue doing what I was doing, hoping that my life would get better by chance. Something had to change.

I decided to take the advice of those close to me and began to look into a full rehab. I found what looked like a good one but the cost was a huge barrier—over $30,000 for two months. There was no way I could afford that. These same friends continued to support me and put me in touch with my church leadership. Thinking I was going to ask for a loan or some sort of payment plan, I talked to my senior pastor about options to pay for rehab, and before I could finish summarizing my shameful story, he interrupted me and asked, "How much is it?" "$30K," I replied. He didn't hesitate, "We'll pay for it." I was shocked. He didn't ask questions, he didn't demand a follow-up plan to make sure he was getting a good return for the money. He extended a gift in grace, and eighteen months later I continue to walk in freedom with a new strength for the daily battle of sex addiction.

It is not easy, but my church's faith in me gives me a strength I didn't have before. It's been a battle, but the support of my church has been overwhelming. It took an unexpected turn of even greater grace when they asked me to consider joining the staff leadership team. I still can't believe it. Not only did they support a recovering sex addict, they hired one. My sin has become my ministry, and I am helping many men with the same problem. I feel I can't do enough to pay it forward. I'm still blown away. Thanks, Michael, for letting me share my story.

R.C.

> *"We make a living by what we get.*
> *We make a life by what we give."*
> ~ Winston S. Churchill

Today, start trying to find your "self" by giving it away. What practical things can you do to bring *hope* to others? What do you have to lose?

SELF-DISCOVERY QUESTIONS

1. If God did a miracle in you that would free you from the thing you struggle with the most, what would He do? What would He heal?

   _____
   _____
   _____
   _____

2. What are you doing to take a risk towards change? See the Hope Formula above.

   _____
   _____
   _____
   _____

3. What have you seen that works in helping people who are self-destructive?

   _____
   _____
   _____
   _____

4. Considering #6 : *"Lay people trained to come alongside special populations needing help and extra support."* What do you think you could do to help others? What is your area of talent and gifting?

_____
_____
_____
_____

PRACTICAL APPLICATION

Considering your answer for the last Self-Discovery Question above, make a commitment to develop some skills and get training to enhance your natural gifting to help others. Ask someone to provide accountability to support you.

CHAPTER TEN

THE FEAR OF GOD

Based on Process Seven in the Change Group Workbook

> **KEY thought** — Knowledge, wisdom and understanding begin with the fear of The Lord.

I know that everything God does will remain forever; there is nothing to add to it and there is nothing to take from it, for God has so worked that men should fear Him. Ecclesiastes 3:14.

The conclusion, when all has been heard, is: fear God and keep His commandments, because this applies to every person. Ecclesiastes 12:13

Some years ago, when I was walking out of church minding my own business, I felt that God spoke to me. He simply said, "Michael, I want you to fear Me." I thought, "OK, that is Scriptural." I didn't think too much about it at the time, as it seemed weird to me. I did a Bible study on it, and got even more confused. I had been taught that God loved me, so why would He tell me to fear Him? When I thought about God all the images of Jesus came to mind, like one with Him smiling with a little lamb in His arms. I went to a Bible scholar friend. He told me not to worry about it because it just means to respect God. However, when I looked up "fear" in Hebrew and Greek, it translated as: "dread or terror, to stand in awe of, be awed." Respect is a different word. I read a commentary on it and it likened the fear of God to being in an earthquake or in front of a tidal wave, to feel very small and overwhelmed by incredible power.

The fear of the Lord is the beginning of knowledge. Proverbs 1:7

The fear of the Lord is the beginning of wisdom, And the knowledge of the Holy One is understanding. Proverbs 9:10

> *To fear God, is one of the first and greatest*
> *Duties of his rational Creatures.*
> ~ Charles Inglis, *Little House on The Prairie*

The Bible states that knowledge, wisdom, and understanding *begin* with the fear of God. I began to realize that the inverse would be, that if you don't fear God you haven't begun. The more I got into it, the more it seemed the fear of God was a very important theme and precept throughout the whole Bible. I struggled for weeks trying to understand how to fear, trust, and love God all at the same time it just didn't make sense. I finally came to the end of myself (the prodigal thing) and gave up. Sitting down at the beach one morning, I said, "God, I give up. I can't figure it out." He spoke to me like I was a small child, saying, "Michael, whatever you fear, you give power to, and will control you." The lights went on, it seemed so obvious. God wants us to fear Him because His control will be benevolent and beneficial. In a life full of insecurity and uncertainty, you are going to have fear. What's important is what you give power and control to. The good news is, what you give control to, you can take back.

> **KEY thought** — What ever you fear you give power to and will control you.

"Do not fear those who kill the body but are unable to kill the soul; but rather fear Him who is able to destroy both soul and body in hell." Matthew 10:28

Jesus tells us in the above scripture what is beneficial to fear and what is not. When you fear the things of this world, including man, you come under the authority and control of the god of this world, Satan. I'm not sure why God let that happen but Matthew 4; 8–9 says; "Again, the devil took him (Jesus) to a very high mountain and showed him all the kingdoms of the world and their splendor. All this I will give you," he said, "if you will bow down and worship me." So the devil is the God of this world and can give power and prosperity to whom he wishes, it only cost you your soul. Fear is the main way we can give him control. Other words for fear are anxiety, worry, stress, insecurity, dread, and panic. The whole sixth chapter of Matthew devoted to the theme of fear/anxiety. Jesus talks about a long list of things not to be controlled by and fearful about. At the end He says to trust God as He wants to show us how He will come through. Although if we choose, He will let us try to be in control, which will result in anxiety.

> The fear of man brings a snare, but he who trusts in the Lord will be exalted. Proverbs 29:25

> *"The reason why many are still troubled, still seeking, still making little forward progress is because they haven't yet come to the end of themselves. We're still trying to give orders, and interfering with God's work within us."*
> ~ A.W. Tozer

Through working with addicts, I discovered two other areas in which this principle is true. They are whatever you love/desire and hate/resentment you also give power to and will control you. All three things—love, hate, and fear—have one thing in common; they produce a focused attention, a need and a craving, towards their object. This focused attention is called an attachment, which can result in dependence. We can put our faith in these things and they can become false gods as we look to them for security.

> **KEY thought** — Whatever you put your faith in can become your god.

The limbic system can begin to equate these attachments with what it believes we need to survival and sets up structures like cravings, anger, anxiety, denial, procrastination, control, and confusion in order to cope and avoid giving them up. Some unhealthy attachments are more powerful than others because they fall into all three areas, like; money, relationships, food, sex, etc. You may have desire, resentment and fear toward these things and others.

Attachments manifest themselves in one of two ways: healthy or unhealthy, helpful or harmful, productive or destructive. One of the keys to personal recovery and growth is evaluating your attachments and getting free of the unhealthy ones. *The Genesis Process* has a whole process devoted to accomplish this re-attachment. David prayed, "Search me, O God, and know my heart; try me and know my anxious thoughts; and see if there be any hurtful way in me, and lead me in the everlasting way." Psalm 139: 23–24 Lets look at all three, starting with the most powerful, fear.

FEAR

> *The only thing we have to fear is fear itself.*
> ~ Franklin D. Roosevelt

Fear is the primary emotion that causes you to give away your power and control. Fear is also the area that the limbic system remembers and reacts to the most. Fear can cause your conscious mind to shut down and your survival brain to take over your thoughts, feelings, and reactions, i.e. you become powerless. Fear can also create cravings for things that in the past have made the fear or the awareness of the fear temporarily subside. Most fear is supported by lies (false belief systems) and can give the "father of lies" access into your life. I believe the enemy mostly controls us by the lies we believe. So replacing a lie with the truth is freedom. The number one command in the whole Bible is, "DO NOT FEAR." I read it is said 365 times, something to be conscious of every day. It is a central message. I think it is interesting that in thirty-five years of being a Christian I have never heard a sermon on the fear of God. The number one promise in the Bible is; "I am with you." They go together. Do not fear, because I am with you. David tells us in the 23rd Psalm: Even though I walk through the valley of the *shadow* of death, I fear no evil, for You are with me. It is not real death; it is the shadow of death. He says he can face it because God is with him. Surrendering the things you fear to the control of God can be the most freeing thing you may ever do. Read Matthew 6.

> "But seek first His kingdom and His righteousness, and all these things (you are so anxious about) will be added to you. So do not worry about tomorrow; for tomorrow will care for itself. Each day has enough trouble of its own." Matthew 6:33–34 (Parentheses are mine)

KEY thought	The areas where you have anxiety/stress are simply areas you don't trust God with.

The areas in which you have fear, anxiety, and stress are basically the areas in which you don't trust God. The areas in which you trust Him are the areas in which you have peace. When you try to control people, life or circumstances you create stress by using your will to get what you think you want or need. You push against life rather than flow with it, which can be exhausting. Constant anxiety/fear usually results in depression. Think about all the things and people you try control that you know you can't; it is a form of insanity. I have worked with so many people who say, "My life is insane, I just can't get all my ducks to stay lined up." When He's in control, you have peace. Acceptance and trusting God is a main objective of most all religions.

As we talked about earlier, anxiety can also be an addiction, creating energy through worry to literally out-run your problems. The simple cure for anxiety is to turn over to, and trust Him with areas you are fearful about. Once again it is a step of faith and you will be more successful if you don't try to do it alone. It is a safe and focused group that makes us able to face and move past our fears.

"Be anxious for nothing, but in everything by prayer and supplication with thanksgiving let your requests be made known to God. And the peace of God, which surpasses all comprehension, will guard your hearts and minds in Christ Jesus." Philippians 4:6–7

Fear is part of your God-given survival system. We all have fears, but what you attach it to is critical, because fear results in control. God wants you to fear Him because His control in your life will be benevolent and beneficial. Again, study the spiritual principles about fear in Matthew 6. In my weekend seminars I talk about what are a man's and a women's greatest fear (belief system) that explains some of our harmful behaviors. For a man I think it is; "I'm not enough, I don't have what it takes." For women I think it is; I'll always be alone, I'll never be loved." Here is a partial list of fears that result in undesirable control; abandonment, rejection, intimacy, poverty, of not being recognized/respected, money, sex, death, pain, inadequacy, success and failure, trusting, and loneliness. I think our greatness and most controlling fear is torture. Regimes have used it to control the masses since the beginning.

ROSE'S STORY

I don't know of a time the fear was not with me. I didn't know that's what it was; all I knew is that I had to control everything and everyone in order to not feel it. Looking back I don't even think I knew it was fear, I would just react, usually with anger. I thought I was coping pretty well until recently, when I got married for the second time. My new husband and I were fairly comfortable with each other before we got married. Not too much passion, just hugging and holding hands. On my wedding night I felt paralyzed when it was time for bed. I just sat there on the edge of the bed unable to move. Gil was so patient; he said, "it's OK, we'll wait until your ready". But it only got worse; I couldn't even be in the bedroom with him without feeling the panic coming on. He would come up to hug and kiss me and I would just brace myself. I told myself I wasn't cold, my family just wasn't very "huggy" nor was I with my children. I went to a friend who knew how to pray though problems when people got stuck. She guided me though the Genesis Process of "healing the protective personality". God showed me the lie that was holding me, "if I am vulnerable to a man, he will hurt me." The Holy Spirit showed me the first time I created that lie to protect me. I was about 4, my step dad had put my younger brother and I down for a nap in the bedroom. He hugged me too much and began to touch me in bad ways. I didn't move so he wouldn't get mad at me and do the same thing to my brother. As we continued in the exercise I saw Jesus there with me, He took me off the bed and held me tenderly and kept me safe in His arms". I was able to turn my self-protection over to Jesus, to be my constant protector. Later that night, I had been reading on my bed, my husband came in and sat beside me. I don't know when, but before I knew it we were cuddling together looking at the book together. I felt so safe and loved. I cried knowing I was free to love and be loved, no longer bound by fear.

Rosie

LOVE AND DESIRE

"All things are lawful for me, but not all things are profitable. All things are lawful for me, but I will not be mastered by anything." 1 Corinthians 6:12

Love and desire play a big part of how God design us as human beings. As we saw in the chapter on Sin and Disease that desire (lust) is a powerful emotion that can motivate us to great good or great harm. You are to love what He loves and hate what He hates. This is where it can get tricky, because religion can create rules about what to desire and hate that are man made. When it comes from His Spirit you will naturally respond to life, people, temptations, and problems in a healthy way. Desire is very powerful because the things you desire for your comfort or to help you cope can become false gods as you put your faith in them rather than in God. For example, money often becomes this kind of god and desiring it can lead to a number of unhealthy emotions and behaviors. Paul tell us: "For the love of money is a root of all sorts of evil, and some by longing for it have wandered away from the faith and pierced themselves with many grief's. (1 Timothy 6:10)

> *When you are discontent, you always want more, more, more. Your desire can never be satisfied. But when you practice contentment, you can say to yourself, 'Oh yes—I already have everything that I really need.'*
> ~ Dalai Lama

Remember, the limbic memory records things that have to do with fear and pain, and pleasure and reward. So when you do something that makes you feel better or more secure, that is, taking away pain and fear, you will naturally have a *desire* to want to do it again. God gave you this system because He wants you to enjoy His blessings, desiring things that are good for you. But when desire becomes distorted or perverted, it can become destructive to you and those close to you. When you become attached to and desire the things of this world to help you cope, you come under the control of the god of this world, Satan (John 12:31). The good news is that what you give power to you can take back and reattach the fear that drives it. All the major religions have a primary goal of overcoming our worldly desires in order to not be controlled by them. For example; Buddha had the realization that all or human pain and suffering is the result of unfulfilled desires, which never really are satisfied. So the goal is to be free of desire, thus at peace. The word Islam literally means submission. The goal is to submit to and please God by following the rules of God, resulting in being free of temptation. So they cover their women up so not to be tempted, it doesn't work. Remember the law excites sin. Some of the most common desires that we give power to are; power, status, money, knowledge, material things, body image, fame, success, sex, and perfectionism.

> *Greed is a bottomless pit, which exhausts the person in an endless effort to satisfy the need without ever reaching satisfaction.*
> ~ Erich Fromm, Social Psychologist,

DESIRE FOR MONEY

Looking back I realize that the desire for money has ruled my whole life. I'm an old man now and I have to say, it didn't get me want I wanted in the end. Like so many people with addictions, (mine is greed) I look back and am amazed at the insanity of my thinking and level of my denial. My obsession with it pushed away the people I care for the most, the very ones I told myself it was all for. It started out with good intentions. I just wanted to give my family a better life than what my parents were able to give me. Along the way I found money gave me power; I was sought after. People came to me for advice and help. I was finally really important. Not only did I know how to fix everyone, I also had the money they needed for the solutions. It gave me another powerful feeling control over other people. They all owed me loyalty, whether I was right or wrong. I had the money and the power. Even after I accomplished my personal financial goals it wasn't enough. I kept worrying and manipulating my portfolio. In the end, the accumulation of work and stress has left me a broken man, which no amount of money can fix. I have also declared bankruptcy three times.

Desire doesn't know when it's "full". Desire for money left me "poor of heart". The people closest to me have built up years of resentments for the way I have treated them, I had no clue. "What doses it profit a man to gain the whole world but loose his soul? I can still try to make amends to my family and say, "I'm sorry, for all the hurt I've caused". The hard part is to not make excuses, that I did it for them. I did it for myself, to feel important, to feel needed and powerful. I didn't count the cost.

Robert

RESENTMENT AND HATE

"See to it that no one comes short of the grace of God; that no root of bitterness springing up causes trouble, and by it many be defiled." Hebrews 12:15

Resentment can be another word for hatred, bitterness, un-forgiveness, criticalness, and judgments. Resentments can be very powerful. In the Big Book of Alcoholics Anonymous (p.64), resentments are identified as the number one cause of relapse. Resentment can be like a cancer, slowly eating you away from the inside. Biblically and neurochemically, un-forgiveness and resentments can isolate you from God and others very much like secrets. Worst of all, it can make you become like the person or object you resent because resentments are driven by judgments.

> Do not judge so that you will not be judged. For in the way you judge, you will be judged; and by your standard of measure, it will be measured to you. Matthew 7: 1–2

Common Areas of Resentments: Family, people who have hurt you that you trusted, e.g., teachers, pastors, leaders, friends, etc. People you envy or are jealous of, e.g., those who possess what you want: skills, fame, money ideas, or beauty. Also things like governments, theology/church wounds, e.g. people who don't agree with you, or any kind of perceived injustice. Even things like food and sex can become a love/hate relationship creating resentments.

> **KEY thought**   You forgive to free yourself.

RESENTMENTS ARE UNFORGIVENESS

Forgiveness is important because it gives you the ability to move on in life. Being unforgiving can tie you to your past hurts and makes it difficult to receive the blessings of new relationships. Forgiveness occurs when the one who was hurt cancels the DEBT owed. When you forgive, you are free from those who hurt you. It doesn't mean you have to trust them again. There is no need for the perpetrator's participation. Reconciliation occurs when the perpetrator changes, apologizes and asks for forgiveness. I have a process in both the Genesis Workbooks on forgiveness and have seen huge changes in some lives by simply forgiving. I think forgiveness is a powerful and much overlooked Biblical principal that God actually puts forth as a command.

> And forgive us our debts, as we also have forgiven our debtors . . . For if you forgive others for their transgressions, your heavenly Father will also forgive you. But if you do not forgive others, then your Father will not forgive your transgressions. Matthew 6: 12, 14–15

We have all been hurt and wounded by others, especially those we trusted. The Bible strongly emphasizes the importance of forgiveness. From Genesis to Revelation, the concept of forgiveness permeates God's message to us. As in the above scripture He even commands us to forgive. This is especially true in the 6th commandment to honor your father and mother so that your days will go well on the earth. It can be hard to forgive parents that were abusive, controlling, critical, condescending, non-communicative (emotionally absent), and any number of other destructive behaviors.

Why does God emphasize that forgiveness is so important? In Matthew 6:15, your forgiveness for others is tied in with His forgiveness of you. I don't want to get into the theology of this verse, but consider it for a moment. What does it mean that He will not forgive you if you have not forgiven others? This is definitely a fear of God thing. I don't know about you, but I'm counting on Grace. A few years ago, I was struggling with this problem of forgiveness. A local pastor and his wife were attacking my wife and me, after we had trusted and confided in them. They were slandering us, and it had spread in the community. There was no opportunity for restoration or repentance. It wasn't the first time we had been hurt by other Christians we had trusted. As missionaries for 10 years, we learned firsthand that the number one reason missionaries leave the field is because of being wounded by other missionaries and unable to get over it.

As hard as I tried to forgive them for what they were doing, the bitter and defensive thoughts were driving me crazy. I call this "going back to court." One way you know you haven't forgiven is that you still are going back to court in your head with all the things you wish you had said, or want to say to them. Of course, in this court scene, you always win; they repent and are punished, and you are exonerated. I was willing to forgive as the Word commands me to do, but found I was not able to forgive.

Darkness cannot drive out darkness; only light can do that.
Hate cannot drive out hate; only love can do that.
~ Martin Luther King, Jr.

> **KEY thought** Forgiveness means canceling the debt.

While on my prayer walk one morning, the Lord began to help me understand what was keeping me from letting go of my resentment and anger. Forgiveness requires canceling the debt. This was so obvious from Scripture that I thought I was the only Christian that didn't understand it. I couldn't forgive because they still owed me things like justice, an apology, restoration, money, understanding, etc. I gave them power over me by my resentments and canceling the debt makes me able to take it back. Judgments and false beliefs (vows) can also keep you from being able to forgive and move on. *The mind will replay what the heart cannot delete.*

CONTROL FROM THE GRAVE

Dear Michael,

I was doing the process on forgiveness and having a hard time. I could do it in my head, but not in my heart. The person I was trying to forgive was my Dad who had done a lot of bad things that had ruined my life, but was now dead. I blamed him for how screwed up I am. Well I was doing the exercise when all of a sudden I saw this picture. I was in a graveyard that looked like and old movie. You know with dead leaves on the ground and the gravestones all tilted. I was at my dad's grave and started walking away when a hand came up out of the grave and grabbed my ankle. I couldn't move. I realized that he was still controlling my life via my un-forgiveness. It gave me the motivation to really let go and "cancel his debt." I can't tell you what a release it was, it was like someone took a huge weight off of my shoulders. Since then I have been able to move on in so many areas especially relationships it was what was holding me back. I had no idea.

Free at last. Janice

Bottom line is that safe and competent churches understand the process of re-attaching the areas that we have given control over to through fear, desire and resentments and are intentional about providing teaching, support and accountability to obtain freedom. A practical Christianity.

SELF-DISCOVERY QUESTIONS

1. What are you most anxious/fearful about and how does it control you?

2. What you most desire, fantasize about, and how does it affect you and others?

3. What or who do you most resent and how does it affect you and others?

PRACTICAL APPLICATION

Identify something or someone in each category and make a conscious decision to re-attach the power and control over to God. Ask for help and accountability.

CHAPTER ELEVEN

THE PASTOR'S ROLE

*"Vision without action is merely a dream.
Action without vision just passes the time.
Vision with action can change the world."*
~ Joel A. Barker [1]

Several years back, I was speaking at a luncheon of about fifty pastors. I was talking about making churches safe for hurting people, and asking the pastors for their help in starting recovery ministries in their church. I was about three quarters of the way through my speech when a pastor raised his hand. He said, "Michael, you don't understand. Most of us here were trained in seminary. In seminary, we were only taught how to administrate, not how to minister. We are afraid to attract the kinds of people you are talking about in our churches, because we don't have the training, the experience, or the know-how to help them." This guy's honesty really opened my eyes to see the problem I was facing in trying to make churches safe and effective for hurting people.

In this chapter, we'll look at why pastors and leaders have a crucial role in the process of restoring broken people and what they can do to be effective.

> **KEY thought** — Healthy churches can help heal family-of-origin wounds.

"When one has not had a good father, one must create one."
~ Friedrich Nietzsche

WE ARE ALWAYS LOOKING FOR A LEADER

Leadership has been described as "a process of social influence in which one person can enlist the aid and support of others in the accomplishment of a common task". For example, some understand a leader simply as somebody whom people follow, or as somebody who guides or directs others, while others define leadership as "organizing a group of people to achieve a common goal". (Wikipedia)

I think for as long as we live we will always be looking for a strong leader. Whether it is in our home, our community or nation, we long for someone that we trust, to put our faith in, to lead us. The role of a great leader is to motivate and challenge people to want to make sacrifices for a just cause. A cause that is bigger and more important than ourselves. I can't think of a time we had a national leader like that. I remember back when I first became a Christian my pastor had a real heart and vision for building churches and orphanages in Third World countries. He was able to motivate us to make sacrifices of our time, money and resources for a cause and mission that was important. It is one of my best memories of my years of being a Christian. We became a group of people each with different talents who worked together to produce something meaningful that help the lives of others. That experience became the foundation of our Christianity. I believe we are all looking for a father figure leader to lead us into discovering our potential in God.

PASTORING AS A FATHER FIGURE

As we learned previously, individuals struggling with addiction and self-destructive behaviors are usually grown-up children who had to learn to meet their own needs because of abuse or neglect from their caregivers—their families of origin. For many hurting people, a pastor may be the first safe authority figure and nurturer that they have ever had. And, the Church may be the first family they have ever tried to belong to since they were children.

This raises an important challenge: Are our churches helping heal family-of-origin wounds, or are we deepening the wounds with legalistic authority, rejection, and conditional performance-based love? The questions to ask are:

- Do we have a focused intention to help wounded people learn to trust again?
- Are we modeling a healthy family?
- Are we like Jesus?

Remember, it is grace and competency that heals and loving acceptance that makes people able to receive our help.

From the perspective of rehabilitation, a pastor functions much like a parent, particularly a father. That pastors are paternal, I believe, is a big part of their spiritual authority. We look to them to guide our lives, encourage us in our gifts, and see our hearts. Like a father, we look to them to help us find our identity. I think most leaders don't fully realize or utilize the fullness of the power and authority God has given them as male authority figures. Having a godly authority figure who is interested in us is the very thing that some of us lacked from our natural fathers.

An effective pastor, just like an effective father, recognizes our natural areas of talents and giftedness, and gives us opportunities to grow and become secure in our true identity. Most of us have a need to be recognized by our pastor, just like the recognition we needed from our father. This can be a critical part of the recovery process. It is a form of re-parenting, which can be a tricky business, because we are most vulnerable and easily wounded in our areas of giftedness—our true identity. It can be a fine line between helpful guidance and control when it comes to "parenting adults." Godly guidance leads to secure independence, whereas control can lead to self-doubt and dependence. That's why I say the process has to be focused and deliberate.

> **KEY thought** To be vulnerable is to show weakness; you must be strong to do it.

PASTORING FROM A PLACE OF SECURITY

A pastor has to be a very a secure person in order to minister to hurting people effectively. He has to be able to lead as an example of vulnerability. In my experience, it is rare to find leaders that are secure enough, and that actually have the time and ability to participate in what God is doing in the lives of those who are under them.

When the pastor begins to effectively mentor hurting people and gives them a chance to serve, several changes can happen. For one thing, those first learning how to exercise their areas of natural or spiritual giftedness are probably going to make some mistakes. This is going to require a lot of grace from the overseeing pastor. He will have to be secure enough to not worry that their mistakes might reflect on him.

Also, the people he releases into areas of ministry may actually be more gifted to do those jobs better than he can do them. He'll have to come to terms with if he's okay with that or not. What if they are better at preaching and teaching than he is? Some may also be prodigals who are always venturing outside the box and trying to improve on everything. Remember, insecurity manifests itself in control, and being controlled is where so many people become wounded and where prodigals rebel. On a practical note, a pastor of a large church will not be able to do this kind of individual mentoring. But as he mentors his leaders, they will naturally *"pay it forward."*

I have a lot of empathy for pastors because they can really never live up to all the needs and expectations of wounded people looking to them for attention and recognition. Most of the people I have worked with over the years came alive when someone helped them identify their true self and mentored them to cultivate it. Many of the stories in this book are about that. Parts of *The Genesis Process for Change Groups* are dedicated to the principle of getting healthy through finding our God-given gifts and using them. Giving to grow. It is a true partnership with God.

However, according to my friend, Gordon Dalbey, who has worked for thirty years with men and churches on healing "father wounds," says there is limit to what most pastors can, or are willing to do. He said, "Michael, the main problem I have found with pastors who are struggling is that they themselves were not fathered well, so they have a hard time meeting the needs and expectations of the people around them who need fathering." 2

> *"If sheep do not have the constant care of a shepherd,*
> *they will go the wrong way, unaware of the dangers at hand.*
> *They have been known to nibble themselves right off the side of*
> *a mountain.... And so, because sheep are sheep, they need*
> *shepherds to care for them. The welfare of sheep depends solely upon*
> *the care they get from their shepherd. Therefore, the better*
> *the shepherd, the healthier the sheep."*
> ~ Kay Arthur [3]

Pastors are human with differing strengths and weaknesses, and they have many hats to wear—preacher, teacher, prophet, visionary, counselor, administrator, husband, and father. In order to be able to help others, they ultimately have to be healthy and secure themselves. The Reverend Ed Khouri, Co-Founder and Director of Equipping Hearts Ministry, and Co-Founder of Thriving: Recover Your Life Program says this:

"Because of the role male pastor's play in the life of their church, it is vital that they have the emotional maturity to have a strong capacity for joy, the ability to regulate their own negative emotions, and an identity rooted solidly in joy. Joy is our most sought after and healing emotion. This is especially true because many in the church—especially those of us who grew up in an environment in which men were absent, addicted, abusive, and the source of significant physical, emotional, and relational trauma—really have no idea what a healthy male looks like, and have internalized a concept of God based on the dysfunction of our dad, fear, and legalism.

As a result, we frequently look to the pastor to help grow a new picture of what is a healthy man, and to develop a new concept of God. This makes it vital for pastors to have grown a strong capacity for joy, joy-based relationships, and a solid, joyful identity. They also need to model regulating their own emotions and reactions effectively. Pastors with these skills are able to create a place for hurting people to belong and connect with a joyful community in which they can grow their own relational and emotional skills—and develop a grace-based relationship with God." [4] We will look deeper into the power of joy in the last chapter.

JOHN'S STORY

Dear Michael,

I was raised in Salt Lake City as a member of the Mormon Church, and religious authority is a critical issue for me. I was a very angry juvenile delinquent with lots of anger towards my very legalistic father. Later, this caused problems with authority figures. I came to Christ at age 18 and joined a wonderful church with young enthusiastic leadership. Within a few years, the church dissolved because of clashes within the leadership. My idealistic expectations and confidence in Christian leadership went tumbling along with the church. I have also had the bad luck of being part of two other churches that also dissolved. My last attempts at church membership and proper submission to leadership have not gone so well.

I still find myself very skeptical, critical, and judgmental. However, I have found some leaders very open to honest relationship. I find that most pastors' doors are open to me if I request time to talk with them about my concerns. I have learned to be aware of my own issues, as I have a hard time trusting the very help I am asking for. Sometimes I think I just want to be noticed. These issues of trust and insecurity are manifested in defensiveness and a need to feel in control. What I really want is a chance to do something meaningful in my church.

Even though I am 35 years old, I realize that I am looking for someone to tell me who I am and where I fit in. I have learned that I may never have an important job within the church, but if I really want to serve our Lord Jesus I can do that every day one-on-one with the people He puts before me. I really feel like I have a purpose and a calling, I just don't know what it is. I feel stupid asking and so I resist the very help I am seeking. I still pray that my deep roots of bitterness are revealed to me. I try to confess and surrender them to the One Perfect Authority everyday. I know I can't do that by myself. I need someone to guide me.

John

> **KEY thought** The gifts of the Spirit are counseling tools.

PASTORING AS A COUNSELOR

Many pastors are well trained as administrators, but lack training as counselors and mentors. Usually administration and counseling are different gifts and most people are either one or the other. Yet, most of the gifts of the Spirit are really counseling gifts—wisdom, knowledge, faith, healing, miraculous powers, prophecy, and distinguishing between spirits (1 Corinthians 12). God wants to partner with us, so He equips us with supernatural understanding, wisdom, and power to help others find a life of meaning, purpose, and value in His kingdom. I believe these gifts are essential to Christian growth and healing. Remember, faith comes from hearing a word from God and most of the time that word comes through people who have "an ear to hear."

> "And I will ask the Father, and he will give you another Helper, to be with you forever, even the Spirit of truth, whom the world cannot receive, because it neither sees him nor knows him. You know him, for he dwells with you and will be in you." John 14:16–17

One of the things I teach in the Genesis Counselor Trainings is about the difference Christian counseling can make versus secular counseling. A Christian counselor, who has the spirit of God and is listening, can get insight into what God is doing in a client's life and participate with it. I have seen that when a client believes a counselor is hearing from God in a natural way, a powerful thing happens. The client's spirit bears witness with the counselor's spirit and the Spirit of God. When the client feels that they are going in the right direction and God is involved, faith increases, which results in an ability to trust more and take risks.

In the Bible, when faith goes up, miracles follow. What hurting, and especially addicted people, really need is a miracle, because they know they can't heal themselves, and the pharmaceutical world can't fix or heal their heart. A godly counselor or pastor who has the ability to become a conduit for God can change lives. I think no matter how old we are, we still long for a strong parental figure to be interested in us and help guide our lives. Our hearts will always long for a father.

> *"My father used to say that it's never too late to do anything you wanted to do. And he said, 'You never know what you can accomplish until you try.'*
> *~ Michael Jordan*

> **KEY thought** Godly counseling should result in healing, action, and change.

Many have lost faith in healing, so they keep going to counseling for years on end. I'm a counselor and have experienced the difference between giving advice and being a part of heart changes. God wants us to partner with Him in healing lives. He can show us what the source of a problem is and join us in the healing process. He gives us gifts; words of knowledge (supernatural understanding of what the problem is), words of wisdom (supernatural understanding of what to do about it), and prophecy (what will happen as a result of our choices), as well as others like the discernment of spirits. Lives can change when we believe our leaders are hearing personally from God on our behalf. The result will be that we will trust and take risks, usually in the area of trusting and giving up control. Remember, change usually requires risk, a step of faith. Of course as Christians, we know that this "hearing from God" thing can get out of hand and even abusive, so we have to be careful to find the genuine.

When counseling, pastors need to keep in mind that healthy boundaries must be in place to avoid slipping into co-dependency and enabling. Pastors can avoid problems by making sure that their church has healthy recovery groups available for ongoing support and account for those he is mentoring. This is important and can prevent unhealthy enmeshments. It takes a focused program that leads to healing, which in turn results in freedom and independence. It may not be practical for most pastors to do this kind of counseling, but their father's heart can establish this kind of ministry in their church and make it safe and effective.

SUSAN'S STORY

Dear Michael,

I don't know if you remember me. I was the one at your last seminar who asked you about what to look for when going to counseling. You said two things. First, if after three or four visits you don't feel some improvement in the issue you came for, try a different counselor, just like you would a doctor. Second, look for a counselor that goes after the root or cause of the problem/ behavior—one who sees the behavior as a symptom rather than the cause.

You said it could be easy to get addicted to counseling. Well I had been in therapy for five years and realized I haven't really made much progress; I am still struggling with constant anxiety. I took your advice and asked around to try and find a counselor that focused on healing. I found someone and my life has changed. He got to the "why" and the root of what I was so afraid of. We found the root memory and he brought the Lord in to bring healing. Because the counselor listened to God and worked with Him, I trusted him and let him go places I didn't think I could. Anyway, thank you for steering me in the right direction. I think every church should have someone that can do this kind Christian counseling.

Susan

> "For the word of God is living and active, sharper than any two-edged sword, piercing to the division of soul and of spirit, of joints and of marrow, and discerning the thoughts and intentions of the heart." Hebrews 4:12

> **KEY thought** — Safe churches have pastors that are open about their own struggles.

PASTORING WITH AUTHENTICITY

A safe home depends on the openness of the father. So, in making churches safe to be able to help wounded people heal, it begins with the pastor. *The strongest love is shown in the willingness to be weak.* In his pioneering book, *Sons of the Father: Healing the Father-Wound in Men Today*, Gordon Dalbey says, "Many pastors have their own deep wounds that affect their ability to minister." Dalbey tells of asking 150 Christian men at a conference, "How many of you had a father who, when you were twelve or so, took you aside and talked to you about girls and sex?" Only two raised their hands—a proportion which Dalbey finds similar around the world. "I'm happy to be in a church filled with honest men," he declares, "as long as they're coming to be open and not to hide from their fears and their brokenness. It is the pastor's openness to deal with his own issues that will set the example and make it safe for the men under him to seek healing. Unfortunately, most of the time at my church seminars for men, the head pastor rarely comes."5 Sex is still a hard subject of most churches to talk about, which is one reason it has so much power.

> *A hero is someone who understands the responsibility that comes with his freedom.*
> ~ Bob Dylan

Many years ago, I was at a Richie Havens concert. He said something that I have never forgotten. He said, "The word *responsibility* means the *ability to respond*." We are naturally willing to take on things we feel able to respond to. When we are given responsibilities that we don't feel we are able or gifted to handle, we "avoid responsibility." Many pastors are not counselor types and don't feel they have the *ability to respond* to the heart wounds of their congregation. I have known pastors who have faced their father-wounds courageously and openly pushed through the shame to move towards healing. The result has been that they have led many others on the same path. God has turned their wounds into healing for others. That's the man I want leading me.

On the other hand, a pastor who doesn't deal with his own issues can have a powerful negative effect on those following him. I was raised by a German stepfather, who communicated to me, "Real men handle their own problems; asking for help is a sign of weakness." I think he didn't have the *ability to respond* to a sensitive boy with emotional needs, so he shamed me for having them. It worked, as I became fiercely independent. Later, I found out that he had a lot of secrets. I think many leaders act the same as a because of having secrets—resulting in legalism. It can be hard for pastors to find a safe place to be open about their struggles, but what are their options?

As we talked about in the chapter on *Secrets*, a pastor's secrets can affect and even infect the whole church. Remember that somewhere between 30 to 50 percent of pastor's struggle with pornography.6 It is common for pastors with secrets to stay very busy, avoiding too much personal contact. Most workaholics I have worked with have multiple shame-based secrets. Their workaholism keeps them from slowing down enough to think and feel how their secrets are affecting their relationship with God and others. Workaholism is a pervasive addiction in Christian ministry.

> **KEY thought** Workaholism can be a way to avoid intimacy.

When I do the counselor training seminars, many of those attending are pastors and leaders of ministries. They are asked to identify something about themselves that they want to work on so they can go through the process. Many of them have a hard time identifying anything they feel they need to work on. I start by asking them, "How many hours a week do you work?" They usually say, "Oh, around fifty or so." So I ask, "What time do you get up and go to work in the morning?" They reply, "Six o'clock." And then I ask what time they actually stop, and they usually say, "Eight or nine at night." I ask how many days a week they work, and they usually say, "Six or seven." When you do the math, it equals eighty-four to one hundred hours a week. "When you're not working, how much time do you spend thinking about work?" I continue, knowing what they are going to say. Nearly all of them admit that they are thinking about work almost all the time. So they're probably working around 100 to 120 hours a week.

They're amazed when we actually add it up. They really don't want to admit they are working that much, and that they actually are workaholics. Of course, the next question—which is one of the primary Genesis questions—"What would happen if you slowed down to forty or fifty hours a week?" They immediately begin to experience anxiety. They can't really identify what would happen if they slowed down, except that they don't want to do it. The underlying issue is usually the same—secrets and avoiding intimacy. Many feel successful and respected at work and a failure at home. They are not very good at being a husband and father, usually because no one ever taught them. So, if you were in their shoes, where would you rather be? Where you feel respected and successful or where you feel inadequate and a failure? The feeling of failure is something men hate and will go to great lengths to avoid.

> *"A lack of transparency results in distrust and a deep sense of insecurity."*
> ~ Dalai Lama

KEY thought: It is identification that leads to honesty versus confrontation that leads to secrecy.

A pastor who is out of touch with his own issues can directly affect the church's willingness and ability to minister. I have learned that a church won't go in a direction if the head pastor doesn't lead. In addition, whether it is sex, work, food, or religion, pastoral problems can result in legalism. Remember in the chapter on *Secrets*, we talked about how self-destructive behaviors isolate us from God and others, resulting in a work-based relationship (legalism). The first step in recovery is accountability, which results in restoring trust from those impacted by the person. Does your pastor have any accountability? Those under him will do what he values.

JIM'S STORY

Dear Michael

You asked us to write about our experiences with going to church seeking help, so here is mine. I have been struggling with alcohol and isolation for a long time. I have wanted to change, but have been looking for the encouragement to get started, if that makes sense. Well, the old pastor at my church retired last year and our denomination sent in a man in his early forties. From the get go he was very open about his own struggles with alcohol and workaholism. He said he had about five years of recovery. His vision is to reach out to help those who are struggling with these kinds of addictive problems.

To make a long story short, after about two months of listening to him be so open and vulnerable, I went to him and shared my problems. I am now in one of his accountability groups getting the encouragement and support I need and I am getting free. It was his openness that gave me the push I needed to begin to seek help. I wish he had been my pastor ten years ago; it might have saved me a lot of pain and loss in my life.

Jim

> "It has always seemed strange to me... the things we admire in men, kindness and generosity, openness, honesty, understanding and feeling, are the concomitants of failure in our system. And those traits we detest, sharpness, greed, acquisitiveness, meanness, egotism and self-interest, are the traits of success. And while men admire the quality of the first they love the produce of the second."
>
> ~ John Steinbeck

PASTORING WITH ACCOUNTABILITY

There is a need for a safe place for pastors to be pastored and have accountability. In my experience, very few pastors have any real accountability with others outside their congregation on a regular basis. Having accountability is a chief component of trusting someone who has destructive behaviors, especially leaders. When you know someone is helping them to see their blind spots, it makes you cut them some slack. Of course it's not safe or healthy to be accountable to people that you pastor. In professional terms, that is called a *dual relationship*. Not only is it unhealthy, it usually results in broken relationships. Pastors need to be accountable to other pastors.

Making churches safe for hurting people must flow down from the pulpit. If not, there will be superficiality and an unconscious awareness of an "elephant" (unspoken vibe) in the church. There will be a resistance to change instead of embracing it. The foundational component for successful personal change is humility. True humility gives us the ability to ask for help, which results in accountability. We will trust and follow a humble man who models openness and vulnerability—in other words, a healthy father.

My heart went out to a catholic priest who came to one of my trainings. He told me how hurt and angry he was about all the sexual abuse that was being exposed in the Catholic Church. He told me people he had ministered to for many years were afraid to have their children around him. If priests had accountability with each other on a regular basis it could have prevented most of it. Remember sin thrives in isolation.

> *"It is easier for a father to have children than for children to have a real father."*
>
> ~ Pope John XXIII

JILL'S STORY

Dear Michael,

I want to tell my story about what changed my life. I am now 33 years old and have been an out-of-control sex and drug addict since I was 12. I had no father, and my mother pretty much ignored me. I never believed I would be someone that anyone would want, so I just gave myself away. Men have always used me and then threw me away. I believed all men are the same. They are nice to me until they get what they want, and then hurt me until I go away.

When I was 28, I was court-ordered to a treatment program in lieu of prison. The only one in town that I could afford was a Christian rehab. I didn't want anything to do with God, but the price was right (free). After a couple of months, I was assigned to one of your Genesis counselors. He was an older man who wasn't intimidated by my defensiveness. He saw something in me that I had sensed, but never understood. He told me that I was a natural-born counselor and that if I was willing to work at it I could help a lot of people. He said I had a gift of "insight." As he took me through the process, he took the time to teach me about what he was doing and why. He believed in me, which totally unnerved me. He never once tried to hit on me or even put out a sexual vibe. He became the first man I had ever trusted.

At my request, he led me to the Lord. I am now working at the rehab and have my state drug and alcohol counselor's certification and a reason to stay clean. I am helping many who were like me. You said at the training that "what works" is when one person invests himself in another. That's me. He is still my "adopted father" and helps guide my life.

Jill

SELF-DISCOVERY QUESTIONS

1. Discuss how your own father's role is still affecting your life today?

2. What role would you like your pastor to play in your life?

3. Write about some people you know who are struggling and why? What would they need to get well? Don't use their names.

4. Think of the pastors/leaders you have had. Which one was the most and least safe to be open and vulnerable with? Why?

PRACTICAL APPLICATION

Ask God to show you someone who is struggling and help them to identify what his or her gifts are. Find a way to encourage them and help them grow in their areas of giftedness.

CHAPTER TWELVE

REVIVAL THROUGH UNITY

"A new commandment I give to you, that you love one another, even as I have loved you, that you also love one another. By this all men will know that you are My disciples, if you have love for one another." John 13:34–35

When I became a Christian, one of the first things I believe the Lord spoke to me was that revival would come through unity. I thought that was a pretty strange thing for God to tell me since I wasn't a pastor or even a leader. I didn't understand why He told me that, so I just put it aside. But when messages are really from God, they don't just go away. He keeps bringing them back to our attention, like a rock in our shoe. I eventually realized that there was something important that I was missing. I started studying about revivals and could see that the broken people I was trying to help really needed the kinds of things that happened in revivals—heart change miracles.

Even though we were fairly new Christians at the time, my wife and I decided to take His word to heart and we attempted to bring revival to our community. We didn't know enough to understand how hard and unrealistic that might be. Because of what He told me, I believed the way to initiate revival was to bring unity into the local churches by breaking down the walls of denominationalism. Looking back, the best thing about being a new Christian was being so naïve, thinking that I could single-handedly break down those walls—I'm still recovering.

Our revival effort began when we took out a second mortgage on our home (at 20 percent interest from a private individual), and purchased a big tent that held 600 people. We built a stage and even bought an organ and a sound system. We got permission from the city government in Santa Cruz, California to put the tent up in the central park, which was a miracle if you know anything about Santa Cruz. We invited seventeen different churches to be involved and asked each church to take the service for one evening over three weeks. The goal was to have Christians experience what other churches believed and how they worshiped. We felt it would build bridges and create cooperation, hoping it would bring the unity that would ignite a true revival.

It was truly amazing what God did in changing hearts and lives during these meetings. He showed us that He blesses unity. Even with all the different worship and preaching styles for those three weeks, all that seemed to be important was praising God and making Him known in our community. Unfortunately, after it was over, everyone went back into their own churches and things went on as usual. We were very disappointed, but I learned a valuable lesson—God blesses unity.

> *"A revival is nothing else than a new beginning of obedience to God."*
> ~ Charles Finney

As we look at the trends in our society, I think we can all agree that things are rapidly getting worse. Sometimes we hear that things are not really worse than they used to be, they are just more out in the open. That is not true. For example, when I was young, we used to hitchhike everywhere—up and down California and around the country. No one gave it a second thought. When was the last time you saw somebody hitchhiking? It's rare these days. Why? Because we realize how dangerous and stupid it is. It's not as safe as it once was. It's risky! I can remember a time when going to the park with my family was safe and carefree. We thought nothing of letting our children go into a public bathroom by themselves. But in today's day and age, it's just not done. It isn't safe.

Most every negative statistic is going up rapidly—sexual abuse, disease, violence, crime, suicide rates (especially among puberty-age girls), self-mutilation, drug and alcohol abuse, divorce, rape, gangs, stress, mental illness, sex addiction, health issues, and obesity are all increasing. It seems like every day we read about some crazy crime where someone "goes postal" and senselessly murders innocent people. There is a persuasive fear that we are not safe anywhere anymore. Terrorism is a fairly new word.

> *"In the Irish Revival of 1859, people became so weak that they could not get back to their homes. Men and women would fall by the wayside and would be found hour's later pleading with God to save their souls. They felt that they were slipping into hell and that nothing else in life mattered but to get right with God… To them, eternity meant everything. Nothing else was of any consequence. They felt that if God did not have mercy on them and save them, they were doomed for all time to come."*
> ~ Oswald Smith [1]

KEY thought — You can't legislate morality.

THE POWER OF REVIVAL

Many believe that the only real hope we have is revival. Historically, real revival brought social change. I think that we can all agree that political solutions to the kind of problems mentioned above are not going to be effective. Many of us hope that a different political party or president is going to halt this momentum of destruction, but history tells us that politics doesn't bring real change to these kinds of negative trends without a total loss of freedom. It is just trading one problem for another. To effect social change, we need moral change. Moral change comes from a change of heart. It comes from the inside out, not the outside in. You can't effectively legislate to stop immorality, so we end up legalizing it, which will increase it and its consequences. Revival, real revival, is not a bunch of Christians jumping up and down for a week getting happy once a year at the community revival meeting. It is an intervening act of The Holy Spirit moving through a community, convicting and restoring people's consciences, and bringing an acute awareness of sin. Brothels close, bars empty, and people swarm into churches and meetings, seeking the peace and freedom of their Creator.

> *"Revival is when God gets so sick and tired of being misrepresented that He shows Himself."*
> ~ Leonard Ravenhill [2]

A TRUE REVIVAL STORY: NEW YORK CITY, 1857–1860

In September 1857, a man of prayer, Jeremiah Lanphier, started a businessmen's prayer meeting in the upper room of the Dutch Reformed Church Consistory Building in Manhattan. In response to his advertisement, only six people out of a population of a million showed up. The following week there were fourteen, and then twenty-three when they decided to meet every day for prayer. By late winter they were filling the Dutch Reformed Church, then the Methodist Church on John Street, then Trinity Episcopal Church on Broadway at Wall Street. In February and March of 1858, every church and public hall in downtown New York was filled.

Horace Greeley, the famous editor, sent a reporter with horse and buggy racing round the prayer meetings to see how many men were praying. In one hour, he could get to only twelve meetings, but he counted 6,100 men attending. Then, a landslide of prayer began, which overflowed to the churches in the evenings. People began to be converted—ten thousand a week in New York City alone. The movement spread throughout New England, the church bells bringing people to prayer at eight in the morning, twelve noon, and six in the evening. The revival raced up the Hudson and down the Mohawk, where the Baptists, for example, had so many people to baptize that they went down to the river, cut a big hole in the ice, and baptized them in the cold water. When Baptists do that they are really on fire![3]

Are we prepared for that kind of revival? Think about it. If God brought revival to one of our largest cities today and a million people were seeking God, where would they go? How would the local churches respond? Will they help the revival or hinder it?

> *"Give light, and the darkness will disappear of itself."*
> ~ Desiderius Erasmus [4]

"I in them and you in me—so that they may be brought to complete unity. Then the world will know that you sent me and have loved them even as you have loved me." John 17:23

"Now I exhort you, brethren, by the name of our Lord Jesus Christ, that you all agree and that there be no divisions among you, but that you be made complete in the same mind and in the same judgment." 1 Corinthians 1:10

PROMOTING REVIVAL

What's the secret to revival, then? It's unity—unity and prayer in the body of Christ. It is when large numbers of people begin to share His heart for the lost and broken. It is when people become more important than doctrine. Galatians 3:26–28 reminds us that we are all one through faith in Christ Jesus, regardless of denomination, ministry goals, belief systems, race, status, etc. Let's take a look at what we need to know in order to promote unity, so that ultimately revival can come.

> *"The Gateway to Christianity is not through an intricate labyrinth of dogma, but by a simple belief in the person of Christ."*
> ~ Norman Vincent Peale [5]

"If you keep My commandments, you will abide in My love; just as I have kept My Father's commandments and abide in His love. These things I have spoken to you so that My joy may be in you, and that your joy may be made full. This is My commandment, that you love one another, just as I have loved you." John 15:10–12

LOVING ONE ANOTHER IS THE KEY

There is a theme that has always bugged me and keeps coming up over and over again in the New Testament, both in the Gospels and Epistles. Jesus tells us that if we ask anything in His name, He will do it. Personally, I haven't seen that in reality very much, and He says it emphatically several times. It is the main theme of John's letters. As I looked deeper into this confusing issue, the lights came on when I read 1 John 3:21-24, "Beloved, if our heart does not condemn us, we have confidence before God; and whatever we ask we receive from Him, because we keep His commandments and do the things that are pleasing in His sight. This is His commandment that we believe in the name of His Son Jesus Christ, and *love one another*, just as He commanded us. The one who keeps His commandments abides in Him, and He in him. We know by this that He abides in us, by the Spirit whom He has given us. I believe this scripture is the key to revival. It basically says that if we keep His commandment, we can ask anything in His name with confidence. *His commandment is that we love one another. John says it over and over.* Sounds so simple, right?

As the secular world looks at the Christian church as a whole, I don't think they are awed by our love for one another. They mostly see how much we criticize and argue with each other. We act a lot like politicians—or worse, Pharisees—where pride creates an "against-ness." I think revival begins by a few people having a burden for the lost and wounded. God begins to change their hearts, bringing a revival of compassion where the pride of being theologically correct seems trivial. There's an old saying: If you want to see revival break out in your community, draw a circle, step into it, and when revival breaks out in that circle, go out and try to help others. It starts with us.

In his book, *From Paths to Power*, A. W. Tozer writes, "God always works where His people meet His conditions, but only when and as they do. Any spiritual visitation will be limited or extensive, depending how well and how widely conditions are met. The first condition is oneness of mind among the persons who are seeking the visitation. 'Behold how good and how pleasant it is for brethren to dwell together in unity! It is like the precious ointment upon the head, that ran down upon the beard, even Aaron's beard; that went down to the skirts of his garments; as the dew of Hermon, and as the dew that descended upon the mountains of Zion; for there the Lord commanded the blessing, even life for evermore' (Psalm 133).

Here the unity precedes the blessing, and so it is throughout the Bible. An individual may seek and obtain spiritual help from God, and that is one thing. For a company of people to unite to seek a new visitation from God for the entire group is quite another thing, and is a spiritual labor greatly superior to the first. The one is a personal affair, and may easily begin and end with a single person; the other may go on to bless unlimited numbers of persons. Revival unity is not the same as doctrinal unity. God will bless a body of men and women who are one in spiritual purpose, even if their doctrinal positions are not identical on every point."

I believe that only when we can lay aside our pride and our differences will true revival come. Like the quote above says, "Revival unity is not the same as doctrinal unity," and, "Unity precedes the blessing." Coming together out of love for hurting people and our love for one another will be what sparks revival. It is not a formula; it is a heart change.

FREEDOM FROM RELIGION

Jesus came to break the power of religion—to set us free from the law. The basis of most religion is thinking that following a set of correct beliefs and rules is pleasing to God, a way of earning His favor. Jesus taught us a better way. He taught us that it is God's love, not His rules, which bring us into right relationship with Him. His favor comes through grace, not through religious works and rituals. God wants relationship, not slavery. I personally believe that God is bigger than our belief systems or any denomination. It is hard to imagine that God would send someone to eternal punishment because they were somehow deceived and didn't quite have the right doctrine. But in reality, most religious people believe that. It is a mystery. No one really knows, do they? Simply admitting that I may not be more right than the next guy is a big step to breaking down walls and becoming a safe person. This can be especially hard for pastors as they are taught never to have doubts and to be strong in what they were taught. We all have doubts, but it's usually not safe to share them.

> "For you do not delight in sacrifice, otherwise I would give it;
> You are not pleased with burnt offering. The sacrifices of God

are a broken spirit; A broken and a contrite heart, O God, You will not despise." Psalm 51:16–17

When I say that Jesus came to set us free from the law, I'm not talking about the law in terms of the Ten Commandments. There are still spiritual and moral natural boundaries that are inherent in His creation with consequences. There are natural consequences for breaking spiritual laws, but what about religious laws? There are so many and they can be so contradictory. Think about how many different denominational interpretations of the Bible there are. Some believe that only a certain type of worship pleases God and edifies. Others have rules about alcohol, food, the day of the week we should have church, baptism, the true version of the Bible, and especially who is saved and how. For centuries, the church has been divided on issues like the rapture, how the Holy Spirit works, and whether we can lose our salvation. All of it seems trivial in the big scheme of things. Historically, denominational correctness becomes trivial and unimportant in times of persecution.

> *"The greatest enemy to human souls is the self-righteous spirit which makes men look to themselves for salvation."*
> ~ Charles Spurgeon

We went to a new church a few years ago and made an appointment to meet the pastor. He told us right up front that if we didn't believe in a pre-tribulation rapture we wouldn't like it there. It is okay to believe that, except when it excludes others who don't. This is an example of someone who was not a safe person to have a different point of view with. These kinds of divisive ideologies have the result of creating disunity, which results in not being able to work together. It is very rare when churches in a community work together on an ongoing basis to affect change—an actual intermingling of congregations. There would be such power in that! A good change question to ask would be: What is the fear or belief system that prevents it? In my experience, the people who are the most argumentative about their beliefs are also the most insecure in them. I was one of them.

> "[Christ] raised us up with Him, and seated us with Him in the heavenly places in Christ Jesus, so that in the ages to come He might show the surpassing riches of His grace in kindness toward us in Christ Jesus. For by grace you have been saved through faith; and that not of yourselves, it is the gift of God; not as a result of works, so that no one may boast." Ephesians 2:6–9

As human beings, it is our nature to want to be in control, so we took the message of Jesus and just created another religion. Religion is about rules and control. If Jesus came back today, I think He would certainly not be part of the Christian religion. Many of us have become the same as the Pharisees, Sadducees, and the scribes, arguing over every little detail about who's right and what is most pleasing to God. We would all be trying to make him fit into our box, just like they did. Jesus would have nothing to do with it. In the New Testament, the only people He had a hard word for were religious people. He had more forbearance for Roman soldiers and prostitutes than for religious leaders. Today, He would more likely be down in a ghetto or at a rescue mission getting his hands dirty with those who need Him the most and are able to receive the Father's love through grace those whose box is empty. He says, "If anyone serves Me, he must follow Me; and where I am, there My servant will be also; if anyone serves Me, the Father will honor him" (John 12:26).

> "For the Law was given through Moses; grace and truth were realized through Jesus Christ." John 1:17

EXAMINE OURSELVES

We can't expect to change the church without first changing ourselves. It is much easier to learn than to unlearn. The goal of this book is to make Christians and churches safe and *effective* to help wounded people heal. God is looking for people through whom He can answer prayer. It begins by courageously examining what we, as individual Christians, believe and why we believe it. The questions are: How does what I believe affect me and my ability and willingness to be used by God to help needy people?

Are there aspects of what I believe that make me self-righteous, critical, and judgmental—all of which boils down to one word, religious? Does what I believe make me inclusive or exclusive?

These are hard, but powerful change questions. Challenging your beliefs can be very unsettling, but if it results in you being more like Christ, then it is worth it.

> *"For the believer, humility is honesty about one's greatest flaws to a degree in which he is fearless about truly appearing less righteous than another."*
> ~ Criss Jami, *Salomé: In Every Inch In Every Mile*

KATHY'S STORY

Dear Michael,

When I was thirty-two, I was in an abusive marriage and seeking help. I was lost and desperate. I didn't believe much in God but decided to try going to church. I didn't believe a word I heard for months. And for months, the pastor listened to my questions (more like accusations), never once flinching. He never once judged me about my current life style. He said those changes were in God's department. He and a few of the people I saw at church seemed to have a joy that appealed to me. It was something deeper than happiness. Pastor always showed grace to everyone. He had the gift of acceptance. I expected to be judged and rejected when the church found out some of the stuff I had done and was still doing. I was looking for rejection but kept running into acceptance.

Once I became a Christian (much to my shock), a woman mentored me and included me in the women's group she led. Her wisdom and grace still affects me now some fifteen years later. Both the pastor and my mentor helped me heal from the abortion I had when I was eighteen and the life I led afterwards. I knew I was forgiven and years of secret shame were lifted. They also both encouraged me in youth ministry, a calling I felt from the beginning of my Christian life. Now I run a ministry for teenage mothers and pregnant girls. This first church experience of acceptance for these girls is the foundation of my ministry.

Thankful for grace,
Kathy

WHAT HINDERS UNITY AND REVIVAL?

When we were setting up our unity tent meetings, I remember going to Los Angeles because some pastors in the inner city had expressed an interest in what we were doing. I was excited because, the *inner city*. The experience educated me into the reality of religion very quickly. At the planning meeting they all agreed on the positive impact that unity and revival could have on the inner city, but after a couple of hours, they all backed out because they couldn't agree on how people who came forward would be baptized. One pastor said, "What if someone gets a word from God or falls in the Spirit? We can't quench the Spirit." Another pastor walked out, saying, "I can't allow my people to be exposed to that sort of circus act." It got very heated.

I was still a fairly new Christian and was dumbfounded by how such seemingly petty theological beliefs were so divisive. That day, pride and denominational walls got in the way of a potential revival that could have had a profound impact on the inner city. It seemed that their hearts were more focused on being right—on religion—than on the hearts of the people they were trying to serve. It still amazes me—it's tragic.

The same principles of what makes people and churches safe and effective apply well to understanding what can promote or hinder revival. Since unity may be the key to revival, and revival can be the key to changing moral issues, then it's natural to conclude that the devil would logically do all that he can to prevent unity. Let's face it! Revival would diminish Satan's control and bring light to areas of darkness. This is why I think denominational beliefs and the walls they create are the main features hindering revival—these walls are built primarily by pride. These same self-righteous beliefs can result in devastating consequences like church splits, violence, disunity, and deep wounds that may never heal. Let's look at some of the tactics that the enemy uses to prevent revival.

CHURCH SPLITS

Have you ever been part of a church split? I often ask this question at seminars. It's interesting to hear the answers. First of all, about two thirds of the audience raises their hands as having been part of a church or a ministry split. Then I ask, "Why did they split?" The most common answer is that the pastor and the elders (or this group or that) couldn't agree on some issue, usually doctrinal.

Another common answer is because of the pastor's moral failure and the disagreement of what to do about it. I keep asking the same question—*Yes, but why did they split?* People begin to look puzzled and realize that they don't really know how the issue caused such a division, but it seemed pretty clear at the time.

There is usually a common denominator of what started the rift. As I asked more questions, most of them realized that just before the rift, their church began to reach out into their community to impact people's lives in a practical way. When you start to see lives that are under the enemy's control become free, he will do whatever he can to stop you. You can turn water into wine, raise the dead, and see a variety of miracles in your church and the enemy will leave you alone. But when you begin to take away what belongs to him, he will attack you. It's called "spiritual warfare" and he usually attacks us from within. For the moment, Satan appears to win by turning our focus on each other. We preach love, grace, and Christian ethics and then people hear stories like this. No wonder the world calls us hypocrites.

Published in the *Sacramento Bee*, September 29, 2012

"A bitter split three years ago in an evangelical group providing Bible studies at California's Capitol has sparked an East Coast lawsuit. Two groups—Capitol Ministries and Capitol Commission—are rivals for the chance to bring Christian teachings to legislators at capitols nationwide. Each nonprofit group blames the other for backstabbing and deceit in the effort to touch lawmakers' hearts through ministries funded by millions of dollars from Christians and sympathetic churches, foundations and businesses. Charges of other ungodly behavior abound, including misappropriation, cyber-squatting, unfair business practices and theft of thousands of emails. Leaders of the two evangelical groups, Ralph Drollinger and Jim Young, respectively, say the battle has tainted a long friendship between them and violates a biblical admonition in Corinthians to settle disputes outside court."

What do you think was behind this confrontation? What do you think happened to their ability and effectiveness to reach the legislators? Can you ever remember being involved in something like this? If so, what were you feeling? If you have been involved in a church split, try and remember what was happening just before the split occurred. In most cases, the church was starting to reach out. Then some issue, problem, or behavior became divisive to such an extent that the people could no longer fellowship with those on the other side of the issue. The effect, of course, was that the outreach stopped.

How did the very people that we were in fellowship with suddenly become our enemies? The source of most church splits is differing beliefs in matters of theology and denominational doctrine—in other words, pride. Incidentally, we see this same phenomenon in marriages. How did the person who God gave us to be our partner, friend, and lover become our enemy? *Remember, just because you believe something doesn't mean you're right.* This simple statement can prevent and heal such divisions if all parties can make unity and love for one another their goal. Or simply ask, "What would Jesus do?"

I remember counseling with a couple, who were leaders, and during the prayer time I saw a picture of them playing tennis. They were criticizing each other for making mistakes and arguing about whose fault it was that they were losing. I saw their opponents on the other side of the net laughing and relaxed knowing they had already won. The point was that they had lost sight of the real enemy on the other side of the net and were attacking each other. A big part of my commitment as a recovering Pharisee is to not let the enemy (or my own pride) undermine relationships, or the ministries of others. I look back now and can see how I slipped into being divisive many times, but I couldn't see it at the time.

> **KEY thought** You can't be humble and self-righteous at the same time.

MARY'S STORY

Dear Mike,

I hit bottom about a year after I had become a Christian and my life was pretty much in shambles. The first place I turned to was 'the church' to find some help. I found a church that offered a recovery group. There were very few women in the women's addiction group. I always thought that was odd with a congregation of several thousand members. Nonetheless, I was surrounded by a good group of women and began understanding what addiction was all about. I felt that the program fell short in answering all the questions that I had. What had led me to this place in my life, and how did I get here?

As a fairly new Christian, I was hungry for information and help. I supplemented the group I belonged to with other groups and material. I realized that once I had some sobriety under my belt, there was lack of connection between the church and the recovery program and its participants. It was very clear that there was a "Them and Us" mentality. There was a lot of infighting between the recovery leaders and the leadership of the church. Eventually the recovery people had a very heated argument with the church board and ended up pulling up stakes and left the church, moving to a church down the street. The situation was really unhealthy. A lot of people got hurt in the process.

I learned early in my walk that I had two secrets: One was that I was a new, middle-aged believer, who had a lot of doubts and questions about God and Christianity, and the second was that I was an alcoholic. I found out that those were two things that were not "safe" to talk about in the church community. We were all encouraged to "tell our story," but it usually came back to bite those that stepped forward. When people got really honest, it felt that they were judged afterwards. It is not easy for Christians to find a safe place to be really honest.

Mary

> *"A belief is not merely an idea the mind possesses,*
> *it is an idea that possesses the mind."*
>
> ~ Robert Bolton [6]

THE POWER OF BELIEF SYSTEMS

There is a basic weakness in human beings that the enemy uses to interfere in God's plans. The weakness has to do with that original sin, pride. Pride comes forward most aggressively when our beliefs systems are challenged. We (mankind) will argue over an idea, but over a core belief system, we will kill you, your family, your dog, and try to wipe out all your generations. Almost all wars are fought over belief systems.

> *War does not determine who is right—only who is left.*
>
> ~ Bertrand Russell, British philosopher

At the core of political ideology there is usually a spiritual belief system. For example, consider Communism versus Democracy. Democracy promotes the belief that all people are created equal and that an individual has intrinsic worth because God has created all of us. Communism, on the other hand, espouses the idea that there is no God and the individual only has intrinsic worth in relation to their contribution to the State. Not believing in God is a spiritual belief. Between sixty and one hundred million people have been killed by communist regimes—many of them because of their spiritual and political beliefs. Many wars and much suffering resulted from the clash of these two beliefs systems. Nazism, fascism, racism, and ethnic cleansing are a few other examples of belief systems that have spiritual foundations. Bob Dylan wrote a famous song back in 1962 called, "God on our Side." He sang about how we justify our hatred of others and military actions by saying, "We have God on our side." Throughout history, both sides of conflicts believe this. He ends his song by saying, "If God's on our side, He'll stop the next war."

Racial prejudice, anti-Semitism, or hatred of anyone with different beliefs has no place in the human mind or heart.
~ Billy Graham

The same power of beliefs can affect us individually by sabotaging our relationships and causing problems in our ability to function. Remember, all our good and bad behaviors have a belief system that drives them. I think the most powerful beliefs are religious and political ones. There are three main areas of human beliefs that don't seem to necessarily correlate with intelligence: addictions, politics, and religion. Humans have said and done some of the most bizarre and insane things in these three areas. These areas of beliefs are in our deep limbic hearts and have to do with our self-worth and identity. They appear as pride and anger, but are mostly driven by fear.

> **KEY thought** Religion is religion and can be used to justify just about anything.

A current example of how beliefs can drive emotions and behavior is the current war on terrorism. Terrorism is a religious war driven by the belief in a Jihad or Holy War. The Islamic Jihadist believes that the time has come to rid the world of infidels—non-Islamic believers. Many also believe that those who die in a Jihad get many rewards in paradise. For the men, they get seventy virgin wives and a castle in paradise.[7] They believe that God (Allah) is pleased and rewards those who blow themselves up along with innocent, men, women, and children, even though the Quran strictly forbids suicide and harming innocents. That Jihad belief helps to explain the frame of mind of the suicide bombers. It may sound crazy to us, but makes perfect sense to them. What kind of deity is that and where did a belief system like this originate? Who taught them that? I saw an interview with a Muslim imam a while back who was being questioned about the abuse of women. He finally got very angry and said, "Women are the property of men." That explains how they justify how they treat women.

Of course, Christians have also committed heinous crimes that they believe were pleasing to God, for example: The Crusades, the Bosnian War, the atrocities during the Inquisition against women, and our own Civil War, a "Biblical" war. Currently the United Nations is trying to step in to stop the genocide in Senegal of thousands of Muslims by Christians. When you see a person, an organization, or even government acting destructively, ask yourself, "What would they have to believe to act that way?" The Nazis had to believe something (Aryanism) to justify what they did. Both sides of most wars believe that God is on their side.

More recently in Oslo, Norway, a man acted out his belief systems violently. Take a look at the article below and ask yourself what you think he believed in order to justify killing innocent people who were not even the Muslims he was protesting against? What did it have to do with his manifesto?

> OSLO —The Norwegian man charged Saturday with a pair of attacks in Oslo that killed at least ninety-two people left behind a detailed manifesto outlining his preparations and calling for a Christian war to defend Europe against the threat of Muslim domination, according to Norwegian and American officials familiar with the investigation. The police identified him as a right-wing fundamentalist Christian. (*New York Times*, July 23, 2011)

There is something deep inside us that rises up when we think our beliefs are being challenged and threatened. It can cause us to react in ways that nothing else can, whether for good or evil. Did you ever feel like you won the argument but lost the relationship? Religion and politics discourages us from thinking too far outside the box. Throughout history those who did were punished. It is also our belief systems that can give us amazing courage to do wonderful things. We will be willing to make great sacrifices if we believe in something strongly enough. It is also our belief systems that the enemy can use to prevent unity and revival. We all have both kinds.

JIM'S STORY

Hello Michael,

I'm not going to lie to you; the church for which I work has had many very talented ministers leave the church without any intention to enter again into ministry. What they all had in common was that they (as you say, Michael) were doing something "outside the box." I may be next.

Jim

One of the main goals of this book is to get you to examine your beliefs. What belief systems are behind how you act and feel? Why do you act and feel the way you do—both constructively and destructively?

Where does what you believe come from and how does it affect yourself and others? Most of these deep beliefs are semi-conscious at best. Remember change comes from asking the right questions and the right questions can challenge your beliefs.

> **KEY thought** — We all believe we are right.

"I gave you milk, not solid food for you were not yet ready for it. Indeed, you are still not ready. You are still worldly. For since there is jealousy and quarreling among you, are you not worldly? Are you not acting like mere humans?"
1 Corinthians 3:2–3

DENOMINATIONAL DIVIDES

The same power of belief systems that can split nations is what the enemy can use to split churches, families, friends, communities, and prevent revival. There is a basic need in us to be more right and superior to others. I think men struggle more than women. The Bible calls it *self-righteousness*. This kind of self-righteousness is evident in the fact that there are denominations. Why are there denominations? Denominations are not really biblical, are they? We are to be one body, in one spirit. The problem is that every denomination believes that what they believe, the way they believe it, and how they worship is better and closer to "God's Will" than everyone else. They are more doctrinally correct; they understand the right way to worship. Even independent churches can believe they are doing it better because they are non-denominational. As a recovering Pharisee I am proud of not being a Pharisee, which of course makes me one. Self-righteous pride is at the core of religion. We believe God will bless us because we are doing it right. The simple fact is that we can't all be right, so we all must (to some degree) be wrong. But of course none of us *believes* that we are wrong. We all "see though a glass dimly." We are all on the same journey of discovery. Who am I, who is God and what is *the truth*? We can feel very insecure and threatened if we are challenged in what we believe. We can react in ways that astonish others and ourselves. Someone might say; Wow, I must have really pushed your button.

> **KEY thought** — If everyone believes they're right, then we have to assume no one is.

"World travel and getting to know clergy of all denominations has helped mold me into an ecumenical being. We're separated by theology and, in some instances, culture and race, but all that means nothing to me anymore."

~ Billy Graham

All denominations, religions, and spiritual seekers think that what they believe is more right and pleasing to God than everyone else. It is the same for politics and almost any area where there is self-justification. Humility and self-righteousness can't exist in the same place at the same time. God works through humble people to do great things. Humble people have an ear to hear. These are the ones who can admit they don't have it all together. You can't change the church, only yourself. So, we go back to asking the right questions. Am I a safe person? Is what I believe a door or a wall? Just because I believe something, it doesn't mean I'm right. When you make room for what others believe without being threatened, it makes you a safe person to help others who are struggling.

> **KEY thought** Safe churches aren't afraid of or threatened by what others believe.

INSECURITY

Insecurity manifests itself in control. It is not doctrine in and of itself that keeps us apart. We can differ on what we believe and still work together. It is our human need to be right that uses doctrine to keep individuals and churches from working together. There is an old saying: "We all need someone to look down on." It is easy to identify the churches that are caught in this mentality because they are against more than they are for. Can you think of a church or person like that? They are constantly criticizing others for what they believe. Most of these kinds of churches are also inward focused. On the other hand, I know of churches that are constantly reaching out to others in loving and competent ways. They are too busy reaching out to others than focusing on pettiness. They bring hope by saying, "Let us help you; come as you are; we have something that works."

I remember when I was a part of the Promise Keepers movement, one denomination held their own events at the same time so their men wouldn't be contaminated with false doctrine. They also don't take part in what other churches are doing because they fear doctrinal pollution. Some members of that denomination have come for counseling feeling guilty, asking me not to tell anyone. They feel ashamed because they think they just don't have enough faith to overcome their problems. There are many churches like this. It is okay to believe differently, but it is not okay to attack others who differ. It is not about doctrine; it is about fear and insecurity—think about the mindset of the Pharisees. What drove them to say and do the things they did? It is so easy to get caught up being like them—we're human.

Churches like the one above sound much like a cult, don't they? Classic signs of a cult are exclusiveness (especially in teaching), control, and isolation. All cults believe they have a deeper insight into the mind of God and that others are deceived, or at least unenlightened. Is our faith so fragile that we can be easily led astray by simply coming into contact with other teachings? Insecurity (fear) manifests itself in control. Pride is the foundational sin that makes us vulnerable to this kind of exclusiveness. The enemy uses it to prevent the unity that will challenge his control. Think of what the church could accomplish if it could truly work together to practically show the love and grace of Jesus in the real world as one united entity. I believe the "gates of hell could not stand against us." I think a sign of a mature person is that they are accepting of others—they are not judgmental. For me and some of my friends it has come with age. There is truth to the saying, "the older I get the less I know."

NICK'S STORY

Dear Michael,

I have struggled with pornography, lust, and depression for many years. I have gone forward for many altar calls, without really revealing what I am struggling with because of fear of rejection. My church doesn't believe in counseling, other than its own form of biblical counseling. We are taught to provide the right scripture to fit the problem and think that faith in the Word will deliver us from every problem. It sounded right, but it didn't work that way for me. I didn't go back because I knew they would tell me I just didn't have enough faith.

I met a guy at church with the same problem who said he secretly went to a 12-step recovery group that was really helping. He said it wasn't Christian, but I went and found that most of the men there were Christian and had the similar experiences with their churches. They were afraid to reveal what they were struggling with. I felt accepted and that it was safe to be completely honest. About a month later I went to my pastor and shared with him my problem and about the group and how much better I was doing. I said that I would like to start a group in the church to help other men. Well, by the next Sunday everyone in the church knew about my problem. The pastor denounced me from the pulpit as an unrepentant sinner who went outside the Word for help. He used Matthew 18. He said I would be welcome back when I was really ready to repent. I thought I was going to pass out from the shame. It will be a long time before I trust going to a church again. I think many churches have good intentions, but are clueless on how to help people like me. It is easier to put us out of sight so everything looks okay. Thanks for letting me share my story.

Nick

CHRIST AND HIM CRUCIFIED

The bottom line is that we can all agree that our society needs revival—a movement of God. I believe we need unity for that to happen. The main thing that prevents unity is what I call the Pharisaical Spirit, which is a dividing spirit whose source is pride. What can we do about it? We can't change others or the church, only ourselves.

As a recovering Pharisee, I am trying to opt out of being used by people or by the enemy to judge, hurt, or divide others. Challenging what I believe and why I believe it has been one of the hardest things I have ever done. I found that so much of my identity was in what I believed. So if some of what I believe is false, what affect do you think that has on my identity?

The process of recovering from religion has been both the most frustrating and freeing experience. So much of what I believed was religious. I have found that the simpler you make something (especially spirituality), the more powerful it is. Now, like Paul, I am down to "Christ and Him crucified." (1 Corinthians 2:2) *When you think about it, what more do we really need to know?* I have asked this question many times. When people try to think of an answer, no one has ever come up with one. I came to discover that much of my studying was about pride. I wanted to impress people with my knowledge. I think the bottom line of what I believe now is that *God is a mystery*. I really don't have a clue about what He does or how He is going to do it. He is so much bigger than my box. I have found that my beliefs are the filter that I see the world through. As I peel off the filters a whole new world I hadn't been able to see comes through. It has also put the adventure back into my Christianity. I keep going back to that little truth that has helped me so much: *Just because I believe something, it doesn't mean I'm right.*

I don't understand why from the beginning God put in our DNA such a strong desire to know Him personally, and yet make it so difficult to do so. I know of only one who really knew Him. I need to just trust Him. Faith is about trusting God outside and beyond our understanding. To trust Him when I don't have a clue to what He is doing and why.

SELF-DISCOVERY QUESTIONS

1. What religious elements can you identify in your beliefs (i.e., denominational/doctrinal)?
   _____
   _____
   _____
   _____

2. What kind of other Christians do you have the hardest time getting along with? Why?
   _____
   _____
   _____
   _____

3. Think in practical terms the answer to the question, "What more do we need to know than Christ and Him crucified?"
   _____
   _____
   _____
   _____

PRACTICAL APPLICATION

Think of something you can do on a practical level to help create unity, like joining an outreach with another church or asking them to join you. The idea is to try something to create cooperation.

CHAPTER THIRTEEN

THE JOY CENTER: HEALING THE HEART

"But now I come to You; and these things I speak in the world so that they may have My joy made full in themselves." John 17:13

"You will make known to me the path of life; In Your presence is fullness of joy; In Your right hand there are pleasures forever." Psalms 16:11

> **KEY thought**   He restoreth my soul.

In this final chapter, we are going to look at another and probably the most powerful tool the church can use to restore a wounded and addicted person—the healing powers of joy. Remember that wounded people have to find a way to cope and function, which usually becomes habitual. That's why I believe it is imperative for churches and individuals to have not only an understanding of human self-destructive behavior, but also an understanding of what brings healing and freedom. It comes down to the power of joy coming through relationships with God and people. Effective programs for healing and recovery must factor in "joy," an emotion critical in the process of restoring a human's brokenness. Let's explore the foundations and power of joy, and how churches can apply it to help hurting people.

> **KEY thought** From birth to death, joy is our most sought after emotion. It makes us feel like human beings.

> *"Find a place inside where there's joy, and the joy will burn out the pain."*
> ~ Joseph Campbell [1]

JOY IMPACTS OUR DEVELOPMENT

Science tells us that the first imprints on our identity begin as soon as we are born (probably before). It is believed that an infant's brain is only able to recognize two emotions—joy and disgust. Joy is our first and most sought after emotion. It is the foundation on which our identity is built. An infant's brain forms its identity constantly from the facial expressions of others, especially their mother. Joy is a unique form of gladness and is mainly produced by someone being glad to see you and be with you. So, as a mother's face brightens up when the baby comes into view, the baby's brain will produce joy, enhancing their foundation of a healthy identity. Their joy center lights up when they perceive that I am welcome, important, and am glad to be here. It's no wonder that this is the first and primary emotion that an infant seeks out on its own.

The development of the joy center in the brain (part of the heart) is foundational to becoming a healthy person. When properly developed, the joy center can have executive control over many of our emotional systems, such as the stress and pain management systems, relational bonding, and even the immune system. It can also be a big part of controlling the impulses of such primary drive centers like sex, food, fear, and anger. This is the primary reason groups of all kinds are so powerful. It is a group of people that are glad to see you, communicating that you are important. The healing and growth of this joy center is an important part of getting free of destructive behaviors, emotions, and relationships. Dr. James Wilder writes, "In order to train the brain to live in joy, we must have face-to-face joy with others. For the brain, joy is amplified and learned when we experience someone who greets us with joy." ² He is saying that an expression of genuine appreciation builds our joy center throughout our life.

THE POWER OF JOY

> Hi, my name is Warren and I am a forty-year alcoholic. I started drinking compulsively in high school. After many years of wreckage I finally got sober when I was 38. AA helped me stay sober for the first few years and then Christ gave me a new life and a ministry. My ministry was to other alcoholics and addicts. I went into the jail and led meetings showing others there is hope by sharing my story and the principals of recovery. I also preached regularly at numerous, different churches. I sponsored many over the years, several coming to Christ. I became sort of leader/speaker and many looked up to me as an "old timer" who new the ropes. Well after 16 years sober I relapsed, and relapsed hard. In nine months I pretty much destroyed 16 years of work, doing severe damage to my family, friends and ministry. When I finally hit bottom (in jail) I didn't know where to go as I felt so much shame, I was such a hypocrite. When I got out I went to an AA meeting as a "new comer." I was so frightened thinking of the looks I would get. Well, when I walked in (trying to be invisible) everyone was so glad to see me, some even cried. It was one of the most life changing moments in my life. I felt that I could be forgiven and restored. I really understand the story of the Prodigal Son now—it was good to be home and loved. People were glad to see me in spite of my failures. It was that moment of grace that restored my life. I remember that when I am tempted to judge others.
>
> Warren

"Do not be grieved, for the joy of the LORD is your strength." Nehemiah 8:10b

That is why recovery (returning to a former healthy state) begins with God. He is the most powerful source of joy. No matter what you've done or how messed up you are, God is always glad to see you and be with you (see Luke 15, the Parables of the Lost Sheep and the Prodigal Son). From eighteen months to about three years, a child is learning to self-regulate. This stage of development is sometimes called "the terrible two's." When children experience anger, sadness, fear, or hurt from those around them, usually because they are not getting their own way, they are learning how to return to joy.[3] They may temporarily hate or fear you, but they are finding an internal way to be glad to be with you again. Those of us who did not experience this important stage of development in a healthy way will probably struggle in the areas of trust, impulse control, and a secure identity. We can have a hard time forgiving and being able to come back to homeostasis (equilibrium) from negative experiences and emotions. I think we all know someone like that—they just get stuck.[4]

> **KEY thought** Joy is when someone is glad to be with you.

> *"I cannot even imagine where I would be today were it not for that handful of friends who have given me a heart full of joy. Let's face it; friends make life a lot more fun."*
> ~ Charles R. Swindoll

I think that one of the reasons we get so attached to our pets is that they are always glad to see us no matter how messed up we are. I read a poster the other day that said, "Lord, help me be the kind of person my dog thinks I am." Children can have the same effect. Think about how good you feel when a small child laughs and holds out their arms when they see you, especially when they don't even know you. We say to ourselves, "I must be a good person," which is a good self-identity statement. The joy center is one of the parts of the brain that can continue to help heal us and grow throughout a lifetime. It affects just about every area of our life. Restoring our ability to experience joy is at the core of Genesis Processes;

we work to bring new energy and healing to this part of the brain (heart). Being in a *safe* group that knows you for real and yet are always glad to see you and be with you is healing. It alone can change /heal negative belief systems and behaviors.

> "These things I have spoken to you so that My joy may be in you, and that your joy may be made full." John 15:11

> "Then some children were brought to Him so that He might lay His hands on them and pray; and the disciples rebuked them. But Jesus said, 'Let the children alone, and do not hinder them from coming to Me; for the kingdom of heaven belongs to such as these.'" Matthew 19:13–15

DISGUST COMMUNICATES REJECTION

The opposite of joy is disgust. Disgust is experienced when someone is not glad to see you or be with you, and can result in rejection and shame, communicating, there is something wrong with me. Shame is our most destructive emotion. Most therapists who work with self-destructive/ addictive clients have concluded that what drives destructive behaviors is shame. Shame is our most powerful heart wounding emotion, resulting in negative distorted beliefs and low self worth. Reprograming these negative self-sabotaging beliefs is primary to real recovery. Some of the most common shame driven beliefs are *"I'm bad—no good, There is something wrong with me, I don't deserve good things, I will always fail, etc."* Reprograming heart/ limbic wounds happens through Gods Love penetrating our heart. Which usually occurs through people who are genuinely glad to see us no matter how messed up we are.

> *"Shame is a soul eating emotion."*
> ~ C.G. Jung

A parent who is struggling with his or her own unmet needs may express disgust with their child when the child has needs or doesn't live up to the parent's expectations. The negative message of disgust can result in shame, which can produce a loss of a sense of self. Loss of self is a loss of worth. A loss of worth usually results in being self-destructive. Disgust felt in our pre-verbal years can do the most damage, as it can go directly into our heart (limbic system) and be very difficult to change. The powerful perception of disgust can come from abuse or feeling judged, criticized, rejected, bullied, slandered, or even from a look that communicates dislike. These self-perceptions later in life—real or imagined—can trigger old wounds and feelings of low self-worth even from our pre-verbal years. We probably don't consciously know they are there, but they can cause us to react in ways that are not what we would like. We all have some of these kinds of hurts. This is one reason the church needs to be safe and free of judgments. People at a safe church are always glad to see you, even when you don't measure up or believe right. A healthy church can create a new joy experience that can help heal the heart. This experience of joy can have a miraculous effect on those struggling with shame-based problems. Once again, it is about love and grace at a heart level. When we genuinely care about people as Jesus did, our joy will naturally result in healing. On the other hand; a person or a church can also amplify these kinds of wounds by communicating rejection. Most of the stories in this book reiterate this theme.

> *"If a person senses that your do not like them,*
> *that you do not approve of their existence, then your religion and*
> *your political ideas will all seem wrong to them.*
> *If they sense that you like them, then they are open*
> *to what you have to say."*
> ~ Donald Miller [5]

Rejection is one of our worst fears. It creates heart wounds that can last a lifetime, because rejection also produces shame. For many years, I have tried to figure out why church wounds can go so deep and be harder to get over than even our childhood wounds. It can be devastating when we take the risk to be vulnerable again, only to be betrayed or rejected by a person or group we trusted. Betrayal or rejection can confirm and reinforce our negative early limbic heart wounds and belief systems. One of my goals for writing this book is to reach out to the large number of un-churched Christians. Most of us know someone who was so wounded by a church or ministry that they will not risk going to church again. Many of the missionaries we worked with felt so betrayed that they left the ministry, saying they will never return. How do you think they cope with having a call to ministry and not being willing or able to fulfill it? Effective recovery ministry in the church can make a safe and competent place for wounded Christians to begin to trust, heal, and grow. They will need to feel welcomed, valued and that others are genuinely glad to be with them without conditions.

> **KEY thought** — Love is action more than words.

"Love to faults is always blind, always is to joy inclined. Lawless, winged, and unconfined, and breaks all chains from every mind."
~ William Shakespeare

JOY EXPRESSES VALUE

How do we typically treat something that has no worth versus something that has great value? In my experience the number one thing that helps those struggling with self-destructive behaviors (including co-dependency) is finding a sense of self-value. It is people who messed us up, and it is through people that healing will come. When those who have been wounded in their joyful identity seek out help, they are very vulnerable (which is most of us, to some degree). They hope to find a group that is genuinely glad to be with them; they look for acceptance, but expect rejection. I say "genuinely" because brain scan research has shown that when someone is genuinely glad to be with us (as opposed to someone who just smiles and pretends), the effect is quite different.6 Even though the facial expression was the same, the energy is different. The scans showed that only the genuine energy lit up the area of joyful identity. In other words, you can't fake it. Joyful love for another has to be from the heart. Jesus says, "Out of the mouth comes that which fills the heart" (Luke 6:45). The vibes we give off don't lie and our hearts sense it.

> **KEY thought** — If you don't know who you are you will end up somebody else.

People have entire relationships via text message now, but I am not partial to texting. I need context, nuance and the warmth and tone that can only come from a human voice.
~ Danielle Steel, Author

JOY IS FACE-TO-FACE

One of the problems we are facing as a society now that the church can help heal is the impact of social media. Approximately 80 percent of what we communicate is non-verbal. It is in our body language, facial expressions, tone of voice, etc. I have read many articles about how we are becoming a socially retarded generation because we rely on social media so much to communicate. Without face-to-face or at least voice-to-voice contact we only see or hear the words and are not learning to read social clues. On Facebook we can pretend to be anyone we want because there is no face-to-face interaction—no eye contact. I have met several people who have become so addicted to Facebook and texting that it's ruining their health and relationships. They go through withdrawal similar to cocaine addiction. Social media communication is a counterfeit for real joy. It can become a temporary anesthetic for loneness and isolation, much like porn. Moderation is the key. Remember, whatever you use to replace love and relationships, you can never get enough of. Church can be a place to heal and replace the counterfeit with the genuine.

I think that this is one reason why secular 12-step groups are so effective. It is a place where face-to-face interaction with real people with real problems who are open and honest takes place; it is a hard place to be phony. Like the prodigal son, when an alcoholic is lost in their addiction and returns to temporary sanity to ask for help, other alcoholics are genuinely glad to see him. They demonstrate it by spending time and energy to help him recover from his time of destructive insanity. Rather than berate him for what he has done, they celebrate his days or even minutes of sobriety. Not many churches or church people are like that. *Love is action more than words.* Remember that grace (an expression of love) is when you have a relationship with someone's heart, rather than her behavior. We can learn a lot about "what works" from the 12-step community.

THE POWER OF ACCEPTANCE

The antithesis of acceptance is judgments. We have to be careful about making judgments. Judgments can negate the healing power of love that comes through grace. Judgments are what Jesus calls the "logs in our eye" (Luke 6:42). Can you see why it is so important that Christians and churches become safe places of grace and effectiveness? Where else on a practical community level can struggling people go? It is a painful world and everyone has a story. Everyone has heart wounds. My challenge to you is this: Can you lay down your theological opinions to see someone healed? This is the message the new pope is challenging the Catholic Church with. It is not easy, but the fruit you see will be worth it. I think getting free of judgments is much harder for Christians than non-Christians, because we have so much theology and denominational doctrines that we view the world and people through (many have been ingrained in us our whole lives). It's hard to break free from lifelong belief systems.

> *"For me, the beginning of sharing my faith with people began by throwing out Christianity and embracing Christian spirituality—a nonpolitical, mysterious system that can be experienced but not explained. Christianity, unlike Christian spirituality, was not a term that excited me. I could not in good conscious tell a friend about something I wasn't experiencing."*
>
> ~ Donald Miller [6]

Ed Khouri, co-author of *Joy Starts Here*, sums up his view of the mission of the church:

"We are all apprentices to joy and healing, and are each somewhere in the process of allowing Jesus to initiate, renew, and continually remove the hindrances that keep us from experiencing the full measure of His relational joy. This is our mission and the mission of the church. As we learn to lay down our claims of strength, power, and perfection—and learn to acknowledge and respond tenderly to our own weaknesses, as well as the weaknesses of others—the fears that can make a church unsafe and hinder healing will diminish. When we share in the joy of Jesus and the wisdom of the generations around us, and allow His peace to rule us in all situations, healing thrives, lives change, and invitations to joy spread contagiously to others outside the walls of the church. This is our call, this is our hope, and this is the mandate that many of us are beginning to see fulfilled. Joy and healing are our birthright, commission, and ministry." [7]

We have consistently observed over and over again from those who have gone through the Genesis Change Groups that when the groups follow the rules to make the group safe, the limbic system (heart) will begin to reveal its secrets. These mostly subconscious secrets, which are belief systems, are the key to healing what drives destructive behaviors and emotions. When a group is safe, we are all glad to be there.

> *"Your success and happiness lies in you.*
> *Resolve to keep happy, and your joy and you*
> *shall form an invincible host against difficulties."*
> ~ Helen Keller

SUMMARY

Believe it or not, my intention in writing this book was not about trying to church bash or tear down Christianity, but to challenge you to rediscover the excitement and power of *Christian Spirituality*. It is my hope that the ideas presented will encourage you to become a more effective emissary for Christ. I believe that God designed the church to be a lighthouse—a hospital—so much more than a social club or a subculture.

In order to be an effective hospital, we need to become safe/competent people. This requires us to ask the right (sometimes hard) questions about how effective we are at helping wounded and addicted people who are seeking help and healing. Healing transformation happens through relationship, rather than religion. Making churches and Christian's safe and effective representatives of Jesus is a process of heart changes and grace. God is in the business of changing our hearts, but we have to ask him, invite Him to do so. Let's summarize the main ideas presented in this book:

1. All self-destructive behaviors are ways of temporarily anesthetizing the awareness of the *Empty Place*. There is a place in us (our heart) that God designed to be filled with relationships. We are designed to get our needs met and resolve painful issues in our lives through our intimate relationships with God and people. We can't change alone. If we could, we would. We need other to complete us.

2. When our willingness or ability to trust, bond, or attach to others gets damaged through the pain of betrayal, we have to learn to meet our own needs. This is self-gratification. All addiction is self-gratification.

3. Addiction is when you simply keep doing something that is not good for you, in spite of knowing better. The logical thing would be just to stop. We all have something. Recovery is to return to a former healthy state—who you were before you were hurt and began a harmful coping behavior. Sobriety is not recovery—it is the first step.

4. Answering the question from Romans 7, "Why do I do the very thing I don't want to do?" is where recovery begins. There is a place in the middle of our brain loosely called the limbic system that the Bible refers to as the "heart." It is this survival brain that has executive control of our emotions, reactions, relationships, and experiential memories. It creates a unique emotion called a *craving* for anything it associates with survival. The limbic system records experiences that have to do with fear and pain and sets up ingenious systems to avoid

them. It also records experiences of pleasure and reward and says, "Do it again" thus the addictive brain. It is relationships that caused our limbic/heart pain. As a result, we set up powerful and mostly unconscious defenses to avoid close relationships. The thing we need the most to heal is relationships, and the thing we avoid the most is relationships. It is this dilemma as human beings that cause us to stay so stuck—a double bind.

5. Spiritual stagnation keeps the church and individuals from being as effective as they can be. What works in healing a broken life is when one person invests himself in another. Church people need broken people to serve in order to mature in their faith, just as much as broken people need others to help them heal. The principle is, "*You have to give to grow.*" God answers prayer through people, and He wants to partner with us to accomplish what He wants to do on earth. This partnership is how we get to know Him personally on a deeper level. A servant learns by serving. Knowledge that you can't apply is useless; it can puff you up.

6. Probably the most hindering and destructive aspect of religion is the *Pharisaical Spirit*. Jesus showed love, tolerance, and compassion for everyone except the religious people of his day. The religious spirit is one of pride and self-righteousness. Pride hinders our effectiveness in all our relationships, especially with God. It thrives through rules and control. To some degree, I think we all have it. The religious spirit always says you have to do something to please God and earn His blessings. It is the opposite of grace. *It is legalism that excites sin*, and the more exciting something is, the more addicting it can be. Relying on legalism to change behavior is like trying to put out a fire with gasoline. Legalism results in judgments, and being judgmental is the main thing that makes us unsafe for God to trust with wounded people. Recovery from being a Pharisee is a process of being free of self-righteous judgments. Remember—you have to believe you are better than someone to judge them. *Just because you believe something doesn't mean you are right.* Recovery from religion is not easy, but worth it.

7. In Chapter 8, we looked at the mystery and power of grace. Paul tells us that grace is nonsense to the Greeks (religious outsiders) and a stumbling block to the Jews (religious insiders). Grace is still the hardest part of being like Jesus. The problem with grace is there are no rules—it is so messy. It is the Holy Spirit's job to convict us and He may do it much differently with each of us. Without rules, we have no power and control. Religion is about rules, power, and control. Grace is simply seeing others and ourselves through God's eyes. His perception is simply the truth that sets us free. Grace is having a relationship with a person's heart instead of his/her behaviors. It is the way we want others to see us.

8. Next, we explored what it takes to heal a broken person. Relationships messed us up and it is relationships that will heal us. Being abused and neglected amounts to being betrayed. Trusting and then being hurt causes the limbic system (heart) to find ways to protect us from being vulnerable. The limbic system finds ways for us to survive and be able to cope, thus feeling normal (momentarily free of stress). *Addiction is not about what you are feeling, but what you are not feeling.* In this false sense of safety, we think we can do life without other people, which feels much "safer." So my "bottomist" bottom line is that *recovery is a process of learning to trust again.*

9. It is not so much that our past trauma is still affecting us today. It is the vows or survival lies (belief systems) that are still controlling us, and keep us from being wounded again in similar ways (e.g., "I will never be vulnerable again"). The formula is: *beliefs create emotions that drive our behaviors.* These survival beliefs are mostly subconscious in our heart (limbic system). Many are formed in our first two years of life. If you want to change destructive behaviors (sin), you have to change your heart through learning to trust again. God starts the process by putting His Spirit in us, but most of the restoration comes from Him working through people. God answers prayers through people. It is a partnership that brings growth and change to both the giver and receiver. We are designed for relationships.

10. Next we talked about *The Fear of God* and how it might be an important and often overlooked competent of Christianity. The key thought is; whatever you fear, love or hate you give power to and will control you. So the challenge is to reattach negative control in each area over to God, as His control will be benevolent and beneficial. It is an ongoing test of or faith. A very practical exercise of our Christianity.

11. In Chapter 11, we talked about the role churches (especially pastors) play in the restoration process. If our parents were not healthy enough to fulfill their part in helping us grow into well-functioning adults, then our ability to give and receive affection and have a secure identity will be compromised. We can also struggle with stress and impulse control. Most of the damage happens early. There is an increasing problem of children growing up without a father. Our father's job is to recognize our gifts and encourage us with loving discipline to help us find our place in life. He helps us find our true identity, which creates a sense of worth. If we don't know our identity and worth, it can become easy to get lost trying to find it in false or destructive ways. It usually takes a male father figure, like a pastor or mentor, to help us find our true selves. We also need women in our lives to teach us what is important, to give and receive love and affection (i.e., how to do relationships). If you don't know who you are, you'll end up as somebody else.

12. We need a miracle in our world to stem the tide of self-destructive behavior. Many believe that our only hope is revival, and that revival will come through unity. What prevents unity is the pride of self-righteous religiosity, both individually and denominationally. It is our vigorous need to defend our beliefs that isolates us and makes us unsafe. We all believe that what we believe and the way we believe is the right way. If we want to be safe people that God can use to help those seeking help, then we need to examine our beliefs and how they affect others and ourselves. The main thing that makes us unsafe is our judgments. Judgments create heart wounds.

13. Lastly, we explored the healing power of joy. There is incredible healing that takes place when we find a safe place where others are genuinely glad to be with us—unconditional grace and acceptance. But remember, grace is not enabling or co-dependency. We all are consciously or unconsciously in the process of healing the wounds created by shame.

FINAL THOUGHTS

I know this book may seem overwhelming for some of you. The path that God has put me on in learning all of this has been overwhelming for me, too. My intention for writing it is to help the church and individuals to become safe and effective so that God can use us to help lost and self-destructive people become healed and whole. With the overwhelming number of people who are struggling (some desperately) in our society, I believe the church is our only hope. It is the only place that has the resources for the kind of one on one investment it takes to restore a broken person. This book is my attempt to build that bridge.

I have learned more from helping people than they have learned from me. Many churches are doing a great job and have many good recovery programs. But there are also a number, who in spite of their good intentions, are wounding more than they are healing. If I were to summarize this book into a "bottom line," it would be this: *It is mostly our religiosity that keeps us Christians and our churches from being safe places for helping hurting people heal—to simply be like Jesus.* My hope is that you will begin the process of becoming a recovering Pharisee. It may be the hardest thing you have ever done. Challenging your basic belief systems can be a journey through the wilderness. But as you begin your own process of recovery, the more real New Testament fruit you will see in your life. It is worth it. The journey begins by having the courage to ask the right questions.

If you are interested in learning more about the practical side of helping people change, you may want to consider starting or being part of a Genesis Personal Change Group, which is designed to bring about the heart changes I have talked about so much. Some of you may want to attend a Genesis

Counselor Training Program, which is also now offered as a web class. You can get more information about Genesis events and trainings on my web site: www.genesisprocess.org. I also have You Tube videos that explain the principles of Genesis and Weekend Personal Change/Healing Seminars for churches interested in helping their community understand the process of personal change. Thank you for considering my ideas in this book. I pray that God will bless you and equip you for every good work.

Michael Dye
www. Genesisprocess.org

OTHER GENESIS MATERIALS

The Genesis Process For Relapse Prevention and Counselors Manual
This is a one-on-one process for relapse prevention for those with relapse-prone self-destructive behaviors. It is a 16-week process to be gone through with a trained Genesis Counselor. The training is for both lay and professional counselors and available through one-week live trainings, and now a 13-week process online web class.

The Genesis Process for Change Groups with accompanying DVD's and Facilitators Guide.
This is a 21-week personal change/healing process for groups. The DVD's have an introduction for each process and a facilitators training guide.

NOTES

INTRODUCTION

1. The Conflict of Two Natures:
   Romans 7:14–25 (NASB)
   14 For we know that the Law is spiritual, but I am of flesh, sold into bondage to sin. 15 For what I am doing, I do not understand; for I am not practicing what I *would* like to *do*, but I am doing the very thing I hate. 16 But if I do the very thing I do not want to *do*, I agree with the Law, *confessing* that the Law is good. 17 So now, no longer am I the one doing it, but sin, which dwells in me. 18 For I know that nothing good dwells in me, that is, in my flesh; for the willing is present in me, but the doing of the good *is* not. 19 For the good that I want, I do not do, but I practice the very evil that I do not want. 20 But if I am doing the very thing I do not want, I am no longer the one doing it, but sin which dwells in me. 21 I find then the principle that evil is present in me, the one who wants to do good. 22 For I joyfully concur with the law of God in the inner man, 23 but I see a different law in the members of my body, waging war against the law of my mind and making me a prisoner of the law of sin which is in my members. 24 Wretched man that I am! Who will set me free from the body of this death? 25 Thanks be to God through Jesus Christ our Lord! So then, on the one hand I myself with my mind am serving the law of God, but on the other, with my flesh the law of sin.

2. Dye, Michael. *The Genesis Process for Relapse Prevention*. (Auburn: Genesis Publishing, 2007).
   The Genesis Process is a systematic program designed to train professional and lay counselors in Relapse Prevention by treating the person first, and the problem second. The core material, which is laid out in a comprehensive, ten-unit workbook, focuses on identifying and working through underlying issues that drive compulsive addictive behavior. *The Genesis Process* is an integration of Biblical precepts for personal change, proven relapse prevention techniques, cognitive therapy principles, and some of the latest brain research relating to human behavior. For the first time in history we can answer the ques-

tion, "Why do we do the very thing we don't what to do?" The Bible tells us that trying to change behaviors without changing internal thought/ belief structures is an exercise in exhaustion that usually leads to relapse (Romans 7:15–23). *The Genesis Process* recognizes that a person's self-destructive behavior is the expression of their beliefs, so along with focusing on changing behaviors, Genesis also concentrates on identifying and changing the faulty belief systems that drive addictive behaviors. Genesis tools have been shown to be effective for anyone stuck in self-defeating behavior patterns that truly want to change. Genesis is not designed as a self-help book. Genesis relies on the insight of a trained Genesis counselor in conjunction with the Genesis workbook to address the client's subconscious relapse patterns resulting in a personal relapse prevention treatment plan that works.

3. More than one-quarter of American adults (28 percent) have left the faith in which they were raised in favor of another religion—or no religion at all—while those Americans who are unaffiliated with any particular religion have seen the greatest growth in numbers as result of changes in affiliation. Based on interviews with more than 35,000 Americans ages 18 and older from May 8 to August 13, 2007. "Pew Forum's U.S. Religious Landscape Survey." Last modified July 26, 2013. http://religions.pewforum. org/reports.

4. Dye, Michael. *The Genesis Process: For Change Groups Book 1 and 2, Individual Workbook and Videos.* (Auburn: Genesis Publishing, 2012).

The Genesis Process for Change Groups addresses biblically a fundamental struggle in all our lives: the struggle to change. Genesis tools can help *those who are willing to change be able to change*. Experience GRACE in a new practical way and practice the healing power of forgiveness; learn the difference between religion and relationship, and how to really hear God's voice.

Whether the issue is anxiety, anger, alcohol, drug or food abuse, a negative, critical attitude, or spiritual stagnation, *The Genesis Process* will help you find new freedom that lasts.

Book 1 examines how unresolved, hurtful experiences sabotage our attempts to change. The Processes are laid out in Book 1, with the goal of establishing safe relationships and understanding what has been sabotaging attempts at success, which will prepare participants for the deeper, inner healing work in Book 2.

Book 2 provides tools for healing old wounds and for letting go of the coping behaviors they produce. Wounds produce subconscious fears that end up controlling our behaviors.

Fear is overcome by faith and faith requires learning to trust again. The Processes are based on the premise that our deepest wounds happened in relationship and are, therefore, best healed through opposite experiences in safe, loving relationships. We cannot change alone.

Genesis blends sound Biblical principles and the latest understanding of the brain with the author's many years of experience as an addictions counselor. These books are written for Christians with the goal of making them and their churches safe for hurting people. This unique and effective process is easy to apply to real life and for churches to implement. For more information, visit our website, www.genesisprocess.org

CHAPTER 1

1. Steve Kroft of *60 Minutes* with CBS News interviewed Tom Brady, All-Pro NFL Quarterback for the New England Patriots. Excerpt aired on *60 Minutes* December 23, 2007, following his third Super Bowl victory for the New England Patriots. http:// www.cbsnews.com/video/watch/?id=1011615n

2. Dr. Vance Havner was a revivalist. He authored nearly forty books during his ministry. His unique style has impacted thousands of God's people through the years. He is considered by many to be the most quoted preacher of the 20th century.

3. Naphtali "Tuli" Kupferberg (1923–2010) was an American counterculture poet, author, cartoonist, pacifist, and publisher.

4. Henry Ward Beecher (1813–1887) was a prominent Congregationalist clergyman, social reformer, abolitionist, and speaker in the mid to late 19th century.
5. Wellins Calcott (*bap.* 1726), religious writer.
6. Elizabeth Jane Howard, CBE (born March 26, 1923, London) is an English novelist.
7. Albert Schweitzer, OM (1875–1965) was a German—and later French—theologian, musician, philosopher, physician, and medical missionary in Africa best known for his interpretive life of Jesus. He was born in the province of Alsace—Lorraine, at that time part of the German Empire. Schweitzer, a Lutheran, challenged both the secular view of Jesus as depicted by historical-critical methodology current at his time in certain academic circles, as well as the traditional Christian view. He depicted Jesus as one who literally believed the end of the world was coming in his own lifetime and believed himself to be a world savior. He received the 1952 Nobel Peace Prize for his philosophy of "Reverence for Life," expressed in many ways, but most famously in founding and sustaining the Albert Schweitzer Hospital in Lambaréné, now in Gabon, west central Africa (then French Equatorial Africa).
8. Cornelia "Corrie" ten Boom (Amsterdam, The Netherlands, 1892, Placentia, California, 1983) was a Dutch Christian. Along with her father and other family members, Corrie helped many Jews escape the Nazi Holocaust during World War II and wrote her most famous book *The Hiding Place* about the ordeal. Her family was arrested due to an informant in 1944, and her father died ten days later at Scheveningen prison. A sister, brother, and nephew were released, but Corrie ten Boom and her sister Betsie were sent to Ravensbruck concentration camp, where Betsie died. Corrie wrote many books and spoke frequently in the post-war years about her experiences. She also aided Holocaust survivors in the Netherlands. Her autobiography was later adapted as a film of the same name in 1975 and starred Jeannette Clift as Corrie.

9. Charles Haddon (C.H.) Spurgeon (1834–1892) was a British Particular Baptist preacher. Spurgeon remains highly influential among Christians of different denominations, among whom he is known as the "Prince of Preachers." He was a strong figure in the Reformed Baptist tradition, defending the Church in agreement with the 1689 London Baptist Confession of Faith understanding, and opposing the liberal and pragmatic theological tendencies in the Church of his day. In his lifetime, Spurgeon preached to around ten million people, often up to ten times each week at different places. Spurgeon was the pastor of the congregation of the New Park Street Chapel (later the Metropolitan Tabernacle) in London for thirty-eight years. He was part of several controversies with the Baptist Union of Great Britain and later had to leave the denomination.

CHAPTER 2

1. Luke Davies is an Australian writer of novels and poetry. He has published two novels, *Isabelle the Navigator*, and the cult bestseller, *Candy*, which was shortlisted for the NSW Premier's Literary Awards in 1998. His novel, *God of Speed*, is about the life of Howard Hughes.
2. Obesity and Overweight (Data are for the U.S.), National Center for Health Statistics through 2009–2010.

- Percent of adults aged 20 years and over who are obese or extremely obese: 42% (2009–2010)
- Percent of adults aged 20 years and over who are overweight (and not obese): 33% (2009–2010)
- Percent of adolescents age 12 to 19 years who are obese: 18.4% (2009–2010)
- Percent of children age 6 to 11 years who are obese: 18% (2009–2010)
- Percent of children age 2 to 5 years who are obese: 12% (2009–2010).

According to the National Conference of State Legislatures, overweight and obese individuals are at increased risk for many diseases and chronic health conditions including the following:

- Hypertension (high blood pressure)
- Osteoarthritis (a degeneration of cartilage and its underlying bone within a joint)
- Dyslipidemia (for example, high total cholesterol or high levels of triglycerides)
- Type 2 diabetes
- Heart disease
- Stroke
- Gallbladder disease
- Sleep apnea and respiratory problems
- Some cancers (pancreas, kidney, prostate, endometrial, breast, and colon)

3. Annual cost of obesity in the US is $190 billion. Reuters is reporting that obesity in America is now adding an astounding $190 billion to the annual national healthcare price tag, exceeding smoking as public health enemy number one when it comes to cost. "Obese men rack up an additional $1,152 a year in medical spending, especially for hospitalizations and prescription drugs, Cawley and Chad Meyerhoefer of Lehigh University reported in January in the Journal of Health Economics. Obese women account for an extra $3,613 a year. Using data from 9,852 men (average BMI: 28) and 13,837 women (average BMI: 27) ages 20 to 64, among whom 28 percent were obese, the researchers found even higher costs among the uninsured: annual medical spending for an obese person was $3,271 compared with $512 for the non-obese." http://www.forbes.com/sites/rickungar/2012/04/30/obesity-now-costs-americans-more-in-healthcare-costs-than-smoking/

4. Amen, Daniel G. *Change Your Brain, Change Your Life*. (New York: Three Rivers Press, 1988). Dr. Amen has several easy-to-understand books about the brain.

5. Seigel, Daniel J. *The Developing Mind*. (New York: Guilford Press, 2012).

6. Excerpt from "Bonding/Attachment and Trust in the First 2 Years of Life," by Dr. Jim Wilder, Author of *The Life Model*. "The brain's relational control center does most of its growth and basic training in the first two years of life. Everything in the brain depends on a secure bond to be trained correctly. One of the most obvious examples involves the governing region of the brain from before birth until about four months of age. This guardian system controls the newborn mind. This guardian has three opinions about everything the baby encounters: good, bad, or scary. For a person to learn trust, it is essential that the people in the baby's life register "good" and not "bad" or "scary." A secure and dependable relationship with parents at this stage builds the bridge to a secure attachment and a brain that is ready to be trained how to love others. This becomes even more important when we notice two other facts. First, the guardian system is subconscious and therefore not subject to our will later on in life. Second, the guardian does not have an erase circuit. Once it learns something it cannot be changed and will always remember what it learned even while you are sleeping or unconscious. So, if a baby learns to fear people, or think that men or women are bad, for instance, that will influence that person's view of others the rest of his or her life—even in dreams. The brain's relational control center completes its main growth by the time a baby is about eighteen months old. By then, a second important structure has grown that was not there when he or she was born. This new leader of the control center is in the executive control for life. On the bottom side of this newly grown executive department are the brain's trust circuits. This system receives its basic programming before the baby is eighteen months old. While the guardian circuits have global opinions like "all women are good" or "my dad is scary," the executive system runs in real time looking for "trustworthy moments." When well trained, this sophisticated part of your brain will notice when others are not paying attention or don't seem to understand and will invalidate what they are saying and doing right then. This keeps a baby from taking in the errors others make and building an identity with the errors. This is an excellent "trust filter," but when the child does not have a secure attachment, this

filter cannot be trained and so the child simply begins to trust his or her own feelings as the basis for reality."

7. According to a 2011 study conducted in New Zealand, self-control is a strong indicator of future success, regardless of intelligence or social status.

- Children who displayed greater levels of self-control were more likely to have better health, greater financial success, and more.
- Those children whose self-control improved as they aged had better outcomes than those whose did not.

    A child's success in his or her thirties in measures of health, wealth, and more can be predicted by how well they can control their impulses as early as age three, says a new study, published in *Proceedings of the National Academy of Sciences.*

    Children with lower self-control scores, the researchers found, were more likely to have a number of physical health problems including sexually transmitted infections, weight issues, and high blood pressure. They were also more likely to be dependent on drugs; to have worse financial planning and money management skills; to be raising a child in a single parent household; and to have a criminal record.

    "Children with low self-control tended to make mistakes while they were adolescents, including starting to smoke tobacco, becoming a teen parent of an unplanned baby and leaving secondary school with no qualification," the researchers added in a summary of their work.

    The study led by Avshalom Caspi of Duke University and colleagues followed 1,000 children from birth to age thirty-two in Dunedin, New Zealand in January, 2011. http://news.discovery.com/human/children-self-control-success-110124.htm

8. Dye, Michael. *The Genesis Process: For Change Groups Book 1 and 2, Individual Workbook.* (Auburn: Genesis Publishing, 2012), 109–122, 213–232. Process 8 is focused on identifying and healing protective personalities. Process 14 works on identifying and healing the false beliefs that drive self-destructive behaviors and emotions.

9. Margaret Atwood was born in 1939 in Ottawa and grew up in northern Ontario, Quebec, and Toronto. She received her undergraduate degree from Victoria College at the University of Toronto and her master's degree from Radcliffe College Throughout her writing career, Margaret Atwood has received numerous awards and honorary degrees. She is the author of more than thirty-five volumes of poetry, children's literature, fiction, and non-fiction and is perhaps best known for her novels.

CHAPTER 3

1. Child Trends is a Washington, D.C. based nonprofit, nonpartisan research center that studies children at all stages of development. Its mission is to improve outcomes for children by providing research, data, and analysis to the people and institutions whose decisions and actions affect children, including program providers, the policy community, researchers and educators, and the media. Founded in 1979, Child Trends helps keep the nation focused on children and their needs by identifying emerging issues; evaluating important programs and policies; and providing data-driven, evidence-based guidance on policy and practice. http://www.childtrends.org/
2. George Herbert (3 April 1593–1 March 1633) was a Welsh-born English poet, orator and Anglican priest. Herbert's poetry is associated with the writings of the metaphysical poets, and he is recognized as "a pivotal figure: enormously popular, deeply and broadly influential, and arguably the most skillful and important British devotional lyricist."
3. Isaac Watts (1674–1748) was an English hymn writer, theologian, and logician. A prolific and popular hymn writer, he was recognized as the "Father of English Hymnody," credited with some 750 hymns.
4. These are the first 5 steps of the 12 steps as published by Alcoholics Anonymous:

   Step 1: We admitted we were powerless over alcohol—that our lives had become unmanageable.

Step 2: We came to believe that a power greater than ourselves could restore us to sanity.

Step 3: We made a decision to turn our will and our lives over to the care of God *as we understood Him.*

Step 4: We made a searching and fearless moral inventory of ourselves.

Step 5: We admitted to God, to ourselves, and to another human being the exact nature of our wrongs.

5. Alexander, Bruce K. "The Myth of Drug-Induced Addiction", a paper delivered to the Canadian Senate, January 2001, retrieved December 12, 2004. http://en.wikipedia.org/wiki/Rat_Park

6. Kurt Vonnegut, Jr. was an American writer. His works such as *Cat's Cradle, Slaughterhouse Five,* and *Breakfast of Champions* blend satire, gallows humor, and science fiction. Born: November 11, 1922, Indianapolis, IN Died: April 11, 2007, New York City, NY.

7. Coursey, Chris M., Khouri, Edward M., Sutton, Sheila D., Wilder, E. James. *Joy Starts Here.* (SAC: Shepherd's House, Inc., 2013), 6.

8. The Taylor Johnson Temperament Analysis Test (T-JTA) is a widely used personality assessment for individual, marital, premarital, and family counseling. The T-JTA measures 18 dimensions of personality (9 bipolar traits) that are important components of personal adjustment and in interpersonal relationships. The T-JTA's unique "Criss-Cross" testing feature identifies pertinent differences between couples, family members, and others in significant relationships. The T-JTA pinpoints for the counselor where to focus counseling time and attention. The T-JTA Profile is a simple yet effective counseling tool designed for use in the counseling session to increase understanding, enhance personal growth and thereby reduce conflict.

CHAPTER 4

1. Quenqua, Douglas. 2011. "Rethinking Addiction's Roots and Its Treatment." *New York Times*, July 10. Accessed August 14, 2013. www.nytimes.com/2011/07/11/health/11addictions.html

2. Daniel G. Amen, M.D., is a physician, double-board certified psychiatrist, teacher and eight-time New York Times bestselling author. He is widely regarded as one of the world's foremost experts on applying brain imaging science to everyday clinical practice.

3. Amen, Daniel G. *Healing the Hardware of the Soul.* (New York: Free Press, 2002).

4. HBO.com's Addiction website brings together many of America's top addiction experts to explain that addiction is a medical condition with real medical solutions. For a better understanding of addiction, watch the HBO series on Addiction at http://www.hbo.com/addiction/. Accessed August 14, 2013.

5. Amen, Daniel G., *Change Your Brain, Change Your Life.* (New York: Three Rivers Press, 1988).

6. William Griffith Wilson (1895–1971), also known as Bill Wilson or Bill W., was the co-founder of Alcoholics Anonymous (AA).

7. Wilson, William G. *Alcoholics Anonymous Comes of Age.* (Alcoholics Anonymous World Services, 1957), 39. "Early AA got its ideas of self-examination, acknowledgement of character defects, restitution for harm done, and working with others straight from the Oxford Groups and directly from Sam Shoemaker, their former leader in America, and nowhere else."

8. Wilson, William G. *The Language of the Heart*, published posthumously, (New York: The AA Grapevine, Inc.1988), 298. "Where did the early AAs find the material for the remaining 10 Steps? Where did we learn about moral inventory, amends for harm done, turning our wills and lives over to God? Where did we learn about meditation and prayer and all the rest of it? The spiritual substance of our remaining ten Steps came straight from Dr. Bob's and my own earlier association with the Oxford Groups, as they were then led in America by that Episcopal rector, Dr. Samuel Shoemaker."

CHAPTER 5

1. Dye, Michael. *The Genesis Process: For Change Groups Book 1 and 2, Individual Workbook.* (Auburn: Genesis Publishing, 2012), 81–94.

This chapter is based on Process 6 in the *Genesis Process for Change Groups Workbook*. You can also watch a YouTube video on this subject that you can access at: www.genesisprocess.org.

2. FASTER RELAPSE AWARENESS SCALE

The heart of the original *Genesis Process for Relapse Prevention* is a tool called the Faster Scale. The Faster Scale is a behavioral, spiritual, and neurochemical model of how we unconsciously descend one step at a time into relapse, doing the things we said we would never do again. In researching how to understand the mystery of relapses over the last thirty years, the hardest part was to determine that first step when people veer from being in recovery and start down the road to relapse. We have found that it takes a minimum of about two weeks and usually about six weeks to deplete our natural coping chemicals before we can no longer cope and relapse by reaching for external chemicals.

This first step in this relapse process is identified as a change in priorities. On the Faster Scale it is called "forgetting priorities." In other words, something has become more important than our commitment to the recovery plan. Our priorities have changed. I came to recognize that this change is part of an unconscious survival response, something that in most cases is below the person's awareness. Brain research has helped us understand how and why the survival or limbic part of our brain creates that primary relapse emotion called a craving. It is a response to the real or imagined feeling of being unable to cope. We have run out of coping chemicals. Once a craving is created, it is very difficult to say no to. Cravings wear us down. Understanding craving is essential, because for the first time in history we understand why Paul and virtually all of us keep doing the very thing that we do not want to do.

FASTER RELAPSE AWARENESS SCALE RECOVERY
(What people in recovery look like.)

No current secrets; resolving problems; identifying fears and feelings; keeping commitments to meetings, prayer, family, church, people, goals, and self; being open; being honest; making eye contact; reaching out to others; increasing in relationships with God and others; accountability.

THE F-A-S-T-E-R
Dry Relapse Pattern

"F" = FORGET PRIORITIES (*Denial; flight; a change in what's important; how you spend your time and thoughts.*)
Secrets; bored; less time/energy for God, meetings, and church; avoiding support and accountability people; superficial conversations; sarcasm; isolating yourself; changes in goals; flirting; obsessed with relationships; breaking promises/commitments; neglecting family; preoccupation with material things, television, or entertainment; procrastination; lying; over-confidence; hiding money.

"A" = ANXIETY (*Getting energy from emotions.*)
Worry; using profanity; being fearful; being resentful; replaying old, negative thoughts; perfectionism; judging others' motives; making goals and lists you can't complete; poor planning; mind reading; fantasy; smoking; masturbation; pornography; co-dependent rescuing; sleep problems; trouble concentrating; seeking/creating drama; gossip; using over-the-counter medication for pain, sleep, and weight control.

= SPEEDING UP (*Out-running depression.*)
Super busy; workaholic; can't relax; driving too fast; avoiding slowing down; feeling driven; in a hurry; can't turn off thoughts; skipping meals; binge eating (usually at night); overspending; can't identify own feelings/needs; repetitive, smoking, negative thoughts; irritable; making excuses for "having to do it all"; dramatic mood swings; lust; too much caffeine; over-exercising; nervousness; difficulty being alone or with people; difficulty listening to others; avoiding support.

= TICKED-OFF (*Getting high on anger; aggression.*)
Procrastination causing crises in money, work, or relationships; sarcasm; black and white, all or nothing thinking; feeling alone; feeling that no one understands; overreacting; road rage; constant resentments; pushing others away; increased isolation; blaming; self pity;

arguing; irrationality, can't handle criticism; defensive; people are avoiding you; having to be right; digestive problems; headaches; obsessive (stuck) thoughts; can't forgive; feeling grandiose (superior); intimidation; feeling aggressive.

"E" = EXHAUSTED (*Out of gas; depression.*)
Depressed; panicked; confused; hopeless; sleeping too much or too little; can't cope; overwhelmed; crying for "no reason"; can't think; forgetful; pessimistic; helpless; tired; numb; wanting to run; constant cravings for old coping behaviors; thinking of using drugs and alcohol; seeking out old unhealthy people and places; really isolated; people are angry with you; self-abuse; suicidal thoughts; no goals; survival mode; not returning phone calls; missing work; irritability; loss of appetite.

"R" = RELAPSE Returning to the place you swore you would never go again. Giving up; giving in; out of control; lost in your addiction; lying to yourself and others; feeling you just can't manage without your coping behavior, at least for now. The result is usually shame, condemnation, guilt, and aloneness.

3. Below are some statistics taken from various surveys and sources to give you an idea of how pervasive and widespread sexual sin is in the church. These are older statistics the numbers are higher now. Do an Internet search on "porn/sex addiction among Christians."

   - 51% of pastors admit that pornography is a possible temptation, 37% say that pornography is a struggle, and 33% have viewed Internet pornography at least once a year.
   - In a 2002 survey of 6,000 pastors visiting the website of Saddleback Community Church in Mission Viejo, CA, 30% admitted viewing Internet pornography in the last 30 days.
   - A survey conducted by Christianity Today of its readership in August 2000 revealed that 33% of clergy have visited a sexually explicit Internet site at least once within the past year, of which 53% have done so "a few times." The survey also revealed that 18% had visited pornographic sites between "a couple of times a month" and "more than once a week."

- A survey conducted by "Leadership" magazine in 2000, showed that 40% of pastors have visited a pornographic Internet site, with over 33% doing so within the last 12 months.
- 75% of pastors do not make themselves accountable to anyone for their Internet use.
- Almost one in seven calls to *Focus on the Family's* Pastoral Care Hotline in the year 2000 dealt with Internet pornography.
- 6.8% of married clergy masturbate to pornography.
- In a 1993 survey conducted of Southern Baptist pastors, 14.1% confessed to "sexual behavior inappropriate to a minister."
- 5 out of every 10 men in the church are struggling with some issue concerning pornography
- 34% of churchgoing women said they have intentionally visited porn websites online
- 54% of pastors admitted to viewing Internet porn in the last year and 30% admitted viewing within the past month
- 50% of all Christian men are addicted to pornography
- 20% of all Christian women are addicted to pornography
- 60% of women admit to having significant struggles with lust
- http://prodigalsinternational.org/

4. Double Binds: Dye. *The Genesis Process: For Change Groups Book 1 and 2, Individual Workbook.* (Auburn: Genesis Publishing, 2012), 57–70.

5. "*1988: TV Evangelist Quits Over Sex Scandal*," BBC, Feb. 21, 1988. http://news.bbc.co.uk/onthisday/hi/dates/stories/February/21/newsid_2565000/2565197.stm

6. Saint Jerome (347–420 AD) was a Roman Christian priest, confessor, theologian, and historian, and who became a Doctor of the Church. He was the son of Eusebius, of the city of Stridon, which was on the border of Dalmatia and Pannonia.

PART III INTRODUCTION

1. "Drug abuse and addiction are major burdens to society; economic costs alone are estimated to exceed half a trillion dollars annually in the United States, including health, crime-related costs, and losses in productivity. However, staggering as these numbers are, they provide a limited perspective of the devastating consequences of this disease," Dr. Nora Volkow, Director of the National Institute on Drug Abuse, Congressional Testimony, 3/1/07

    - The costs of drug abuse and addiction to our nation are staggering.
    - Fourteen percent of patients admitted to hospitals have alcohol/drug abuse and addiction disorders.
    - Almost 20 percent of all Medicaid hospital costs and nearly
    - $1 of every $4 Medicare spends on inpatient care is associated with substance abuse. 70 percent of individuals in state prisons and jails have used illegal drugs regularly.
    - Drug offender's account for more than one-third of the growth in state prison population and more than 80 percent of the increase in the number of prison inmates since 1985.
    - The economic burden in the United States for addiction is twice that of any other disease affecting the brain, including Parkinson's and Alzheimer' Disease, as well as all the others.

CHAPTER 6

1. Aelred of Rievaulx (1110–1167) was a twelfth-century Cistercian abbot and well-known spiritual writer, whose treatise "Spiritual Friendship," is widely considered a classic of Christian spirituality. Inspired by Roman statesman and orator Marcus Tullius Cicero's philosophical dialogue, "On Friendship," Aelred approaches his subject from a decidedly religious standpoint, examining both the theoretical and practical aspects of friendship in the light of faith in Christ. Christian friendship, he maintains, is all about extending the fellowship of Christ to another. The more two persons grow as friends, the more they should sense the gentle, unobtrusive, yet abiding presence of the quiet third

partner in their lives. He affirms this belief when talking to his friend Ivo at the outset of Book One, stating, "Here we are, you and I, and I hope a third, Christ, in our midst." "Spiritual Friendship: The Classic Text with a Spiritual Commentary by Dennis Billy, C.S.R." (Notre Dame, IN: Ave Maria Press, Inc. 2008. https://www.avemariapress.com/product/0-87061-242-5/ Spiritual-Friendship/).

2. At the 2003 meeting of the American Academy of Matrimonial Lawyers, two-thirds of the 350 divorce lawyers who attended said the Internet played a significant role in divorces in the past year, with excessive interest in online porn contributing to more than half of such cases. http://www.psychologytoday.com/ blog/inside-porn-addiction/201112/is-porn-really-destroying-500000-marriages-annually. Last Accessed January 17, 2014.

3. A list of the parables and metaphors of Jesus:
   - The Bridegroom and His Attendant (John 3:29)
   - The Builder (Matthew 7:24–27; Luke 6:47–49)
   - The Dragnet (Matthew 13:47–50)
   - The Friend at Midnight (Luke 11:5–13)
   - The Good Samaritan (Luke 10:25–37)
   - The Good Shepherd (John 10:11–16)
   - The Great Banquet (Luke 14:15–24)
   - The Growing Seed (Mark 4:26–29)
   - The Hidden Treasure (Matthew 13:44)
   - The Laborers in the Vineyard (Matthew 20:1–16)
   - The Lamp (Matthew 5:15; Mark 4:21–23; Luke 8:16–18)
   - The Leaven (Matthew 13:33; Luke 13:20–21)
   - The Lost Coin (Luke 15:8–10)
   - The Lost Sheep (Matthew 18:10-14; Luke 15:4–7)
   - The Mustard Seed (Matthew 13:31–32; Mark 4:30–32; Luke 13:18–19)

- The Pearl of Great Price (Matthew 13:45–46)
- The Pharisee and the Tax Collector (Luke 18:9–14)
- The Pounds (Luke 19:11–27)
- The Prodigal Son (Luke 15:11–32)
- The Rich Fool (Luke 12:16–21)
- The Salt That Loses Its Savor (Matthew 5:13; Luke 14:34)
- The Sheep and the Goats (Matthew 25:31–46)
- The Sower (Matthew 13:1–9; Mark 4:1–9; Luke 8:4–8)
- The Talents (Matthew 25:14–30)
- The Thief and Sheepfold Door (John 10:1–5)
- The Ten Bridesmaids (Matthew 25:1–13)
- The Tree and Its Fruits (Matthew 7:17–20; 12:33; Luke 6:43–44)
- The Two Debtors (Luke 7:41–43)
- The Two Sons (Matthew 21:28–32_
- The Unforgiving Servant (Matthew 18:23–35)
- The Unrighteous Judge (Luke 18:1–8)
- The Unrighteous Steward (Luke 16:1–9)
- The Vine and the Branches (John 15:1–8)
- The Wedding Banquet (Matthew 22:1–14)
- The Weeds among the Wheat (Matthew 13:24–30)
- The Wicked Tenants (Matthew 21:33–46; Mark 12:1–12; Luke 20:9–19)

4. Edmund Burke was an Irish statesman, author, orator, political theorist, and philosopher, who, after moving to England, served for many years in the House of Commons of Great Britain.

5. We look at recovery rates in two ways: 1) The percentage of those who complete the program, stay clean and sober, and, more accurately, 2)

The number of how many seeking help enrolled in the program, graduated, and remained sober. Many programs I have visited have almost no recovery success, while others are in the seventy percent range.

6. Change Group Format
    1. For the first few weeks one person tells their story, about 400 to 500 words, 5 to10 minutes, using the format of; 1. What happened to them? 2. How did it affect them, i.e. how did they cope? 3. What and who help them get free or brought healing, i.e. the wisdom learned.
    2. After all have shared then the weekly format begins with one person sharing a scripture or a story that has special meaning to them and how they practically applied it to their life. About 10 minutes.
    3. Each person shares what they are struggling with and the group prays asking for insight and wisdom from God, trying not to give advice. For example; a scripture, a personal word, a picture, etc., with the emphasis on application. Then the person commits to what they are going to doing about it, i.e. take an action and the group finds practical ways to support them and hold them accountable. The groups job is to help them be successful.
    4. At the beginning of the next meeting each shares what they did as to their commitment and the result.
    5. The goal is to identity problems and fear and move towards them with support and accountability which produces change.

CHAPTER 7

1. Source: *Encarta Dictionary*
2. James Russell Lowell (1819–1891) was an American Romantic poet, critic, editor, and diplomat. He is associated with the Fireside Poets, a group of New England writers who were among the first American poets to rival the popularity of British poets.
3. Garrison Keillor (born Gary Edward Keillor on August 7, 1942 in Anoka, Minnesota) is an American author, storyteller, humorist, col-

umnist, musician, satirist, and radio personality. A 1999 study by the *Barna Research Group* showed that divorce rates among conservative Christians were significantly higher than for other faith groups, and much higher than Atheists and Agnostics experience. Barna released the results of their poll about divorce on December 21, 1999. They had interviewed 3,854 adults from the 48 contiguous states. The margin of error is ±2 percentage points.

4. The American Academy of Matrimonial Lawyers determined that Internet pornography and sex addiction were significant factors in two out of three divorces. http://www.psychologytoday.com/blog/inside-porn-addiction/201112/is-porn-really-destroying-500,000-marriages-annually. Last Accessed January 17, 2014.

5. USA average: Internet-filter-review.com reports 10 percent of men admit to having an Internet sexual addiction. It can more than likely be assumed that this number in relation to the statistics above is much higher. The National Council on Sexual Addiction and Compulsivity estimates that 6 to 8 percent of Americans—or 18 million to 24 million people—are sex addicts. And 70 percent of sex addicts report having a problem with online sexual behavior. Here are a few more statistics on sex addiction in the Church:

- April 6, 2007: 70 percent of Christians admitted to struggling with porn in their daily lives. (From a non-scientific poll taken by XXX Church, as reported by CNN.)

- August 7, 2006: Fifty percent of all Christian men and 20 percent of all Christian women are addicted to pornography. Sixty percent of the women who answered the survey admitted to having significant struggles with lust; 40 percent admitted to being involved in sexual sin in the past year; and 20 percent of the church-going female participants struggle with looking at pornography on an ongoing basis. (From the results of a Christian Net poll reported by Marketwire.com).

- In his book, "The Sexual Man," Dr. Archibald Hart revealed the results of a survey of some 600 Christian men, on the topic of masturbation: 61 percent of married Christian men masturbate.

Eighty-two percent of these have self-sex an average of once a week; 10 percent have sex with self 5 to10 times per month, 6 percent more than 15 times per month, and 1 percent more than 20 times a month. Thirteen percent of Christian married men said they felt it was normal.

- Thirty-four percent of female readers of Today's Christian Woman's online newsletter admitted to intentionally accessing Internet porn in a recent poll.

- In March of 2002, Rick Warren's (author of *The Purpose Driven Life*) Pastors.com website conducted a survey of 1351 pastors on porn use: 54 percent of the pastors had viewed Internet pornography within the last year, and 30 percent of these had visited within the last 30 days.

- Forty-seven percent of families said pornography is a problem in their home (Focus on the Family poll, October 1, 2003).

- In a survey of over 500 Christian men at a men's retreat, over 90 percent admitted that they were feeling disconnected from God because lust, porn, or fantasy had gained a foothold in their lives.

- Porn Sites Get More Visitors Each Month Than Netflix, Amazon And Twitter Combined. The Huffington Post. Posted: 05/04/2013 10:45 am EDT

- For more information on sex addictions statistics, visit http://www.safefamilies.org/sfStats.php; http://internet-filter-review.toptenreviews.com/internet-pornography-statistics.html; http://www.covenanteyes.com/

6. Science Daily Dec. 13, 2007: Some hair-raising statistics from Newsweek's "*The Sex Addiction Epidemic*": 40 million people a day are logging into porn websites, (about 13 percent of the US population). Up to 9 million may qualify under the strict clinical definition of a "sex addict." Psychologists specializing in the disorder have multiplied from 100 a decade ago to over 1,500 today. November 30, 2011. http://www.thedailybeast.com/ Newsweek/2011/11/27/the-sex-addiction-epidemic.html

7. Google, the world's most popular Internet search engine, has found in a survey that mostly Muslim states seek access to sex-related websites and Pakistan tops the list. Google found that of the top ten countries searching for sex-related sites, six were Muslim, with Pakistan on the top. The other Muslim countries are Egypt at number 2, Iran at 4, Morocco at 5, Saudi Arabia at 7, and Turkey at 8. Non-Muslim states are Vietnam at 3, India at 6, Philippines at 9, and Poland at 10. From WikiIslam, the online resource on Islam.

8. Tullian Tchividjian is the grandchild of Reverend Billy Graham & Ruth Bell Graham & the son of Gigi Graham Tchividjian.

9. Bell, Rob. *Love Wins*. New York: Harper Collins Publisher, 2011. 78.

CHAPTER 8

1. Thomas Brooks (1608–1680) was a nonconformist preacher. Born into a Puritan family, he was sent to Emmanuel College, Cambridge. He soon became an advocate of the Congregational Way and served as a chaplain in the Civil War. In 1648, he accepted the rectory of St. Margaret's, New Fish Street, London, but only after making his Congregational principles clear to the vestry.

2. Al-Anon was formed in 1951 by Anne B. and Lois W., wife of Alcoholics Anonymous (AA) co-founder, Bill W. They recognized the need for such an organization, as family members living with AA members began to identify their own pathologies associated with their family members' alcoholism. The group's purpose is to "help families of alcoholics by practicing the Twelve Steps, by welcoming and giving comfort to families of alcoholics, and by giving understanding and encouragement to the alcoholic." http://en.wikipedia.org/wiki/Al-Anon/Alateen

3. Khalil Gibran (Arabic pronunciation: born Gubran Khalil) was a Lebanese American artist, poet, and writer. Born in the town of Bsharri in modern day Lebanon (then part of the Ottoman Mount Lebanon), as a young man he emigrated with his family to the United States, where he studied art and began his literary career. He is chiefly known in the English speaking world for his 1923 book *The Prophet*.

CHAPTER 9

1. Suicide Facts (www.save.org)

   - Suicide takes the lives of nearly 30,000 Americans every year.
   - Many who attempt suicide never seek professional care.
   - There are twice as many deaths due to suicide than HIV/AIDS.
   - Between 1952 and 1995, suicide in young adults nearly tripled.
   - Over half of all suicides occur in adult men, ages 25 to 65.
   - In the month prior to their suicide, 75% of elderly persons had visited a physician.
   - Suicide rates in the United States are highest in the spring.
   - Over half of all suicides are completed with a firearm.
   - For young people 15 to 24 years old, suicide is the third leading cause of death.
   - Suicide rates among the elderly are highest for those who are divorced or widowed.
   - 80% of people that seek treatment for depression are treated successfully.
   - 15% of those who are clinically depressed die by suicide.
   - There are an estimated 8 to 25 attempted suicides to 1 completion.
   - The highest suicide rate is among men over 85 years old: 65 per 100,000 persons.
   - 1 in 65,000 children ages 10 to 14 commit suicide each year.
   - Substance abuse is a risk factor for suicide.
   - The strongest risk factor for suicide is depression.
   - By 2010, depression will be the #1 disability in the world. (World Health Organization)
   - In 2004, 32,439 people died by suicide. (CDC)
   - Suicide is the 11th leading cause of death in the U.S. (homicide is 15th). (CDC)

- Suicide is the 3rd leading cause of death for 15- to 24-year-old Americans. (CDC)
- According to the Violent Death Reporting System, in 2004 73% of suicides also tested positive for at least one substance (alcohol, cocaine, heroin or marijuana). (National Institute of Mental Health (NIMH))

2. Dye, Michael. *The Genesis Process: For Change Groups Book 1 and 2, Individual Workbook.* (Auburn: Genesis Publishing, 2012), 25–26.

3. Dye, *The Genesis Process: For Change Groups Book 1 and 2, Individual Workbook*, 236–240. (Also refer to Chapter 5 endnotes, #2 about the Faster Scale.)

4. W. E. Vine. *Vine's Expository Dictionary of New Testament Words*, (Nashville: Thomas Nelson, 1997), 970. <Righteousness: 1, 1343,dikaiosune> *Dikaiosune* is "the character or quality of being right or just." This meaning of *dikaiosune*, right action, is frequent also in Paul's writings, as in all five of its occurrences in Rom. 6; Eph. 6:14, etc. But for the most part he uses it of that gracious gift of God to men whereby all who believe on the Lord Jesus Christ are brought into right relationship with God. The man who trusts in Christ becomes 'the righteousness of God in Him,' 2 Cor. 5:21 (i.e., becomes in Christ all that God requires a man to be, all that he could never be in himself).

5. "The law is only a shadow of the good things that are coming— not the realities themselves. For this reason it can never, by the same sacrifices repeated endlessly year after year, make perfect those who draw near to worship. If it could, would they not have stopped being offered? For the worshipers would have been cleansed once for all, and would no longer have felt guilty for their sins. But those sacrifices are an annual reminder of sins, because it is impossible for the blood of bulls and goats to take away sins.

> Therefore, when Christ came into the world, he said: "Sacrifice and offering you did not desire, but a body you prepared for me; with burnt offerings and sin offerings you were not pleased.

Then I said, 'Here I am—it is written about me in the scroll— I have come to do your will, O God.'" Hebrew 10:1–7 (NIV)

6. Creflo Dollar is the founder and senior pastor of World Changers Church International (WCCI) in College Park, Georgia, which serves nearly 30,000 members.

7. The United States Department of Justice tracked the re-arrest, re-conviction, and re-incarceration of former inmates for 3 years after their release from prisons in 15 states in 1994. Key findings include:

- Released prisoners with the highest re-arrest rates were robbers (70.2%), burglars (74.0%), larcenists (74.6%), motor vehicle thieves (78.8%), those in prison for possessing or selling stolen property (77.4%), and those in prison for possessing, using, or selling illegal weapons (70.2%). http://www.bjs.gov/content/pub/press/rpr94pr.cfm; last accessed September 9, 2013.

- 67.5% of prisoners released in 1994 were rearrested within 3 years, an increase over the 62.5% found for those released in 1983; The re-arrest rate for property offenders, drug offenders, and public-order offenders increased significantly from 1983 to 1994. During that time, the re-arrest rate increased: From 68.1% to 73.8% for property offenders, from 50.4% to 66.7% for drug offenders, and from 54.6% to 62.2% for public-order offenders. http://www.bjs.gov/content/reentry/recidivism.cfm; last accessed September 9, 2013.

8. Ray Douglas Bradbury (1920–2012) was an American fantasy, science fiction, and mystery fiction writer. Best known for his dystopian novel *Fahrenheit 451* (1953) and for the science fiction and horror stories gathered together as *The Martian Chronicles* (1950) and *The Illustrated Man* (1951), Bradbury was one of the most celebrated 20th-century American writers. Many of Bradbury's works have been adapted into comic books, television shows, and films.

9. "In the name of our Lord Jesus, when you are assembled, and I with you in spirit, with the power of our Lord Jesus, 5 *I have decided* to deliver such a one to Satan for the destruction of his flesh, so that his spirit may be saved in the day of the Lord Jesus. 6 Your boasting is not

good. Do you not know that a little leaven leavens the whole lump *of dough?*" —1 Corinthians 5:4–6 (NASB)

"Brethren, even if anyone is caught in any trespass, you who are spiritual, restore such a one in a spirit of gentleness; each one looking to yourself, so that you too will not be tempted." — Galatians 6:1 (NASB)

10. Dye, *The Genesis Process: For Change Groups Book 1 and 2, Individual Workbook*, 57–67. The Double Bind Worksheet is one of the main tools in the Genesis Process to help people resolve problems that they are stuck with. It helps bring the mostly loose / loose unconscious belief systems into the light where people can make a choice to move forward.

11. Genesis Meditations for Relaxation and Reprograming Negative Self Image and Beliefs

Purpose/ Goal: Reducing stress is a survival skill for everyone, especially addicts. Most relapses happen because of stress overreactions. More importantly: most therapists who work with self-destructive/addictive clients have concluded that what drives destructive behaviors is shame. Shame is our most powerful heart wounding emotion, resulting in negative beliefs and self worth. Reprograming these negative self-sabotaging beliefs is primary to real recovery. Some of the most common shame driven beliefs are "*I'm bad—no good, There is something wrong with me, I don't deserve good things, I will always fail, etc.*" Reprograming heart/limbic wounds happens through Gods Truth penetrating our heart. This meditation is designed to help replace shame based lies with The Truth. To reduce stress the goal is live here—stay in the now. Try to stay out of the future—the land of anxiety.

Steps

1. Sit quietly in a comfortable position. Try to do this exercise before meals on and empty stomach, first thing in the morning and at bedtime are best.

2. Close your eyes.

3. Deeply relax all your muscles (while breathing deep and slow) beginning at your feet and progressing up to your face. Keep them relaxed.
4. Breathe through your nose. Become aware of your breathing while extending your arms and flexing your hands (open and closed) rapidly about 50 times. Breathe filling the bottom, then sides and top of you lungs. Hold for a few seconds at the top and bottom of each breath.
5. I suggest you use positive affirmations like the Fruits of the Spirit, using this three-part format.

   a) Breathe in slowly saying *I receive*, then breathe out saying *Gods Love*,

   b) Breathe in slowly saying *I feel*, then out saying *Gods Love*. Try to pause for a few seconds and feel the emotion.

   c) Breathe in slowly saying *I give* or *exude*, then out saying *Gods Love*.

   d) Continue with; joy, peace, kindness, goodness, patience, etc. Let God bring to your mind different things you need.

   e) You can also be creative with the things you struggle with like; *forgiveness, humility, trust, acceptance, etc.*,

   f) You can also breathe in saying, I release of, breathing out saying, *resentments, bitterness fear, judgments, control etc.*

7. Do not worry about whether you are successful in achieving a deep level of relaxation. Maintain a passive attitude and permit relaxation to occur at its own pace. When distracting thoughts occur, try to ignore them by not dwelling upon them and return to repeating the next word.
8. Continue for 15 to 20 minutes. Then sit quietly and ask God if there is anything He wants to show you or say.
Michael Dye / Genesis Processes

CHAPTER 11

1. Joel A. Barker is one of the best known futurists in the world. His videos on the future have been translated into 20 languages and have been seen by more than 100 million people. His book on paradigms is a standard text in more than 100 universities and has been translated into 20 languages.

2. Dalbey, Gordon. *Healing the Masculine Soul.* (Folsom, CA: Civitas Press, 2012). See also www.abbafather.com.
3. Kay Arthur is an international Bible teacher, four-time ECPA Christian Book Award winning author, and co-CEO of Precept Ministries International. http://en.wikipedia.org/wiki/Kay_Arthur
4. Rev. Ed Khouri, Co-Founder and Director, *Equipping Hearts for the Harvest*, and Co-Founder: *Thriving: Recover Your Life Program.*

- *Equipping Hearts for the Harvest* provides education about addiction and other life controlling problems that is biblical, as well as firmly grounded in an understanding of Physiology, the brain, and Neuroscience. *Equipping Hearts* trains workers, leaders, and churches to serve the addicted community and hurting people worldwide. They have worked with numerous students and leaders from Africa, the Middle East, Asia, North America, South America, Europe, and Australia. http://equippinghearts.com

- *Thriving: Recover Your Life* brings people of all levels of maturity together to build a joyful healing community. Participants heal and grow by building joy in the context of secure, healthy relationships with God and others. As joy builds, participants are better able to handle distress and increasingly able to live from their heart. http://www.thrivingrecovery.org

5. Dalbey, Gordon. *Sons of the Father: Healing the Father-Wound in Men Today.* (Folsom, CA: Civitas Press, 2011).
6. Refer to Chapter 5 endnotes on *Secrets*, #3 in *The Genesis Process for Change* book.

CHAPTER 12

1. Oswald Jeffrey Smith (1889–1986) was a Canadian pastor, author, and missions advocate. He founded The People's Church in Toronto in 1928. He was a leading force in Fundamentalism in Canada.
2. Leonard Ravenhill (1907–1994) was an English Christian Evangelist and author who focused on the subjects of prayer and revival. He is

best known for challenging the modern church to compare itself to the early Christian Church as chronicled in the Book of Acts.

3. Orr, J. Edwin. *The Role of Prayer in Spiritual Awakening*. Video by Randolf Productions, Inc., Irvine, California. May 27, 2009.

4. Desiderius Erasmus (1466–1536) was born at Rotterdam the illegitimate son of a physician's daughter by a man who afterwards turned monk. On his parents' death, his guardians insisted on his entering a monastery and in the Augustinian college of Stein near Gouda he spent six years. It was certainly this personal experience of the ways of the monks that made Erasmus their relentless enemy. In 1519 appeared the first edition of his Colloquia, usually regarded as his masterpiece. The audacity and incisiveness with which it handles the abuses of the Church prepared men's minds for the subsequent work of Martin Luther. Erasmus stands as the supreme type of cultivated common sense applied to human affairs. He rescued theology from the pedantries of the Schoolmen, exposed the abuses of the Church, and did more than any other single person to advance the Revival of Learning.

5. Norman Vincent Peale (1898–1993) went on to serve as a Methodist clergyman who would later join the Dutch Reformed Church. He gathered a large following with his preaching style, sharing radio, and TV sermons, and editing the popular newsletter *Guideposts*. His book *The Power of Positive Thinking* became a huge best seller.

6. Robert Bolton (1572–1631) was an English clergyman and academic, noted as a preacher.

7. Suicide is clearly forbidden in Islam, but the permissibility of martyrdom operations (Istishhad) is an altogether different topic, with scholars being split on the issue. Notable scholars and apologists such as Shaykh Yusuf Al-Qaradawi, the world's most quoted independent Islamic jurist, Dr. Zakir Naik, known for his advocacy of "Qur'anic science", and Tahir Ashrafi, the Chairman of the All Pakistan Ulema Council, have justified the use of suicide bombing in Islam. Opinion polls have further shown that an extremely large number of Muslims from around the world support the practice. The Qur'an states that

all Muslim males, not only martyrs, will be rewarded with virgins. However, the Qur'an does also mention that those who fight in the way of Allah (jihad) and get killed will be given a "great reward," and there are also hasan (good) hadith which refer to 72 virgins as one of the "seven blessings from Allah" to the martyr. This has led to the 72 virgins concept being widely used as a way to entice other Muslims into carrying out "martyrdom operations" for Islam. This is witnessed in Palestine, where the actions of a mother who sends her son to die as a martyr is sometimes seen as "marrying him off" and where the concept is used in Friday sermons and music videos, both airing on official television. It has even been used in the United Kingdom, where, in one event, Muslim teens were told to train with Kalashnikov rifles with the promise that the would receive 72 virgins in paradise if they died as religious martyrs. Contrary to what the Qur'an, hadith, scholars and Muslims themselves say, a Western author named Margaret Nydell in a book that "promotes understanding between modern day Arabs and Westerners," states that mainstream Muslims regard the belief of 72 virgins in the same way that mainstream Christians regard the belief that after death they will be issued with wings and a harp, and walk on clouds. However, both the Qur'an and Muhammad in the hadith literature discuss the issue of virgins being provided for men in Paradise. So, unless the Bible, and more specifically Jesus in the four Gospels, claims Christians will indeed be issued with wings and a harp upon their arrival in Heaven, this claim is inaccurate and misleading.

CHAPTER 13

1. Joseph John Campbell was an Irish American, writer and lecturer, best known for his work in comparative mythology and comparative religion. His work is vast, covering many aspects of the human experience.

2. Dr. Jim Wilder is the Director of Shepherd's House, an international speaker, and author of *The Life Model* and many others books on joy, the brain, and the Bible.

3. For more reading on early trauma and the brain:

- Wilder, Khouri, Coursey, and Sutton. *Joy Starts Here*, The Life Model Works. 2013.
- Allan N. Schore. *Affect Regulation and the Repair of the Self.* (New York, NY: W.W. Norton, 2003).
- Allan N. Schore, *Affect Dysregulation and the Disorders of the Self.* (New York, NY: W. W. Norton, 2003).
- Erik H. Erikson, *Growth And Crisis, Theories of Psychopathology and Personality*. Edited by Theodore Millon. (Philadelphia: W. B. Saunders Co., 1973). Pages 136–156.
- Bessel van der Kolk, *Psychological Trauma*. (Washington: American Psychiatric Press, 1987).
- Daniel J. Siegel, *The Developing Mind: Toward a Neurobiology of Interpersonal Experience*. (New York: Guilford Press, 1999).
- Daniel G. Amen, *Healing The Hardware of the Soul*. (New York: The Free Press, 2002).
- James G. Friesen, E. James Wilder, Anne M. Bierling, Rick
- Koepcke, Maribeth Poole, *The Life Model: Living From The Heart Jesus Gave You—The Essentials of Christian Living Revised 2000*. (Pasadena: Shepherd's House Inc. 2000). Distributed by C.A.R.E. Packaging Baldwin, MI. www.CARE1.org.
- Gerald M. Edelman, Guilio Tononi, *A Universe of Consciousness*. (New York: Basic Books, 2000).
- Ronald A. Ruden and Marcia Byalick, *The Craving Brain*. (New York: Perennial, 2000).

4. Brain and shame / we are all in recovery.

Understanding what's broken in self-destructive people is essential to effective recovery. Our ability to bond trust that attach is what is broken, so the challenge is how to come up with effective treatment to heal these destructive self-messages from the preverbal period in our life. What works is an effective partnership between God and people. Remember, recovery is to return to a former health state. Negative and positive self-worth messages from the beginning of our life will dictate who we are and how we behave—for good or bad—until they are changed. There are some excerpts from some of the experts in the field about early attachment and their conclusions.

It's a more nuanced view of the nature vs. nurture debate. Not only is it nature and nurture, as most of us already believe; an individual's particular genetic makeup (nature) also continues to evolve during the first two years of life under the influence of the environment (nurture). In other words, what happens to you, emotionally and psychologically, during those first two years, and especially in the first nine months of life, will powerfully influence your neurobiological development, determining how your brain takes shape in lasting ways. Most important among the brain parts that develop during these early months are those that involve the "emotional and social functioning of the child." And if those parts of the brain are to develop appropriately, "certain experiences are needed. Those experiences are embedded in the relationship between the caretaker and the infant." A deeply sobering thought. You can call it what you like—bad parenting, failure of attunement, insecure attachment—but when things go wrong between parent and child in the first two years of life, you are permanently damaged by it in ways that cannot be entirely erased. The awareness that you are damaged, the felt knowledge that you didn't get what you needed and that as a result, your emotional development has been warped and stunted in profound ways—this is what I refer to as basic shame. The concept lies at the heart of the work I do.

Do a YouTube search for videos by Daniel Shore.

Two other lecturers in this video link the experience of secure\ attachment during this critical period to the development of both a fundamental sense of self-esteem and the ability to feel empathy for others. The relationship to shame and narcissistic defenses against it is implicit. Either you get what you need from your caretakers during those early months and your brain develops in such a way that you have a fundamental self-confidence and security in the world; or you don't get what you need and the residue—the neurological damage—is basic shame. Either your caretakers are emotionally attuned to you and you develop (neurologically) the capacity to empathize with other people; or those caretakers let you down and as a result, your constant struggle for a sense of your own worth and importance powerfully limits your ability to empathize with other people. Near the end of the video, Schore stresses the importance of joy in the attachment experience—that is, the infant's attunement with its mother in the experience of her joy and interest in her baby is crucial for optimal development. If you don't have that experience, if you don't feel that your mother experiences joy in your presence and finds you beautiful—it will permanently damage your brain as it develops. In an earlier post on my website, After Psychotherapy, I wrote that the baby whose mother doesn't adore it (or feel profound joy and interest in her baby) "never gets over it, not really." Now I can say why: it's because the neurological development of its brain was permanently altered by the failure to get what was needed during the first year of life. Toward authentic self-esteem by Joseph Burgo, Ph.D.

The Insecurely Attached Child. Children who do not develop secure attachment during early childhood are most often found to have social difficulties throughout the rest of their development and up into early adulthood. Dr. William Sears, MD, who some claim to be the man most responsible for the development of Attachment Parenting (a way of parenting geared toward fostering secure attachment in children), reports a number of characteristics often observed in insecurely attached children as they grow:

- Misbehavior/receive constant reprimands (school & home)
- Constant dissociation or 'tuning out'
- Aggressive and/or manipulative behavior towards others
- Bullying or easily bullied
- Defensive response to authority figures (teachers, parents, etc.)
- Unwilling to share
- Shunned by peers
- Shallow later friendships

- Less curious or more hesitant to learn
- Difficulties with empathy
- Distrust of adults leading to not asking for help when needed
- Low Self-Confidence
- Difficulties regulating emotions (example: calming self down when upset)

  Dr. Sears' research also found that insecurely attached adults were morally immature, still having difficulty understanding the concepts of 'right' and 'wrong.' There were also links found between severe levels of insecure attachment and later addictive tendencies as well as violence and sociopathic behaviors (Sears).

5. Donald Miller, *Blue Like Jazz*. (Nashville: Thomas Nelson, 2003), 220.

6. The brain has a control center that has as its major function, maintaining a joyful and peaceful sense of our true identity. At the heart of this control process is the training our brain requires to develop loving relationships with others. When we are living in loving relationships, our joy and peace are full. This life of love, joy, and peace is to be the main characteristic of the people remade in God's image, also known as the "church." We are told in Romans 14:17 that Gods whole kingdom is one of peace and joy, "For the kingdom of God is not food and drink, but righteousness and peace and joy in the Holy Spirit." In fact, Jesus made joy the reason for his teaching, "These things I have spoken to you, that my joy may be in you, and that your joy may be full" (John 15:11). Also, "But now I am coming to thee; and these things I speak in the world, that they may have my joy fulfilled in themselves" (John 17:13).

   In order to train the brain to live in joy, we must have face-to-face joy with others. For the brain, joy is amplified and learned when we experience someone who greets us with joy. Again we are told in Romans 12:15 to "Rejoice with those who rejoice, weep with those who weep." No only is the church a source of mutual joy, but it is a place where people are willing to be with us and share our grief until we are at peace again.

Our brain's control center is damaged when we have a failure of either joy-building (rejoicing with those who rejoice), or grief-sharing (weep with those who weep). If our relationships of love do not include both of these ways to bond, we will develop subhuman and unstable brains that lose control when we are upset and do not build joyful and peaceful relationships with others. By following the instructions in Romans 12:15, the church has the ability to restore and retrain people whose brains were badly trained when they were younger. Dr. Jim Wilder

7. Miller, *Blue Like Jazz*, 115.
8. Coursey, Chris M., Khouri, Edward M., Sutton, Sheila D., Wilder, E. James. *Joy Starts Here*. (SAC: Shepherd's House, Inc., 2013).